MOBILISING CLASSICS
Reading radical writing in Ireland

Edited by

Fiona Dukelow and **Orla O'Donovan**

Manchester University Press
Manchester and New York
distributed in the United States exclusively by Palgrave Macmillan

Published by Manchester University Press
Oxford Road, Manchester M13 9NR, UK
and Room 400, 175 Fifth Avenue, New York, NY 10010, USA
www.manchesteruniversitypress.co.uk

Distributed in the United States exclusively by
Palgrave Macmillan, 175 Fifth Avenue, New York,
NY 10010, USA

Distributed in Canada exclusively by
UBC Press, University of British Columbia, 2029 West Mall,
Vancouver, BC, Canada V6T 1Z2

British Library Cataloguing-in-Publication Data
A catalogue record for this book is available from the British Library

Library of Congress Cataloging-in-Publication Data applied for

ISBN 978 0 7190 8017 3 *hardback*
ISBN 978 0 7190 8018 0 *paperback*

First published 2010

Typeset by Special Edition Pre-press Services
www.special-edition.co.uk
Printed in Great Britain
by CPI Antony Rowe, Chippenham, Wiltshire

Contents

Notes on contributors

Fiona Dukelow is a lecturer in the School of Applied Social Studies at University College Cork. Her research and teaching interests include Irish social welfare policy, the impact of globalisation on the Irish welfare state, and social theory and social policy. Her publications include *Irish Social Policy – A Critical Introduction* (2009), which she co-authored with Mairéad Considine.

Mark Garavan lectures in sociology in the Galway and Mayo Institute of Technology. He is primarily concerned with nursing degree programmes, but also teaches youth work and social care. He is actively involved in environmental justice politics. He has acted as spokesperson for the Rossport Five and for the Shell to Sea campaign. He has written widely on the issue of the Corrib gas project and also on wider issues of sustainability and democracy. In 2006, he published *The Rossport Five – Our Story*.

Fintan Lane is a historian and left-wing activist. He is the author of a number of books including a study of Irish socialism entitled *The Origins of Modern Irish Socialism, 1881–1896* (1997). He is the editor of *Saothar*, the journal of the Irish Labour History Society. In recent years he as been actively involved in the Irish Anti-War Movement.

Bernadette McAliskey, an active civil and human rights campaigner since 1968, describes herself as a socialist republican, feminist, and free thinker. She currently manages STEP, a local community development organisation in Dungannon, Co. Tyrone. She also teaches part-time on the Community Development Degree course at the University of Ulster and on the Women's Studies programme at the North West Regional College.

Orla McDonell is a lecturer in sociology in the University of Limerick. Her teaching and research interests include health, medicine and science, bio-ethics, and the sociology of the body. Her publications include *Sociology for Health Professionals in Ireland* (2004), which she co-authored with Abbey Hyde and Maria Lohan.

Robbie McVeigh is a researcher and activist. He has taught on racism and anti-racism at Queen's University Belfast, the University of Ulster and University College Dublin. He has researched racism and sectarianism in Irish society and is the author of *The Racialisation of Irishness: Racism and Anti-Racism in Irish Society* (1996), *Theorizing Sedentarism: The Roots of Anti-Nomadism* (1997) and *Travellers, Refugees and Racism in Tallaght* (1998). With Ronit Lentin he is the co-author of *After Optimism? Ireland, Racism and Globalisation* (2006).

Rosie Meade is a lecturer in the School of Applied Social Studies at University College Cork. Her research and activist interests include alternative media, social movements, the state, grassroots globalisation, community development, corporatism, adult and community education and community arts. She has edited a special issue of the *Community Development Journal* on community arts. Other recent publications include a critical analysis of media constructions of anti-globalisation activists and a critique of community development professionalism.

Eileen O'Carroll teaches with the Waterford City and County Vocational Education Committees and has recently been awarded a M.Ed. on 'William Thompson and the Radical Tradition in Education'. She was one of the co-founders of the William Thompson Weekend School, established in Cork in 1999 to facilitate radical critique and create space for dialogue, discussion and joint action among progressive forces in Irish society.

Orla O'Donovan is a lecturer in the School of Applied Social Studies in University College Cork. Her teaching, research and activist interests centre on the politics of health and medicine and on struggles to democratise the production and use of science and technology for public purposes. Recent publications have focused on interactions between pharmaceutical companies and patients' organisations, conflicts of interest in pharmaceutical regulation, and patients' organisations involvement in knowledge production. She co-edited *Power, Politics and Pharmaceuticals: Irish Medicines Regulation in a Global Context* (2008).

Tina O'Toole is a lecturer in the School of Languages, Literature, Culture and Communication in the University of Limerick. Her research interests include Irish and British literature of the nineteenth and twentieth centuries, specifically the literature and cultural and social activism of Victorian and Edwardian writers. A long-standing activist herself, she has focused many of her publications on women's activism, including *Documenting Irish Feminisms* (2005), co-authored with Linda Connolly.

Hilary Tovey lectures in sociology in Trinity College Dublin. Her interests include environmental knowledges and conflicts, food and society, social movements, the politics of the rural and rural development, social theory, and the sociology of animals. She is an ex-president of the European Society for Rural Sociology, a council member of the International Rural Sociological Association, and a board member of the European Sociological Association Research Committee on Environment and Society. In 2004–6 she coordinated an EU Framework 6 twelve-country research project 'CORASON a Cognitive Approach to Rural Sustainable Development'. Amongst her recent publications is *Environmentalism in Ireland: Movement and Activists* (2007).

Acknowledgements

With thanks to the National University of Ireland and the College of Arts, Celtic Studies and Social Science, University College Cork, for publication assistance funding.

Introduction
Orla O'Donovan and Fiona Dukelow

Ideas and radical politics

[E]very revolution has been preceded by an intense labour of criticism. (Gramsci, 1977: 12)

Radical feminist consciousness spirals in all directions, dis-covering the past, creating/dis-closing the present/future. (Daly, 1991: 1)

Ideas and intellectual activity have long been recognised as crucial to radical politics. Extending far beyond pacifying formal schooling, education in its broader conception is an essential part of the diverse and sometimes overlapping long revolutions of socialism, republicanism, feminism and environmentalism, to name just a few. 'Cognitive praxis' is the term used by Ron Eyreman and Andrew Jamieson (1991) to refer to the thinking of new thoughts and interrogation of taken-for-granted knowledge in the public spaces provided by social movements. Other theorists of social movements point to the significance of 'framing' or 'meaning work' in legitimating, mobilising and sustaining activism, whereby social conditions once seen as unfortunate but inevitable are redefined as unjust and immoral, and amenable to change (Snow and Benford, 2000). This ideological work entails not only efforts in persuasion to win the hearts and minds of others to draw them into movements striving to effect structural change, but also processes of self redefinition. Illustrating the importance of frames of understanding, Nick Crossley (2002: 134) notes that the 'individual who reads the beggar as proof of the evils of capitalism is more likely to be mobilized into anti-capitalist actions ... than the individual who sees only individual fecklessness'. Likewise, if we interpret all the hardships and sufferings in our own lives as evidence of personal failings, we are less likely to challenge them politically than if we viewed them as system failings. Social movements are thus seen to develop alternative ways of defining social situations, and alternative meanings and interpretations of our own lives and the world around us. To appreciate the significance of this work, which provides us with new ways of thinking, talking, feeling and being in the world, imagine a woman who suffers 'sexual harassment' prior to the time when the feminist movement forged that conceptual tool; 'she cannot properly comprehend her own experience, let alone render it communicatively intelligible to others' (Fricker, 2007: 6). These shared meanings, 'discursive repertoires' and 'fighting words' (Steinberg, 1999) are highly dynamic and shaped by the contexts in which movements emerge and activists learn how to protest. Indeed, within a particular field of activism, there may well be multiple and even competing frames offering different situational definitions, different diagnoses of the problem and different ways of remedying it.

Even though ideas and movement frames are inherently social phenomena, certain individuals are nonetheless instrumental in their articulation and elaboration, often in texts that become mobilising classics. 'Organic intellectuals' is the term used by the influential Italian theorist Antonio Gramsci (1977) to refer to the individuals he regarded as playing a pivotal role in the organising and influencing the 'war of position' necessary for social transformation. For him, everyone is an intellectual and philosopher, as we all try to make sense of the world, but certain individuals specialise in articulating counter-hegemonic ideas that inspire collective action. Emerging from or assimilated into subaltern groups and in response to particular historical developments, he saw organic intellectuals as different from the traditional variety; they do not feign political independence but align themselves with working-class struggles, and further because they aim to educate and learn, rather than impress (Mayo, 2008).

Variations on the concept of organic intellectuals have been coined, including 'framing specialists: women and men who develop, borrow, adapt, and rework interpretive frames that promote collective action and that define collective interests and identities, rights and claims', and 'popular intellectuals' characterised by, amongst other things, their acknowledged status 'as producers of meaning and as representatives of collective interests by a popular group or local society' (Baud and Rutten, 2004: 7–8). Some popular intellectuals are actively involved in the movements they inspire, but this is not always the case. Others may be more distant, including those whose lives predate struggles informed by posthumous readings and interpretations of their ideas. Notwithstanding the pivotal role of organic or popular intellectuals, it is only through the reading and acting upon their texts by movement activists that these texts become mobilising classics. Readers too are pivotal. As Fiona Dukelow emphasises in her essay in this volume, Simone de Beauvoir's *The Second Sex* was not 'a ready-made feminist text but became a feminist text through women's reading of it in the context of second-wave feminism'.

There is by now an exciting and substantial body of literature that considers the relationship between organic intellectuals and social movements, and how certain texts have become mobilising classics. One example is the supplement to the *International Review of Social History* edited by Michiel Baud and Rosanne Rutten (cited above), which focuses on eight popular intellectuals and considers the impact of their work on the global flow of ideas. Furthermore, a number of publishing houses have book series dedicated to classic social movement texts.

Reading and acting on mobilising classics in Ireland

What is distinctive about the contributions presented in this volume is that they provide rich reflections on how radical ideas have been circulated, read and acted upon specifically in the Irish context, and how they offer analytical tools that can serve as resources for contemporary social movement activity. Collectively the essays consider selected mobilising classics and their dynamic contributions to the generation of Irish social movements' discourses, contentious vocabularies, interpretations of the world, norms, identities, symbols and strategies. Rather than rendering the book of interest to only those concerned with things Irish, the intention is to offer insights into how the interaction between ideas (or social theory) and social action is rooted in time and place, or, to borrow from Gramsci, how it is 'organic'. The book also sheds light on the international diffusion of social movement frames. As emphasised by Tina O'Toole in her contribution to the volume, in the case of Irish lesbian organising this did not entail wholesale importation of ideas from abroad, but processes whereby texts and ideas published elsewhere were taken by Irish activists who made their own of them. As discussed by Mark Garavan in his contribution, Paulo Freire cautioned against the simplistic adoption of political slogans and templates forged elsewhere which results in political action based on propaganda rather than pedagogy. Also drawing on Freirean ideas, in her contribution to the volume Rosie Meade approaches her selected text as a 'problem posing' one that, instead of prescribing easy solutions, alerts us to particular tensions that beset activism on the left.

Our aims for the volume are twofold. Firstly, we aim to provide insights into how selected mobilising classics have framed or have the potential to frame Irish social movement discourses and oppositional activity. In addition to tracing the political legacies of the inspiring texts, many of the contributions consider how the texts have been read in multiple ways and reinterpreted at different historical moments. Because the material injuries inflicted by the most recent crisis in capitalism (such as a return to high rates of unemployment in Ireland and effective reductions in the minimum wage) became apparent during the period when this book was being written, many of the contributions provide timely commentaries on what the selected radical treatises have to offer at this time and why they should be read now. Many of them highlight how reading radical writing can serve to offset the current widespread resignation that there are no alternatives to capitalism as we know it, despite all its flaws.

Secondly, because many mobilising classics are known but now rarely read, we want to 'open up' the texts and entice students (not just in the formal sense) to read them. Many people, including political activists but particularly students (in the traditional sense) rely on second-hand encounters with the concepts, ideas and arguments offered by classic texts. The names and perhaps even the faces of popular intellectuals such as Simone de Beauvoir, Paulo Freire and James Connolly may be familiar to many, but it seems that few venture to read the original works of these influential writers. James Connolly, along with Thomas Paine and William Thompson, may have been encountered by many Irish people when learning history, but few appear to be familiar with their intellectual legacies and how their ideas have influenced and been used (and abused) in various political struggles. 'Fighting words', such as patriarchy, alienation and institutionalised racism, may be familiar, but possibly encountered in distorted or diluted forms, and emptied of their original subversive purpose. The volume thus seeks to counter the speedy and superficial fast-food style of reading, which is increasingly a feature of academic learning, and entice readers to read and be enlivened by the 'real thing'.

The texts

The texts that provide the focal point for each of the chapters in this volume were selected by the individual contributors, many of whom straddle the boundaries between academia and activism. Reflecting their individual optics and styles, each essay provides an account of the contributor's personal encounters with the classic text, some by word of mouth from their parents, others through copies passed around in activists' groups, and others still through serendipitous reading. Contributors also reflect on how the text has the potential to nourish and invigorate the political imagination of contemporary oppositional politics. Together with a commentary on the key ideas elaborated in the text, the historical context from which it emerged, and a biographical profile of the popular intellectual who penned it, many contributors temper their celebration of the texts with critical reflection on the ideas it expounds but also on the movements and cognitive praxis they have informed. The selected texts are considered by many contributors in light of the widespread disparagement of radical thinking and activism, but also of the potential for much social movement resistance to be limited and largely ineffective, constrained by its own imaginative capacity to a generalised 'being against', incapable of transcending the very systems it resists (Duncombe, 2007a). Reflection on the various dilemmas faced by activists features in many of the chapters, as does consideration of the profound challenge facing contemporary radical mobilising – the apparently all-pervasive and unassailable worldwide regime of consumer capitalism.

As will be seen in the pages that follow, while all the selected texts are considered as mobilising classics, they are highly diverse in many respects. Most obviously, they were published over a period that spans three centuries; Thomas Paine's *The Rights of Man* (discussed in the essay by Bernadette McAliskey), published in 1791, is the oldest text considered, whereas *Our Common Future*, published in 1987 by the UN-established World Commission on Environment and Development (discussed in the chapter by Hilary Tovey), is the most recent. The texts also vary significantly in their form: they include a novel, a set of letters, a report from an official commission, a short essay, a progress report on conversations, and a lengthy philosophical tome.

In keeping with Gramsci's argument that not only must the contemporary dominant culture be transformed but 'history too needs to be confronted, mastered and transformed' (Mayo, 2008: 430), a number of the essays consider how the selected texts can be read to gain an understanding of, and take courage from, the frequently ignored, obliterated and denied traditions of Irish radicalism. In his discussion of James Connolly's *Labour in Irish History*, Fintan Lane notes that for him the text has served 'as "proof" that socialism historically had a place within the republican tradition' and that 'socialist ideas had powerful and well-regarded advocates in the Irish past'. Regarding the Irish republican tradition, Bernadette McAliskey's consideration of the ideas of Thomas Paine underscores how it is part of a political project that extends far beyond the struggle to get 'Brits Out' and stretches back to the French Revolution. Likewise, Eileen O'Carroll's essay on William Thompson's *Practical Education for the South of Ireland* traces early Irish articulations of socialist feminism. It also shows how in the early nineteenth century curriculum reforms were championed that strongly resemble those still advocated by critics of conventional schooling who oppose rote learning in favour of 'useful' experiential learning. The importance of social movements 'dis-covering' their history, to use Mary Daly's (1991) words, is emphasised by Tina O'Toole in her essay on Adrienne Rich's essay 'On Compulsory Heterosexuality and Lesbian Existence'. She argues that when the history of a movement is unrecorded or silenced (as in the case of lesbian resistance in Ireland), once people become politically active, they join 'a collective state of unknowing'. The past, therefore, is not just of historical interest but a usable political tool to groups as they connect it with the present and construct collective identities.

Attention is drawn to the importance of historical analysis in several of the contributions that trace how certain concepts and ideas, and even personas of popular intellectuals, have been appropriated by diverse political groupings in the 'afterlife' of the classic texts. Other essays shed light on the tensions within the texts and how they are flexibly interpretable. For example, in Hilary Tovey's commentary on *Our Common Future*, the work of a committee, she reveals tensions within the text and argues that its key concept 'sustainable development' is an inspirational but confused one. Tracing competing ways in which the text, also known as 'the Brundtland Report', has been read and acted upon in Ireland, she points to its appropriation by ecological modernisationists and 'alternative' environmental activists.

Some of the selected mobilising classics are primarily concerned with 'diagnostic framing', the identification and attribution of blame for the injustices social movements seek to redress, whereas others are more oriented towards 'prognostic framing', the articulation of possible strategies for effecting change (Benford and Snow, 2000). For example, Orla McDonnell's essay on *The Myth of Mental Illness* by Thomas Szasz considers his ideas about the huge social costs of the medicalisation of 'the problems of living', especially in respect of the liberty and dignity of those diagnosed with a psychiatric illness. In contrast, Orla O'Donovan's reflections on Ivan Illich's *Tools for Conviviality*, consider how his ideas can springboard our thinking beyond the prisons of visionlessness or circumscribed political imaginations, and provide us with a methodology for distinguishing 'convivial' from 'non-convivial' social arrangements. As discussed by Eileen O'Carroll, William Thompson's writings on social transformation also placed considerable emphasis on 'how to set about it'. That said, to varying degrees, all of the texts discussed in this volume are 'doubly coded', tools that can be used for analytical and practical purposes. As explained in his commentary on *Black Power: The Politics of Liberation* by Kwame Ture and Charles Hamilton, Robbie McVeigh says that the text is 'simultaneously scholarly sociopolitical analysis and radical treatise', aimed at impelling critical reflection but also political action.

From the biographical accounts provided in each chapter in respect of the popular intellectuals who penned the selected texts it can be seen that these authors' social positions varied considerably and they endured reprobation because of their ideas and actions to varying extents. Some of them are organic intellectuals in the sense that Gramsci used the term, emerging from subaltern groups. Examples include Robert Noonan (aka Robert Tressell), whose *Ragged Trousered Philanthropists* is discussed by Rosie Meade, and Kwame Ture and Charles Hamilton, whose theorising of racism, Robbie McVeigh notes, 'proved that the subaltern could speak'. That said, manifesting the patriarchal relations of power and authority in which social movements are embedded, and oftentimes reproduce, only two of the selected texts were written by women, both of whom are framing specialists within the feminist movement – namely, Simone de Beauvoir and Adrienne Rich. Another, *Our Common Future*, was the outcome of deliberations of a commission chaired by a woman. Some of the authors of the selected mobilising classics could be considered traditional intellectuals who were disloyal to their own class interests and assimilated into subaltern politics. Many of the popular intellectuals, and activists inspired by their writings, were or continue to be at the receiving end of the fury of elites. In its milder forms this entailed isolation and vilification for being, amongst other things, irrational and mad, but for others it was more severe, resulting in imprisonment, exile and even death. However, as noted by Robbie McVeigh, 'dangerous' texts cannot be repressed, censored or destroyed in the way their authors can.

In our concluding remarks at the end of the volume we focus on how the mobilising texts considered within it can serve as (to take a phrase from Rosie Meade's essay) 'reservoirs of identity, hope and imagination' for contemporary movements against oppression. While acknowledging the severe and unjustly distributed hardships associated with the most recent crisis in capitalism in Ireland and globally, we note the political opportunities potentially afforded by this crisis. In Ireland the collapse in authority, public confidence and legitimacy of institutions that once seemed all- and ever-powerful, such as the major banks and the Catholic Church, has the potential to open up spaces for new ways of thinking and acting. It is also an encouraging reminder of the provisional nature of power and authority. We reflect on how the essays point in different ways to the potential for us individually and collectively to cultivate new frameworks of thought, and imagine new social possibilities and ways of taking part in history-making.

Read on, and to borrow from Bernadette McAliskey's essay, read avidly!

1

Thomas Paine's *The Rights of Man*
Bernadette McAliskey

Introduction – Making the acquaintance of Thomas Paine

'These are the times that try men's souls.' So said Barack Hussein Obama, the first Black president of the USA, in his 2009 inauguration speech. He continued: 'Let it be told to the future world ... that in the depth of winter, when nothing but hope and virtue could survive ... that the city and the country, alarmed at one common danger, came forth to meet [it].' Though eloquent and well chosen, these words were not his own. They belong to Thomas Paine. He wrote them on 23 December 1776 in his essay *The Crisis*. Maybe Mr Obama's script writer, in search of a good quote, sourced Paine on the internet; maybe the young Obama grew up with Paine, or met him while studying at college. These things are possible when the people write and read, parents pass on their knowledge by word of mouth, and students go back to original texts for inspiration.

My affection for Paine stems partly from the fact that I grew up with him until I was nine years old, and then he died. Actually my father died, but he must have read Paine avidly as he quoted him liberally and instilled his sense of individual right and responsibility into his children. My father was a joiner, a skilled carpenter and member of the Amalgamated Union of Woodworkers. His union card still remains among the family heirlooms. He was educated through the trade union and workers' education movements, having started school at about five years of age and left at seven to become a grocer's bicycle boy. He had printed books, and he had hard-backed exercise books into which he copied poetry, prose, songs and quotations that were meaningful to him, including some from *Common Sense* and *The Rights of Man*. After my father's death, his books remained, but I do not recall reading any volume of Thomas Paine's work at home. I lost him when I lost my father.

I would become re-acquainted with Paine in the middle of the revolting sixties, when I spotted a paperback copy of *The Rights of Man*[1] on the bookshelf of a fellow student. I borrowed it, scanned it eagerly, looking for the words I had heard spoken but never really read, and soon became acquainted with Thomas Paine in my own right. There was that great emotive word 'usurpation'. 'All power exercised over a nation, must have some beginning. It must either be delegated or assumed. There are no other sources. All delegated power is trust, and all assumed power is usurpation. Time does not alter the nature and quality of either' (Paine, 1987: 153). Uncompromising stuff in a Europe full of monarchs! Then there was the powerful resonance of 'the band of robbers ... [who plundered and] parcelled out the world.'

My mother opined that the queen (Elizabeth II) was a noble and gracious lady; my father that, gracious or not, she was a receiver of stolen goods and inheritor of a butcher's apron. Paine is unequivocal about the claims of monarchy to ownership and power.

> Those bands of robbers having parcelled out the world, and divided it into dominions, began, as is naturally the case, to quarrel with each other. What at first was obtained by violence was considered by others as lawful to be taken, and a second plunderer succeeded the first. They alternately invaded the dominions which each had assigned to him, and the brutality with which they treated each other explains the original character of monarchy. It was ruffian torturing ruffian. The conqueror considered the conquered, not as his prisoner, but his property. He led him in triumph rattling in chains, and doomed him, at pleasure, to slavery or death. As time obliterated the history of their beginning, their successors assumed new appearances, to cut off the entail of their disgrace, but their principles and objects remained the same. What at first was plunder, assumed the softer name of revenue; and the power originally usurped, they affected to inherit. (Paine, 1987: 137)

It is the breathtaking directness and irreverence of Paine which enthral and engage reason with passion. The language flows on the page like the spoken word of the orator and agitator. You feel the intellectual and emotional pull of revolutionary change and sense the writer is in the thick of it. However, Paine makes no reference in the context of colonialism to the rights of displaced indigenous people. Understanding this glaring omission takes us into the realms of understanding the construction of 'scientific racism' within the European Enlightenment. I will return to this.

So apart from the nostalgia of childhood and sympathy with the radical democratic content and energy, why recommend Mr Paine and *The Rights of Man* to the modern student? Let me say at the outset, the recommendation is not based on dogmatic assertion of his philosophy being without tensions, contradictions or limitations. I would argue that while the core tenets remain valid, Paine's weakness is twofold and reflects his location in time. This too will be revisited later.

The debate between Messrs Paine and Burke

The latter half of eighteenth-century America may have tested men's souls, but it excited and challenged their intellect, and that of women. Thomas Paine is writing, arguing and formulating his ideas of democracy, representation, social contract, civil rights and the relationship between the citizen, society and the state in an environment of rapid and often revolutionary change in the old imperial Europe and the 'new territories' of North America. He predates John Mill's treatise *On Liberty* by some seventy years and Ferdinand Tönnies on community versus society by eighty, and it will be a hundred years before Karl Marx, who in the same vein of advancing theory for the purpose of effecting social change, addresses the alienation of labour and makes an argument for dialectic materialism and socialism. From the social science perspective, modern state theory cannot effectively be understood if you have not entered into the thrust of that seminal debate between Mr Edmund Burke and Mr Thomas Paine. It might be worth adding a note of modern Irish interest at his point. While Thomas Paine stands tall in my line of intellectual giants, John Hume proclaims Edmund Burke as his hero. *Plus ça change!* There may be a dissertation lurking here for some brave soul.

The Enlightenment may not by twenty-first century standards have been all that enlightened, but the new thinking, the challenge to the old order, and the resulting social change make the literature of this era compulsory and compulsive reading. The story goes something like this. Edmund Burke published a damning criticism of the French Revolution, to which among others both Thomas Paine and Mary Wollstonecraft responded. Paine's response motivated William Godwin to join the debate with his own perspective, *Enquiry Concerning Political Justice, and its Influence on General Virtue and Happiness.* Godwin's treatise was probably the first clearly articulated argument for anarchy. Unlike the revolutionary activism of Paine, *Political Justice* was more abstractly philosophical and in turn inspired the radicals amongst the 'romantic' poets, particularly Shelley. Ironically, Godwin developed his theory from reading an earlier treatise of Burke's which the author later repudiated. The whole saga included charges of treason and men fleeing the country and might well have the makings of a BBC costume drama!

Edmund Burke had, in modern parlance, been 'outed' as the author of a philosophical treatise in support of radical political theory published in 1756 – *A Vindication of Natural Society: A View of the Miseries and Evils Arising to Mankind.* This was penned under the name of Lord Bolingbroke.[2] Between writing the essay, when he was eighteen, and being discovered as the author years later, Burke had become a statesman of some significance and respectability. He declared the work to have been a satire on Bolingbroke's philosophical perspective and disowned the intellectual ideas it contained. Too late! Burke's *Vindication* had already inspired Godwin (who obviously missed the satirical intent) to further develop the theoretical anarchist perspective. Godwin's pamphlet *Political Justice*, despite its 'outrageous price', is recorded as having sold some 4,000 copies in a predominantly illiterate England. In it Godwin acknowledged the contribution of Burke's earlier disowned work. In light of Burke's sticking to the satire story, Godwin is acknowledged as the first of the English anarchist theorists. There seems little reason why Burke had not at some point voluntarily declared his authorship of and satirical intent in *Vindication* in order to challenge the concepts argued in the work, particularly when it was universally accepted as a serious treatise, thereby defeating his claimed purpose in writing it. Whether or not *Vindication* was a satire or Burke's new position required him to disavow its standpoint, he was certainly sympathetic to the American cause, and so his vitriolic attack of the French Revolution took many of his contemporaries by surprise.

Reflections on the Revolution in France was published in 1790 and his arguments were used and adapted to support classical liberal analysis and form the baseline of criticism of communism in theory and practice. In essence, *Reflections* still stands today as the first manifesto of modern conservatism and it lays the ideological ground for nationalism as opposed to national identity as cultural artefact. Burke, whose origins were in Ireland, was essentially an 'English nationalist' and a monarchist. Paine was an internationalist and a republican. *Vive la différence!*

Many people, whose knowledge of Paine is derived from third-hand references or mythology, mistakenly associate him centrally with nationalism, particularly in the Irish context. This may be because of the nature of the alliance made by the Irish republicans with the Hibernian nationalists in the Irish Home Rule movement in relation to both the land and Ulster questions. Much of the internal dynamic of these tensions are lost to the modern student of such matters unless you are lucky enough to get your hands on another original text published in 1927, *The Irish Revolution and How It Was Lost* by William O'Brien. This work may well have circulated in the reading rooms of rural towns in Tyrone as my father was not alone in his generation in describing the English nationalist philosophy of Burke as adapted by Irishmen as 'hibernianism' and despising it with bitter and vindictive contempt. Marx (1979: 925–6) was equally contemptuous, and wrote of Burke, 'This sycophant ... in the pay of the English oligarchy ... was a vulgar bourgeois through and through'. However, it is not the function of this work to vilify Burke or eulogise Paine. Both were formidable thinkers and passionate advocates of social change and social justice in their time. I am resolutely on the side of Paine in the argument with Burke. I merely set out my own prejudice and preference so that the reader may take them into account in my advocacy of reading his rather than Burke's work.

Paine had been actively involved in formulating the ideas and processes of both the American and French constitutions, so his philosophy is echoed in these documents and other earlier tracts and pamphlets, but the series of 'chapters' which make up the 1791 work *The Rights of Man* are the most complete articulation of his social and political philosophy. Burke's treatise was itself a response to an earlier set of sermons by Richard Price (1789) that had linked the French Revolution with the English 'Revolution' of 1688, much to the annoyance of Burke who was opposed to the one and a devotee of the other. (If you skipped history at school, the Glorious Revolution of 1688 was when James II was deposed as King of England by the Dutch William of Orange. Irish students will be more familiar with

1690, when the brawl spilled over to the banks of the Boyne in Ireland. The English consider this violent change of dynasties to have been revolutionary). In a nutshell, Price and Burke had conflicting constructions of authority, national identity and democracy. Price had cited the example of the French Revolution in revisiting the gains of the earlier English experience and essentially argued the latter to be a development of the former. Burke was outraged and castigated the French Revolution to make his case for prejudice against reason, heredity against democracy, and the general superiority and continuity of state and government authority against the rights of people who make up society. The intellectual debate on the French Revolution raged for six years, with pamphlet and counter pamphlet being produced furiously and circulating widely, and authors fleeing the country as the readership were tried for treason. For publishing and circulating *The Rights of Man* Paine had to flee to France in 1792 and was never able to return. Godwin avoided a similar fate because the court considered that his pamphlet was too expensive and too philosophical for anybody vulnerable to its ideas to actually read it and so the public could not be corrupted by it. When the excitement had subsided the ground was laid for nationalism, prejudice and the authority of property and inheritance on one hand, against an articulation of ideas that would inform the future development of radical and working-class-based movements on the other.

Consider the dismal, parochial and petty-minded self-absorption of the hoards inhabiting 'blogger space' on today's internet, twittering back and forth about everything and nothing, with scarcely a radical new thought to be shared amongst the whole self-imaging spectrum. It could be said, to quote Leonard Cohen, that in the particular discourse around the constitutional relationship between the individual, society and the state 'nothing much has happened since but closing time'. Current discourse on constitutional democracy and participative citizenship, active citizenship, and earned citizenship seems to circulate in ether, seeking no clarity of terminology and recognising no contested construction of the concepts on which the discussion is based. While gender and 'race' have been added to the rights debate, the infrastructure of state power has remained beyond equitable integration of either. So, at least you now get a second layer of meaning to Mr Obama's inaugural opening remarks. I have no idea if he did. Imagine if Thomas Paine and Edmund Burke had conducted their debates via the internet, Wollstonecraft and Godwin challenging both, and we could all witness and participate in the exchange, waiting for the next riposte and you get an idea of the immediacy and excitement. Maybe not, if you haven't the slightest idea what ideas I am talking about, so permit me to introduce you to the man and the thinking that was Thomas Paine, the first international revolutionary.

Born in rural England in 1737, Thomas Paine was a common man, one of Gramsci's 'organic intellectuals'. He worked at a number of trades and professions before emigrating to America in 1774, complete with a recommendation from Benjamin Franklin. In 1776, he wrote *Common Sense* as a pro-independence pamphlet for the American colony. Originally published anonymously, presumably because it was seditious, it ultimately ran to 100,000 copies, circulated to meet popular demand. Paine wrote in plain English and in concrete terms of the real life experience of his readers. The more restrained discourse of modern academia might require a more objective framework of 'case studies', but Paine is also an activist and his thinking emerges from experiential knowledge of the social realities he seeks to change, and the purpose of his theorising is to argue for and effect social and political change. He was perhaps the first to effectively use a clearly political style of writing to express his philosophical thinking. Sadly, despite the impact of the 1960s, this is still frowned upon in academia as lacking scholarly tone and whatever masquerades as objectivity. Paine both weaves and critically appraises the fascinating tapestry of the evolving context of social and political change as the eighteenth century ends in revolution on two continents. All of his works reflect his belief in natural reason and natural rights, political equality, tolerance, civil liberties and the dignity of humanity.

The text I have chosen to discuss is, however, not *Common Sense*, though common sense would suggest it too should be read. I have chosen the somewhat lengthier *The Rights of Man* because it sets out more comprehensively the core philosophy of Paine's republicanism. In my view, it articulates the finest statements of eighteenth-century democratic philosophy ever formulated, the core principles of which I believe remain valid three centuries later, pointing out the pathways and processes required of democratic constitutional government.

The Rights of Man

You will be pleased to know that the original text can be read on the internet. Thomas Paine would have liked that idea. The introduction consists of two letters of presentation of his work. One is to George Washington, as president of America. 'I present you a small treatise in defence of those principles of freedom which your exemplary virtue hath so eminently contributed to establish. That the rights of man may become as universal as your benevolence can wish, and that you may enjoy the happiness of seeing the New World regenerate the Old' (Paine, 1987: 9). The other is to the Marquis de La Fayette, a kind of bourgeois revolutionary Che Guevara who fought in both the American and French revolutions, and who Paine clearly encouraged to become further involved in supporting the developing revolutionary actions in Germany: 'Should the campaign commence, I hope it will terminate in the extinction of German despotism and in establishing the freedom of all Germany' (Paine, 1987: 122). These would be seen today as 'dedications' and demonstrate Paine's internationalism and involvement in both revolutions.

The second section titled 'Applying principle to practice' sets out the author's rationale for the work and the context in which it is written – the 'battle royal' with Edmund Burke. It might be a good point to identify the need when reading it to abandon the modern lazy usage of terminology in theoretical and practice-based discussion which interchanges usage of words – the people, nation, society, country, state, government, and more recently the community – as if they are all referring to the same thing, the same phenomenon. From Paine's perspective they are not the same thing, and much of his theory of democracy centres on the dynamic tension and interaction between these constructions. It is that core understanding of the need for transparent, open, accountable and reversible process to manage the interaction that stands the test of time and continues challenging the processes of democracy.

Ironically the validity of Paine's theories in the twenty-first century can only be understood by recognition of the limitations of practice or application of principle of his own theory in his own time. Perhaps it is this paradox which excites me more than anything else. How can Paine be simultaneously right and wrong? What caused him to miss the different context of the American and European Revolutions in relation to the indigenous people of North America not being included amongst the individuals who had a natural right to participate in designing the society of which they were a part, or the government which regulated their affairs? The explanation lies somewhere in an unquestioning acceptance of the social construction of race. The indigenous people of other lands were not viewed as rational and social animals. They were viewed as subhuman, lacking the intellectual and social capacity of fully developed rational human beings. The racial construction of society as a rational theory is buried here within the mixture of empire-building, proselytising and development of 'natural science'. The absence of any reference to the destruction of civilisations and the slaughter and enslavement of indigenous people cannot be attributed to an assumption of unspoken inclusion in the rights equation.

White European Christian men were at the top of the human tree, second only to God and equal before God with each other, but superior to the less rational, uncivilised and dependent humans who, not being in full possession of rational capacity, were not part of the decision-making processes. They were all 'the white man's burden' and duty of care. White European women (of a class) were considered socially developed, but not rational, animals. They were emotional beings, requiring both protection and regulation in the interest of their own well being and that of society. These issues could have been raised at this time, within this discourse. The key driver in gender inequality is in patriarchy, but this modern inquisitive mind asks why Paine's clarity of thought on the idiocy of monarchy and hereditary power was not moved to challenge patriarchy itself.

The journey to find these answers encourages even more reading of original texts from Wollstonecraft to de Beauvoir to Marx, Engels and Luxembourg. Arguably the question of class and the alienation and exploitation of labour required the development of the concept of recognition of the core integrity of individual humanity and the right of the people to form collective agreements before the human being's right to their own labour value and collective agreement and organisation against exploitation could be effectively argued. The democratic rights of those with disability and those without 'citizenship' status are even more modern developments. Paine has no excuse, other than the limitations of his gendered thinking in relation to women. He could have taken some advice from Wollstonecraft.

Nonetheless, Paine's central construct stands the test of time. It begins with the individual human as a rational and social animal who interacts with others to create groups of shared interest which make up communities and society, and then of his or her own free will agrees with others what limitations should be placed on individual liberty. These limitations are necessary in order to effectively manage the complexities of the interactions to ensure equal access to the benefits of society while maximising the protection of the rights of both the individuals and the collective society. One might describe this as the original 'bottom-up' approach much lauded in modern community development approaches and British New Labour social policies, although even a cursory reading of Paine leaves Blair and Brown exposed as a pair of 'Burkes'.

If this is already proving too laborious a journey, might I suggest you seriously consider taking up Accountancy, combined with Business Studies or even Computer Programming, with or without Japanese. You will be happier in the new environment, and those tasked with broadening your thinking will be happier in being spared the dreaded tutorial question, 'Is this reading really necessary for the module assignment?' If you won't study mathematical disciplines because you don't understand the underlying principles of mathematics or they simply bore you, what makes you think society is less complex, without core principles and insights from great social thinkers?

For those of you still reading after that little aside, allow me to take you even further back with an excerpt from another original text, or more correctly, an English translation of one. Long, long before Hobbes, Locke or Paine, in his poem *Metamorphoses* Ovid[3] writes the following in 8 AD.

> The golden age was first; when Man yet new,
> No rule but uncorrupted reason knew:
> And, with a native bent, did good pursue.
> Unforc'd by punishment, un-aw'd by fear,
> His words were simple, and his soul sincere;
> Needless was written law, where none opprest:
> The law of Man was written in his breast:
> No suppliant crowds before the judge appear'd,
> No court erected yet, nor cause was heard:
> But all was safe, for conscience was their guard.

... The mountain-trees in distant prospect please,
E're yet the pine descended to the seas:
E're sails were spread, new oceans to explore:
And happy mortals, unconcern'd for more,
Confin'd their wishes to their native shore.

The human being is understood in the natural state to be first and foremost accountable to and for itself. This natural state is presumed to exist from the origins of the species before socialisation. A person's natural rights, like their needs and capacities, were basic but unfettered. Men and women could do what they had the resources and capacity to do, limited only by the consequences of their actions. In this natural state, at its worst, it was every one for themselves against every other; at its best, each person guided by conscience or reason (both of which, it was believed separated humanity from other species) engaged in a crude form of social contract – each caused as little aggravation as they received. Then the complications set in. Ovid continues:

Truth, modesty, and shame, the world forsook:
Fraud, avarice, and force, their places took.
Then sails were spread, to every wind that blew.
Raw were the sailors, and the depths were new:
Trees, rudely hollow'd, did the waves sustain;
E're ships in triumph plough'd the watry plain.

Then land-marks limited to each his right:
For all before was common as the light.
Nor was the ground alone requir'd to bear
Her annual income to the crooked share,
But greedy mortals, rummaging her store,
Digg'd from her entrails first the precious oar;
Which next to Hell, the prudent Gods had laid;
And that alluring ill, to sight display'd.
Thus cursed steel, and more accursed gold,
Gave mischief birth, and made that mischief bold:
And double death did wretched Man invade,
By steel assaulted, and by gold betray'd,
Now (brandish'd weapons glittering in their hands)
Mankind is broken loose from moral bands;
No rights of hospitality remain:
The guest, by him who harbour'd him, is slain ...

So it begins to look as though Hobbes, Locke *et al.* may have read Ovid as translated by Garth, Dryden *et al.* and laid the ground for Paine. How easily we forget where our understanding of the world around us comes from! Ovid, translated into English in the seventeenth century, could be next on your reading list, once you get into the spirit of discovery. Before you know it, you will be thinking and linking and finding the chinks for yourself. Meanwhile, back to *The Rights of Man*!

Paine argued that since each human being already possessed natural and therefore inalienable rights, it was irrational to argue that legislation gave the people these rights. On the contrary, the setting out in legislation of who had particular rights would imply that the rights of others were limited or removed. According to Paine, only those to whom the rights naturally pertained had the authority to collectively agree to their limitation. Where such consent did not exist then the right had been usurped and not conceded. He further argued that such an enforced breach of the natural right and social contract could ultimately be sustained only by force or superstition. This led to the logical conclusion that the people from whom the right had been usurped retained an alienable and continuing right to retrieve it, by force if necessary.

The context of this argument is not interpersonal relationships between individuals, or the competing exercise of individual rights which Paine believed made up the informal social contracts of society. It relates to the formal relationship of the individual with the administration of that society through the machinery of government. Paine's differentiation between the nation, made up of individuals sharing common cultural artefact, identity and purpose who form society, and the state as represented by the legislature and apparatus of state authority is reflected in how he juxtaposes these in his arguments.

> Man did not enter into society to become worse than he was before, nor to have fewer rights than he had before, but to have those rights better secured. His natural rights are the foundation of all his civil rights. But in order to pursue this distinction with more precision, it will be necessary to mark the different qualities of natural and civil rights.
>
> A few words will explain this. Natural rights are those which appertain to man in right of his existence. Of this kind are all the intellectual rights, or rights of the mind, and also all those rights of acting as an individual for his own comfort and happiness, which are not injurious to the natural rights of others. Civil rights are those which appertain to man in right of his being a member of society. Every civil right has for its foundation some natural right pre-existing in the individual, but to the enjoyment of which his individual power is not, in all cases, sufficiently competent. Of this kind are all those which relate to security and protection.
>
> From this short review it will be easy to distinguish between that class of natural rights which man retains after entering into society and those which he throws into the common stock as a member of society.
>
> The natural rights which he retains are all those in which the Power to execute is as perfect in the individual as the right itself. Among this class, as is before mentioned, are all the intellectual rights, or rights of the mind; consequently religion is one of those rights. The natural rights which are not retained, are all those in which, though the right is perfect in the individual, the power to execute them is defective. They answer not his purpose. A man, by natural right, has a right to judge in his own cause; and so far as the right of the mind is concerned, he never surrenders it: but what availeth it him to judge, if he has not power to redress? He therefore depos-

its this right in the common stock of society, and takes the arm of society, of which he is a part, in preference and in addition to his own. Society *grants* him nothing. Every man is a proprietor in society, and draws on the capital as a matter of right. (emphasis in original) (Paine, 1987: 43–4)

Others had argued that the existence of government in nation states superseded the concept of natural rights. All rights and duties were dictated by the state, which in a sense had become the collective individual. This line of thought also developed the theory that the state and only the state had the right to use violence in managing this relationship. Again, this related to the individual relationship with the collective. The violence of interpersonal relationships was not considered a matter of any philosophical interest, and men merrily duelled and beat their women for centuries to come. The governments legislated on behalf of the monarchs, who usurped the right of government to themselves for their own benefit – a usurpation of the rights of common men (no mention of common women).

Paine argued that individuals who make up the citizens of the territorial state should, of necessity, first agree the principles by which they would regulate their rights and limit their individual liberty in order to collectively protect themselves from their own excesses. These principles needed to be written and agreed by each citizen. The nation (i.e. the people) by this process created the constitutional basis on which they could delegate and retrieve their responsibilities to and for each other. The next step was to set in place the mechanism of regulation, government, legislature, courts, etc., and the means of removing those delegated to regulate and enforce if they failed in their obligations. Without this clearly defined social contract, written and consented to by each citizen, democracy was a sham. This was the core of the republican argument.

For the moment a temporarily blind eye is being turned to the limitations of the concept of 'citizenship' which informed the eighteenth-century debate. Burke argued that the nature of the government and its authority had been established in 1688 for posterity. Paine writes:

> There never did, nor never can exist a parliament, or any description of men, or any generation of men, in any country, possessed of the right or the power of binding and controlling posterity to the 'end of time,' or of commanding forever how the world shall be governed, or who shall govern it; and therefore all such clauses, acts, or declarations, by which the makers of them attempt to do what they have neither the right nor the power to do, nor the power to execute, are in themselves null and void. Every age and generation must be as free to act for itself, *in all cases*, as the age and generations which preceded it. The vanity and presumption of governing beyond the grave is the most ridiculous and insolent of all tyrannies. Man has no property in man; neither has any generation a property in the generations which are to follow. (emphasis in original) (Paine, 1987: 16)

Paine had argued that the decision to mutually limit individual rights by forming governments, police, tax offices, armies, etc., was required to protect the people from each other. The constitution was to protect the people from the government they created. In relation to individuals, he argued that every citizen should retain the same and equal rights. While this may seem tame stuff in the second millennium, it struck fear in the rulers of eighteenth century Europe and forced Burke to formulate and articulate the fundamentally racist and prejudice-based construction of nationalism which underpinned government authority in eighteenth-century Europe and laid the foundations of European and American 'democracy'.

> But it will be first necessary to define what is meant by a *constitution*. It is not sufficient that we adopt the word; we must fix also a standard signification to it.
>
> A constitution is not a thing in name only, but in fact. It has not an ideal, but a real existence; and wherever it cannot be produced in a visible form, there is none. A constitution is a thing antecedent to a government, and a government is only the creature of a constitution. The constitution of a country is not the act of its government, but of the people constituting its government. It is the body of elements, to which you can refer, and quote article by article; and contains the principles on which the government shall be established, the manner in which it shall be organized, the powers it shall have, the mode of elections, the duration of parliaments, or by what other name such bodies may be called; the powers which the executive part of the government shall have; and in fine, everything that relates to the complete organization of a civil government, and the principles on which it shall act, and by which it shall be bound. A constitution, therefore, is to a government what the laws made afterwards by that government are to a court of judicature. The court of judicature does not make the laws, neither can it alter them; it only acts in conformity to the laws made; and the government is in like manner governed by the constitution.
>
> Can, then, Mr. Burke produce the English constitution? If he cannot, we may fairly conclude that though it has been so much talked about, no such thing as a constitution exists, or ever did exist, and consequently that the people have yet a constitution to form. (Paine, 1987: 46–7)

It is Paine's adherence to an uncompromising intellectual concept of democracy in theory and practice that makes him challenging in the twenty-first century. He argued that, since it is citizens, not governments, who actually go to war, the decision to go to war is for the nation, not the government. That is to say, a referendum and not a parliamentary vote is required before a country can go to war. He further argued that the people required a constitutional mechanism for effectively firing the government, as it stood to reason the government was unlikely to fire itself, and the people retained the right, if all else failed, to remove the government by force.

Paine does not set out social or economic ideologies which should inform the policy and practice of society but merely the baseline for the foundation of democratic structures of self-government. I have alluded to the weakness in the concept of citizenship. If the process by which the state is created excludes the interest and perspective of those marginalised due to class, gender, 'race', and more, then every state in Europe needs a new constitution (mind you, the British still don't have one).

The core limitation goes beyond that to the limitation of republicanism as a concept. Paine cannot be held accountable for that. His argument is made within the limitation of structure for the purpose of self-government, the construction of the democratic state. But you cannot simply have a democratic republic, which is objectively removed from the differentiated interests of its unequal citizens. The state will have an ideology and culture that reflect the 'nation' – the collective expression of the citizens. It will of necessity be a democratic republic of the left, right or centre, which will in turn create new dynamics and tensions. This raises questions about other forms of power; economics, and the state's social policy; the role of the state in welfare, capitalism and socialism in relation to political structures of state, but the concept of republicanism all starts with knowing that the people are the only legitimate source of authority. They have the right and the capacity to exercise power, where each person is accountable to themselves and for themselves in the final analysis, and no power has the right to exercise authority where there is no consent or concession of an inalienable right. It is one of history's ironies that whereas Paine's revolutionary concept was not fulfilled in the new democratic republics which absorbed the nationalisms and prejudices lauded by Burke, the volume written by Burke is by and large forgotten, while Paine's answer to it has become a classic. Read it.

Read Ovid, read avidly. Read 'til your eyes hurt, think 'til your head hurts, then do what you think needs to be done to change what you see and doesn't make sense. This will make you an informed, educated and better human being, and with any luck, lead you to want to read, experience and know more.

Notes

1 The version of *The Rights of Man* to which I refer in this discussion was published by New York-based Prometheus Books in 1987.
2 It should be noted that Bolingbroke was safely dead when Edmund Burke usurped his identity for the purpose. He had died some five years previously, so the 'discovery' of this posthumous work would have excited considerable interest.
3 You can read Ovid's *Metamorphoses*, translated by Samuel Garth, John Dryden *et al.* online at http://classics.mit.edu/Ovid/metam.html.

2

William Thompson's *Practical Education for the South of Ireland*

Eileen O'Carroll

Introduction

In the unconsecrated portion of Kensal Green Cemetery in London stands the Reformers' Memorial, which has the following inscription:

> Erected to the memory of men and women who have generously given their time and means to improve the conditions and enlarge the happiness of all classes of society. They have felt that a far happier and more prosperous life is within the reach of all men, and they have earnestly sought to realise it. The old brutal laws of imprisonment for free printing have been swept away, and the right of selecting our own law-makers has been gained, mainly by their efforts. The exercise of these rights will give the people an interest in the laws that govern them, and will make them better men and better citizens.

Thomas Paine, John Stuart Mill and Robert Owen are but a few of the legendary radicals whose names are recorded for posterity on this monument. In a prominent position near the top of the plinth is the name of William Thompson.

William Thompson (1775–1833) is one of the most important Irish intellectuals of the nineteenth century. A renowned political economist, he invented the term 'social science' and developed a theory of socialism originating in Ricardian political economy and Bethamite utilitarianism. His treatises on economic and social organisation are widely studied, and his work on feminism, with collaborator Anna Doyle Wheeler, has been the subject of excellent intellectual archaeology and subsequent restoration. In contrast, Thompson's interest in education is not the first thing that comes to mind in any discussion of him, but it was a huge passion of his and the focus of his first ever published work, *Practical Education for the South of Ireland* (1818a).[1] Reading this short first text of Thompson's provides a jumping off point for understanding his ideas elaborated in subsequent and much lengthier texts.

Highlighting the overarching themes in the work of William Thompson, Dolores Dooley contends that

> It is possible to speak of a dominant project, an all-consuming life task that absorbed Thompson's energies. It is the critique of exploitative

power ... Thompson concentrated on three forms of power: the power of systems, institutions and men to rob women of the means to happiness and independence; the power of capitalists and the idle rich to deprive the working classes of an equitable share of the fruits of their labour; finally the power of lawmakers and leaders of social institutions to enhance their own powers at the expense of the uneducated, the poor and the politically powerless. (Dooley, 1996: 37)

This concentration on power is directly linked to his belief in the liberating power of education and the value of education in improving the lives of both individuals and communities. Indeed, the idea of educated, independent, self-regulating community living as a means of social revolution is a thread woven throughout Thompson's work and the importance of education in the formation of such communities is underlined throughout.

Thompson was born into a wealthy Cork Protestant family in 1775. At that time the city was flourishing as a centre of commerce, and traditionally wealthy families such as Thompson's were at the summit of genteel society. John Thompson, William's father, was conferred as Lord Mayor of Cork in 1794, a testament to the position he occupied in the life of the city. When his father died in 1814, William inherited a significant estate, including a shipping fleet and a large tract of land in West Cork. He was aware from an early age that the privileges afforded to him were not the norm, and that the majority of people lived in conditions wholly alien to his own. He would dedicate his life to using his wealth and education to help outline alternative visions of justice and equality.

Practical education

Of the inherited privileges William Thompson was to receive, proprietorship of the Royal Cork Institution was one he truly valued. Following in the wake of the much earlier Royal Dublin Society, the Institution became a valuable focus of education for the wealthy in Cork, specialising in the natural sciences. It housed a museum and a library, provided public lectures and helped lay the foundations for many of the third-level educational institutions in Cork today. The charter under which it was established in 1807 allowed for a grant of £2,000 per annum, but a system of proprietorship also operated whereby patrons could part-fund the Institution and in return could, for a limited period, influence and monitor its functioning. William Thompson was one such proprietor.

His interest in education, economics and science found outlet in this arena, but his tenure there was not without controversy. In 1817 an internal dispute arose regarding certain perceived shortcomings in the management of the Institution. In 1818 Thompson embarked on a letter-writing campaign in the *Southern Reporter* (1818b) where he drew attention to deficiencies in the Institution's management, which provoked responses by other proprietors who found themselves targets of his admonishment. These letters also outlined his vision of the *raison d'être* of such a centre of learn-ing – what it should teach, the type of person who should teach there and how it should be governed. It encapsulates his earliest vision of education and describes the type of people he envisaged being students at what could become, in his opinion, a vibrant contributor to 'practical' education in Cork and surrounding districts. His views in these letters formed the basis of *Practical Education for the South of Ireland*.

The pamphlet outlines in great detail Thompson's philosophy of educa-tion. Along with other thinkers of the late eighteenth and early nineteenth centuries, he held distinctly radical views on the subject and his uncompro-mising belief in the necessity of cheap and useful education for boys *and girls*, men *and women*, formed an integral part of his philosophy of equality and inclusion. His flowery address to the managers belies the concrete nature of what was to follow, but it does provide an insight into Thompson's idea of the 'gift' of knowledge and the social benefits that would arise if the proprietors 'would unlock the stores of knowledge' (Thompson, 1818b: 16 May). His almost utopian view of education was a broad one; he was as convinced of the merits of mechanics as he was of literature in the making of a gentler, wiser, more egalitarian society. A 'cheap and liberal system of Education adapted to active life' would contribute to 'peace and good order, and happiness of society' (Ibid.). The paternalist utilitarian is evident in a call for benevolence, but so is the much more forward-thinking analyst of social organisation; 'the minor morality of politeness' along with 'litera-ture, poetry, and eloquence' have as great a role in the making of a 'useful' member of society as they make for easier 'social intercourse'. There can be common communication across the class divide provided there is a basis in education.

If we consider Thompson to be a utilitarian at this point in his life, we have to consider him in the broader utilitarian tradition, and what exactly that means in the history of education. According to David Wardle,

> [t]hinkers of this school are often referred to as 'utilitarians' because when considering the value of an institution they asked the question, 'what use is it?' The test applied was that an institution ... contributed to 'the greatest happiness of the greatest number', and 'happiness' was generally inter-preted rather crudely as physical well-being. Clearly this was a reforming doctrine and was particularly destructive when applied at the beginning of the nineteenth century to many institutions which had little to recommend them but a long history. (Wardle, 1970: 3)

Though Thompson can be categorised as a utilitarian on the above grounds, he was to wholeheartedly break with utilitarianism as his ideas progressed towards utopian socialism. It is not always easy to understand how one of the earliest theorists of democratic socialism could have been aligned so closely with the utilitarian project, as this position clearly had its blind-spots. Eric Hobsbawm, succinctly, if caustically, encapsulates the difficulties of utilitarianism:

> Arithmetic was the fundamental tool of the Industrial Revolution. Its makers saw it as a series of sums of addition and subtraction: the difference in cost between buying in the cheapest market and selling in the dearest, between cost of production and sale price, between investment and return. For Jeremy Bentham and his followers, the most consistent champions of this type of rationality, even morals and politics came under these simple calculations. ... The accountancy of humanity would produce its debit and credit balances, like that of business. (Hobsbawm, 1987: 79)

It is not unreasonable to surmise that Thompson and Bentham had different notions of what exactly was meant by 'the greatest number'. It became clear through his later writings that Thompson saw the greatest number being near the total population of a community, as that community was to be built on agreed policies and would be joined voluntarily only by those who thought similarly. Bentham's greatest number could be as little as fifty-one per cent of a population, as it was concerned not with building a new society but establishing a seemingly democratic apparatus in a distinctly undemocratic world. However, Thompson's *Inquiry* of 1824 (discussed below) 'marked an advance from Benthamite thought towards socialism' (Simon, 1960: 204).

The subjects which Thompson believed should be taught in the Cork Institution were listed under 'six general heads of knowledge' and divided into moral and physical sciences. The moral sciences included ethics, the political sciences and general literature; the physical sciences encompassed natural history, natural philosophy, chemistry and agriculture. He went on to point out that only two chairs were then filled (natural philosophy and chemistry) and that the committee should immediately fill the other vacancies, and reminded them of their purpose as proprietors of the Institution:

> The object of your Institution is not to make linguists, nor mathematicians, nor astronomers nor antiquarian dilettanti, but to make useful citizens for active life, to make intelligent & respectable, & let me add benevolent, tradesmen & merchants & country gentlemen, and to make their wives and daughters equally intelligent, respectable and useful. (Thompson, 1818b: 16 May)

Summarised here is his vision of education's purpose: to prepare 'citizens for active life'. The benefits of this utilitarian education are not ephemeral or aesthetic but are grounded in normal commercial activity. He is not blind to the non-industrialised Ireland of his time, however, and seeks to include agriculture and country-living among the areas that will be catered for in this view of education. A further (and perhaps more surprising for its time) inclusionary measure is his unequivocal recognition of the place of the 'wives and daughters' of these intelligent and respectable citizens. This is his earliest plea for sexual equality in education and is a precursor to much of his later work in which he outlines a complete rationale for viewing women as 'citizens' with all the legal, financial and social rights accorded to men, while also arguing for an extensive revisioning of the rights of all human beings, from all classes.

Much of the letter is taken up with rebukes to the committee of the Cork Institution regarding the mismanagement of funds and the tendency to lose sight of the true purpose of such a centre of learning. Thompson is quick to see bourgeois ideas take hold and warns:

> Keep always, Gentlemen, steadily in your eye the whole map of useful infor-
> mation and let no subordinate district, however endeared to you by early
> association, or attractive in its present pursuit, distract your minds from
> those extensive empires of science which every young man and woman,
> that wishes to share the civilization and happiness which the 19th century
> can cheaply give, should be familiarly acquainted. (Thompson, 1818b: 16
> May)

Having listed the subjects he wished to see provided, he went on to make 'a few observations' on moral philosophy, general literature, natural philosophy, chemistry and agriculture. It is possible to see keywords emerging: 'practical' of course is one, 'happiness' is another. Through his language his utilitarian credentials are firmly in place:

> Moral philosophy I would make practically useful, would apply its original
> principles to practice in all the details of life, would show that the ways of
> virtue, and of every particular virtue, are the ways of pleasantness, would
> justify with Paley the ways of God to man, and from the tendency of every
> moral command, which is known to produce human happiness of mankind
> must guide us where no positive precept is given ... But not a word of the
> principles of Locke, or Paley, or any other author would I quote which
> could clash in the remotest degree with the peculiarities of faith or doctrine
> of any religious sect. (Thompson, 1818b: 16 May)

The efforts to teach ethics in a scientific way, that is, without recourse to religious zealotry, had been a touchstone of scientific and radical education going back to the Lunar Society. Thompson was part of this tradition, but his argument for the inclusion of moral science in the curriculum of the Cork Institution had been misunderstood, or had been used to discredit him in some way. He was himself without religious belief and was an avowed secularist, but there is a hint here that he may have been considered in con-travention of the bye-laws of the Institution which prevented any discussion of religion or politics:

> Hincks [the founder of the Institution] had decided to keep the Institution
> free of political and religious rancour, and it was to this that he attributed
> the widespread support that he enjoyed at its initiation. 'We have persons
> of all religions amongst us, Protestants, Catholics, Presbyterians and
> Quakers; in fact there is not a word ever mentioned about religion,' stated
> Thomas Cuthbert in evidence to the Commissioners of Irish Education in
> 1826. (*Freeman's Journal*, 19 May 1825 in Byrne, 1976: 53)

The 'dead languages' of Latin and Greek, the regular objects of radical rancour, came in for attack, this time with an added local dimension in the form of the 'commercial city' of Cork:

> How absurd that, in a commercial city, all the efforts at education should be directed and almost confined to the acquisition of a dead or even a living language, to the learning how to express by two or three combinations of letters those scanty ideas of folly, by the expression of which any one language, any one combination of letters would be disgraced. (Thompson, 1818b: 16 May)

Even if it is difficult to imagine the young merchant princes of Cork spending hours at their Latin when important commercial matters awaited them, Thompson finds himself in the company of most radical theorists in his castigation of the overwhelmingly classical curriculum. One can discern echoes of Edgeworth in his discussion of these subjects, often learned by rote with very little understanding on the part of the pupil:

> The principal defect in the present system of our great schools, is that they devote too large a portion of time to Latin and Greek. It is true, that the attainment of classical literature is highly desirable; but it should not, or rather need not, be the exclusive object of boys during eight or nine years. (Edgeworth cited in Lyons, 2003: 47)

Literature was seen by Thompson as a useful subject, in recreation. This type of learning has an added bonus in that it is a pleasure by means of which women and men may interact socially, as an alternative to the evenings 'spent in stupid disease: engendering gluttony or drinking, where ladies are savagely driven from table that men may without blushing, turn themselves into brutes' (Thompson, 1818b: 16 May). Thompson's 'improving' view of education is of course a cornerstone of the radical tradition, but his insistence on women's rights to education set him apart.

Natural philosophy and chemistry were subjects for which the Cork Institution had been very well appointed but Thompson insisted that all the materials and facilities in the world are worth nothing if the teaching is not of the highest standard:

> Burn the ... innumerable works on which dust is accumulating in your library on this universally amusing and instructive science, or make them useful by appointing an enlightened and really efficient lecturer to explain and invite attention to them. – Put up to auction your useless minerals, and shells, and insects, and fishes, and birds, or let mind be called forth and awakened by you to study their properties and uses. (Thompson, 1818b: 16 May)

Going beyond the subject in question, it is clear that in Thompson's view, to achieve high standards in teaching it is imperative that lecturers themselves always analyse their methodologies. He expressed very strong views on teachers at various points, at times valuing their contribution much less than other 'practical' professions, notably draughtsmanship. Education for him stemmed primarily from real, lived experience and instruction aimed at learning, not displays aimed at gratifying teachers' personal vanities.

His next letter was long and detailed, focusing on the management of the Institution. He advised on appointments and salaries, on timetabling and on various economising measures deemed necessary. A long passage is devoted to the advantages of students undergoing intensive learning while still living at home; boarding schools were described as wholly unsuited to the moral formation of young people.

> Who, that values the virtue, the sobriety, the health of his child, does not tremble at the dangers of sending a lad of 15 to 19, into a scene, much as all overgrown Colleges must present, where every temptation to extravagance, to sensuality and debauchery, in their most seductive forms of lying promise, awaits him ... By the union of a domestic abode and domestic guidance with the course of education pointed out, these deplorable evils would be avoided by means of the Cork Institution ... Let us not regret that our Institution aspires not to be a College: it will be more moral, it will be more useful. (Thompson, 1818b: 19 May)

Thompson clearly believed that day schools not only were cheaper and more efficient but also provided more moral and social instruction through the continued influence of parents and the general community. These views are in line with many commentators on education at this time. It was widely held that many of these boarding schools were centres of excessive discipline, poor management and insufficient moral authority.

Accounts of the debate within the Cork Institution appeared again on 21 May 1818, and another letter from Thompson was published on 23 May 1818. In this letter it is possible to feel his utter disbelief at the disrespect with which the management had greeted his objections, compounded by the fact that they were now pursuing further physical alterations to the building, thereby reducing even further the amount of money available for truly 'useful' purposes. Thompson believed that the ordering of such work directly contravened the constitution of the Cork Institution, which set out that only necessary renovations or improvements be made, and in his opinion, this was clearly not a necessary development. In a letter published on 26 May 1818, Thompson directly confronts John Lecky, manager of the Cork Institution, regarding Lecky's questioning of Thompson's credentials and consequent silencing of him and his objections at a meeting of the proprietors. Thompson became almost emotional at the implied slight on his character and for the first time personalised the debate. He accused him of gross mismanagement of public funds and of a 'jobs for the boys' approach to lectureships.

On 28 May 1818 Thompson addressed a letter to the Chief Secretary for Ireland, Robert Peel, which constitutes the lengthy dedication to the pamphlet in published form. In it he recounts his misgivings about the running of the Institution and asks the Chief Secretary to withhold the annual grant if the administrators are not held to account. His confidence in the abilities of Peel and his judiciary are evident:

> For all the details I refer you, Sir, to the following pages; and have the honour to be, with sincere respect for your attention to the internal economy of Ireland, and anxious anticipation of future practical resources of usefulness, expected from you; – particularly the arrangement of our minor sessions, judicature, diffusing a cheap and frequent, and accessible administration of justice thro' the country, to improve and humanize the people, and interest them in the execution, by affording them the protection, of the laws. (Thompson, 1818b: 28 May)

It is surprising to find Thompson so complimentary towards a member of the ruling class, as his work is generally much more suspicious of the motives of those who govern, but it is interesting to see how his views were subject to change over the years.

Further accounts are provided of the machinations of the committee in subsequent editions of the *Reporter*, all drawing attention to the fact that meetings are taking place behind closed doors, where no journalist is allowed. Consequently, reports were based on information provided by anonymous sources. The letters from Thompson continued to appear over the next weeks, mostly expanding on points already made or replying to issues raised in the *in camera* meetings of the committee as reported by the newspaper. In them he enlarges on his views on the subjects listed earlier and refutes the contentions of the committee that: 'the people of Cork and the South of Ireland had no need of moral Philosophy'; 'General Literature, and Rhetoric and Elocution had nothing to do with science'; and 'there would be no pupils to attend such lectures'. On the latter question he announced on 5 November 1818:

> To supply this supposed deficiency of pupils, it is proposed to establish in Cork, the beginning of the ensuing year 1819, a Day School, on an enlarged plan of instruction, for the children of the middling and higher classes of society. (Thompson, 1818b: 5 November)

This 'New Juvenile Institution' was proposed as a place where children 'beginning from 7 to 12 and ending from 14 to 18 years of age' can attend for basic education before going on to benefit from the specialised scientific education provided at the Cork Institution. It would, of course, be open to boys and girls and the '"means" of conveying such a body of useful elementary knowledge ... will be found in the admirable system ... of Dr. Bell and Mr. Lancaster, and the many judicious improvements of Miss Edgeworth' (Thompson, 1818b: 5 November). There was to be no corporal punishment in the school. Bell and Lancaster, well known for their adoption of the monitorial system, were also initiators of alternatives to corporal punishment, resulting in ticket and rank systems of reward. However, the punishments meted out alongside these reward systems were of sufficient degree to be deemed crimes today, and many were abandoned, but corporal punishment continued to be the norm in most schools for at least another century.

Like Robert Owen who advocated a humanitarian approach in his infant schools, Thompson was at least a century ahead of his time in relation to the vision of education he espoused, and in highlighting the failure of the state to reach anything like that vision in terms of provision for both boys and girls, choice of subjects and facilities. If one takes adult education into account, it would take even longer for the state to recognise the need or desirability of educating those who had been failed by the system in their formative years.

According to Pankhurst (1991: 8), 'what Thompson desired was an institute which would provide an education nearly equivalent to that of a modern secondary school, but which would also devote attention to the social sciences and the ethics of citizenship'. Thompson planned to open the school in 1819 as soon as fifty pupils were registered to attend, but as with many of the practical attempts at fulfilling his educational vision, the school never materialised. His plans did, however, form the impetus for contacting Jeremy Bentham, and that connection helped Thompson to refine his views on education and other matters in subsequent years, though he did outgrow his mentor in many ways.

Thompson's later works

In 1824, the year after his visit to Bentham, Thompson published his *Inquiry into the Principles of the Distribution of Wealth*. As described by Dooley, the *Inquiry*

> includes detailed arguments for a philosophy of labor and a sustained cri-
> tique of wealth; critiques of political economists; searing commentary on
> the negative impact of many social institutions in the task of disseminating
> knowledge to all people. In this 1824 work we also get Thompson's first
> detailed proposals for the formation of small communities of mutual co-
> operation. (Dooley, 1997: 27, n 21)

The *Inquiry* is his best-known publication and runs, in the original edition, to six hundred pages. It was adopted as a fundamental textbook in political economy by the co-operative movement, and established Thompson as one of that movement's leading theoreticians. As Pankhurst (1991: 17) asserts, the *Inquiry* 'revealed that in Thompson the Co-operative Movement had acquired a leader who equalled Owen in stature and who offered a refreshingly democratic alternative to the latter's rather arrogant and often dictatorial lead'. Its basic thesis, the overhaul of wealth distribution in favour of the producers of the wealth, the working classes, was well received by co-operators, but it also makes clear that a revised vision of society was necessary, where women were seen as full and equal citizens. The belief in equality lies at the heart of Thompson's philosophy. This belief is extended in all directions, and encompasses the contested terrains of class and gender. A fundamental and unshakeable belief in the injustice of inequality between rich and poor is embedded in all his work, and he is supported in this endeavour by a great body of literature emanating from radical philosophy and the co-operative movement.

On equality for women, he and his close friend and colleague, Anna Doyle Wheeler, were on lonelier terrain. Their *Appeal* of 1825 is the culmination of a close friendship and sharing of ideas, particularly on the treatment of women in society. Dooley (1996: 17) outlines how the *Appeal* 'is the first detailed statement of socialist feminism'. The title page tells us that it was written 'in reply to a paragraph of Mr. Mill's celebrated "article on government"'. That article was utilitarian James Mill's treatise *On Government* (1819–20), in which he denied the need for universal suffrage on the grounds that 'women, children and idiots' did not need to be part of the electoral process as their needs would be met by male relatives who would use their votes in the best interests of those dependent on them. Wheeler and Thompson were outraged that these views could be promulgated by a utilitarian (who should believe in the greatest happiness for the greatest number), and were deeply disappointed that fellow disciples remained silent on this immensely important matter. The *Appeal* is their joint response, even though, ironically, Thompson is the only named author.

The *Appeal* is an exercise in democracy in its construction and in its content. At a time when Irish society was governed by a few landed and moneyed families, and indeed by the male lineage within these families, it provided a radical statement in support of women's rights, and by extension in human rights. Continuing in the vein of Wollstonecraft's *A Vindication of the Rights of Woman* (1792), it placed sexual equality centre-stage in the attempts at societal reform being made by the likes of Robert Owen, who disagreed with Thompson and Wheeler on issues relating to marriage and women's rights (Dooley, 1996: 50).

Another of Thompson's later texts, *Labor Rewarded* (1827), is revolutionary in its vision of oppression and how society should be reorganised on the basis of equality, with capitalism being replaced by co-operative communism. It was undertaken as a rebuttal of Thomas Hodgskin's *Labour Defended*, which propounded the free market view of economics combined with various reforms to better the conditions of the poor. Tackling every aspect of the unfair society in which he lived, Thompson's work of political economy was a more accessible work than the *Inquiry*, and it laid down his vision of a democratically controlled society organised as a collection of co-operative communities, or communes, where every citizen would be equal. Religion would be tolerated, as a democratic society would not outlaw it, but the existing form of marriage would be radically revised to guarantee the equality of men and women. Education would be available to all, and each citizen would partake in the democratic process. Remuneration would be equal no matter what the type of job, and a classless society was the ideal espoused.

Thompson explained that the greatest trend visible in early eighteenth-century society was the transformation of a society based on a domestic economy to one governed by competitive capitalism, but he was no Luddite. Ever open to the progress of science, he believed that technology could be harnessed to help the working classes gain more freedoms from the toil to which they were subjected by fate of birth.

In *Labor Rewarded* Thompson 'provides a sketch of an ideal system of government which aimed at obtaining the maximum of freedom with the minimum of coercion and bureaucracy' (Pankhurst, 1991: 80). He outlined a blueprint for democratic representation within the commune, and from there the province, the state and national legislatures where every holder of official office would be answerable to universal suffrage.

Having elaborated on the new society which would emerge after the adoption of co operative principles in the organisation of society, Thompson turned in his last publication to the intricacies of such a world. An 'amazing work', *Practical Directions* (1830) was

> filled with a thousand and one pieces of information carefully arranged and indexed. There are arguments for Co-operation and against competitive Capitalism; 'practical directions' for communities discussed with infinite care and an almost incredible attention to detail; estimates of the time required to complete each stage of the project, production targets, lists of necessary machinery with their prices and recommended suppliers, monthly instructions for gardening, crop rotation, and other agricultural work; dietary tables showing the comparative value of divers foods, and an examination of the theory and practice of earlier communities with reasons for their success and failure. (Pankhurst, 1991: 101)

Underscoring once again the importance of democracy as a means of running society, he categorically stated that all adult members and 'children capable of forming an opinion' should agree to any deviations from the adopted plan once a community had been established.

With the publication of *Practical Directions* Thompson and Owen once again differed, this time on the subject of the commencement of building communities and on some elements of their running once formed. The co-operative experiment at Ralahine in County Clare had been visited by Thompson, and he was encouraged to find that a community could be established along the lines he had envisaged. Despite the difficulties in the Owenite experiments at New Harmony, New Lanark and Orbiston, Thompson was adamant that Owen should not prevent new communities from being initiated. The co-operative community voted with Thompson at the third Co-operative Congress of 1832 and Thompson offered his lands at Rosscarbery in West Cork if the members wished to make use of them.

Thompson died before any substantial effort could be made in Rosscarbery. The chest ailment that had afflicted him for most of his life finally could be resisted no more. Despite his well-known rejection of religion his funeral was conducted according to normal Anglican rites, and he was buried in a churchyard near Glandore. When his will was read it was found to contain strict instructions that no religious ceremony be held, and that his body be donated to medical science. Thereafter he wished his skeleton to be donated to the museum of the first established co-operative community in Britain or Ireland. These were not the only wishes of his that were not carried out. The will also instructed that after making an annual allowance to Anna Doyle Wheeler, the bulk of his estate was to be assigned to the co-operative movement.

> Funds were to be lent to assist the establishment of communities, and to reprint the *Appeal*, *Labor Rewarded* and the whole or such parts of the *Inquiry* as his trustees might 'deem most useful.' Shares in Co-operative communities were to be purchased and given to 'industrious persons, particularly young females' who could not otherwise afford to enter. (Pankhurst, 1991: 130)

Thompson's family did not share his political views and were not about to let go of what they perceived to be their rightful inheritance. They contested the will first on the grounds of insanity, which was later retracted, then on those of bankruptcy, and even on the grounds of immorality. A legal battle ensued for twenty-five years, at the end of which the main beneficiaries seem to have been the lawyers.

Thompson's legacy

As Thompson's will was contested so too has his intellectual legacy been the subject of debate in the works of political and economic theorists and commentators. James Connolly, the Irish socialist and republican leader, was certain of the place of Thompson in the history of socialism. In *Labour in Irish History* (see Chapter 3 by Fintan Lane) he described Thompson as 'an original thinker, a pioneer of Socialist thought superior to any of the Utopian Socialists of the Continent, and long ante-dating Karl Marx in his insistence upon the subjection of labour as the cause of all social misery, modern crime and political dependence, as well as in his searching analysis of the true definition of capital' (Connolly, 1922: 110–11). Of Marx, Connolly concluded that Thompson anticipated him in 'most of his analyses of the economic system' (Connolly, 1922: 116), but he believed that putting the two in competition did neither justice: 'Rather we should say that the relative position of this Irish genius and of Marx are best comparable to the historical relations of the pre-Darwinian evolutionists to Darwin' (Connolly, 1922: 117).

In his biography of William Thompson, Richard Pankhurst reinstated him in the history of Irish political thought and made the case for 'one of the two outstanding leaders in the Co-operative Movement in these islands, from which the Socialist ideal had its birth': 'He anticipated Marx in many of his theories, and even coined some of the definitions and terminology of politico-economic phenomena which the 'founder of scientific socialism' subsequently employed' (Pankhurst, 1991: 1). Other commentators take a different view of Thompson's influence on Marx. Cormac Ó Gráda (1983: 193) believes that Thompson 'must have been an exceptional individual, at once respected, if not revered, by the London circle of utilitarian philosophers, and idolized by the labourers and smallholders of Glandore and Rosscarbery. However, while his works continue to be studied and reissued, his influence on later social thinking, particularly that of Karl Marx, has been somewhat exaggerated'. Another commentator, Terry Eagleton, contends that

> Thompson can be seen as the founding father of the so-called Dublin school of nineteenth-century economics, which unlike its English counterpart refused to abstract a skeletal entity called 'the economy' from its complex embedment in social, cultural and spiritual life. And where Thompson is immeasurably Marx's superior is in his feminism. *An Appeal* ... is a magnificent work of political theory and polemic, in the finest traditions of the radical Enlightenment. (Eagleton, 2000: 80–8)

Even though Pankhurst's biography was first published in 1954, Thompson and Wheeler's feminist tract, the *Appeal*, was 'still largely understudied despite their anticipations of so much in contemporary feminist debate' (Dooley, 1997: 5). Dolores Dooley has placed this work on the international agenda with her work in reissuing the *Appeal* and with her critical study of that same volume.

Thompson's legacy to social science more generally is less contested, as it is more widely accepted that the very term 'social science' is his invention.

> For Owenite political thought, the most significant concept to be derived from the vocabulary was 'social science', which by the 1830s became synonymous with a socialist programme generally. Probably first introduced into English in the Irish Owenite William Thompson's main work, *An Inquiry into the Principles of the Distribution of Wealth Most Conducive to Human Happiness* (1824), 'social science' carried a distinctly Owenite connotation in many quarters until well into the 1840s, when it gradually took on the more neutral meaning of the largely statistical examination of civil society which would be popularised by the Social Science association. (Claeys, 1989: 61)

One of the great benefits of reading *Practical Education*, Thompson's first publication, is the impression one gets of him. He was a committed idealist striving to reform an organisation as a means to establishing long-term change in the provision of education in Cork and its environs. His knowledge of educational matters ran deep, and his political outlook, while still in development, was firmly rooted in the radical tradition. He did not draw a veil around disagreements with his peers and was willing to incur the wrath of the respectable middle classes (his natural social circle), while uncovering what he considered to be cosy little arrangements in the running of a publicly-funded body. He took the position of observer and reporter, as well as that of philosopher, which more or less guaranteed his outsider status. This single-mindedness would later provide him with another social circle in which he could feel more comfortable, but that would necessitate travel abroad and correspondence with many leading radicals and reformers. It would not, however, be the last time he showed the courage to follow a different path from that expected of him.

Thompson's work forms a link in the chain of radical politics which challenged firmly held views of human nature and society. This radicalism was based on a belief that people are formed by the world in which they live; if the circumstances of a person are improved, so too is the person. The importance of science and scientific education was high up the agenda of this radical enlightenment movement, as was the need to develop a secular morality. These views provided a direct challenge to the political, economic and religious establishment and formed part of a vision of a democratic and egalitarian future. One can see many reflections of these beliefs in the efforts of those who strive to provide alternatives to the state- and church-controlled education systems in Ireland that have remained largely unchanged since the introduction of the national school system to Ireland in 1831, two years prior to William Thompson's death.

The period 1818–30, from the time of William Thompson's first publication to his last, was a time of horrendous poverty and suffering for many people in Britain and Ireland. Thompson, along with other radicals and reformers, could see a correlation between a lack of education and the ability to live a life well. He believed that education, along with changes in people's material circumstances, could enhance and improve people's lives immeasurably, and he devoted his life to developing both practical solutions and a theoretical framework to allow this happen. Whether he was successful in his endeavours is debatable: beyond the basics of material improvements in individual lives, one can ask if Thompson and his radical co-workers were successful in presenting alternative views of how people might live. In *Industry and Empire* Hobsbawm addresses these pertinent questions:

> Whether the Industrial Revolution gave most Britons absolutely or relatively more and better food, clothes and housing is naturally of interest to every historian. But he will miss much of its point if he forgets that it was not merely a process of addition and subtraction, but a *fundamental social change*. It transformed the lives of men and women beyond recognition. Or, to be more exact, in its initial stages it destroyed their old ways of living and left them free to discover or make for themselves new ones, if they could and knew how. But it rarely told them how to set about it. (Hobsbawm, 1987: 80)

Thompson was interested in 'more and better food, clothes and housing'. He was also interested in science and secularism, agriculture and atheism, labour and industry, profit and reward, sexual equality and class indistinction. In short, he was interested in 'fundamental social change', and was one of the rare few who actually addressed the question of 'how to set about it'.

In tracing the connection between Thompson and the radical tradition in education, perennial questions surrounding the ability of education to change society remain of the utmost importance. Surveying the period from the Corresponding Societies in the 1790s, through to the Owenite socialist and the Chartist movements in the late 1830s and 1840s, Brian Simon believes that

> whole generations of working people (or at least their leading representatives) educated themselves, in many cases consciously, in order the more effectively to transform society – the outer world – to their desires. (Simon, 1985: 20)

Thompson was part of this tradition, and therefore is part of the history of education both in Britain and in Ireland, and he deserves to be better known for his work in developing alternative visions of education, as well as for his more widely known contribution to economics, social science and his more recently rediscovered work on feminism.

From this short consideration of Thompson we find evidence of his wide engagement with early nineteenth-century radical politics. His analysis of the society created by the industrial revolution began with a strong connection with Bentham and utilitarianism, but gradually left strict utilitarianism behind in a search for a more thorough reorganisation of society, in the form of co-operative socialism. Not content to be a mere Owenite, he surpassed Robert Owen to become a leading theorist in his own right. He was widely known and respected by members of the mechanics' institutes and was a frequent contributor to their journals. He constantly encouraged efforts at self- and social improvement and was known to show support to striking workers and other movements aimed at the amelioration of poverty and injustice. His extensive philanthropy was not simply a nineteenth-century case of 'cheque-book socialism' but was part of his overall philosophy of social change. His feminism was integral to his vision of an egalitarian future.

Practical Education for the South of Ireland, as well as Thompson's later works – all of which elaborated his views on the value of education – also reflect the developing views on how education should be provided, and for whom. His valuing of democracy in education places him in the long tradition of radical educationalists who promoted the complete overhaul of the classical education system, which in their eyes benefited only the idle aristocracy. Beginning with the Cork Institution arguments, we see a persistent belief in the value of universal and lifelong education, and of the central importance of education in the new society created through the redistribution of wealth. Adult education is central to this plan, as it is only possible to create this societal change through education. Education will be changed, but education is first required to bring that change about.

Practical Education for the South of Ireland is mostly ignored and under-valued. It suffers from having a focus that is not as 'hard' as economics nor as imaginative as the commune and so has not been the subject of much comment by academics or activists, as Thompson's œuvre is seen almost exclusively in economic or feminist terms. What one gets from a reading of Thompson that puts an emphasis on education, is how vital education is to any attempt at societal change. Education leads to greater decision-making abilities, greater inclusion and therefore greater participation in democratic frameworks. Maybe the greatest value in re-reading *Practical Education* is regaining such a simple wisdom. One cannot draw direct parallels with contemporary education provision and that espoused by Thompson (who was writing in the era before state provision), but certainly his idea of 'cheap and useful' education can be adapted to fit current needs. In Ireland 'free' education should fulfil his criterion of 'cheap', but every family is aware of the true cost of sending children to school, from transport to books to exam fees. The extent of third-level attainment by working-class students raises the question of who benefits most from so-called free education. One area that does come close to his ideal is seen in the recent developments in the adult education sector and the emphasis on 'lifelong learning'. Programmes such as the Vocational Training Opportunities Scheme provide life-changing opportunities to people in receipt of social welfare, albeit in very limited numbers. Such schemes combine practical subjects, chosen for their relevance to the current jobs climate (and so 'useful' in Thompson's terms), with education basics using materials chosen to reflect the students' own life experiences, resulting in an enriched experience that is sometimes greatly at odds with students' earlier experiences of the education system. The relationships between participants and teachers in this type of education often challenge the idea of the teacher as controller and supplant it with the idea of teacher as collaborator and facilitator. Mainstream secondary education has much to learn in term of tailoring the system to individual needs and could well look to the adult education sector for guidance. This is the sector of modern education which owes much to mechanics' institutes and worker-led provision, with which Thompson and his theoretical descendants had many ties. More directly, Thompson has consistently inspired activists, from the co-operators to the present day. The William Thompson School was inaugurated in 1999 as a forum for left-wing writers, artists and activists to help cultivate a culture of opposition in the moribund political climate of Celtic Tiger era Ireland. Its educational and practical focus would have suited Thompson well.

The entirety of Thompson's philosophy and his practical guidelines for establishing a new society can usefully be examined through the lens of his education philosophy and practice, which as we have seen began with a local row, in his home town of Cork.

Notes

1 The full title of the pamphlet (which is a collection of the *Southern Reporter* letters with a long dedication to Robert Peel) is: *Practical Education for the South of Ireland in Letters Addressed to the Proprietors of the Cork Institution on the Propriety and Necessity of Directing its Funds to their Proper Object, the Diffusion of Knowledge, by a Useful and Practical System of Education, Applying Science to the Common Purposes of Life* (Cork: West and Coldwells, 1818). This publication was thought to be lost, but following the publication of her *Equality in Community*, Dolores Dooley was sent a copy by a gentleman from Japan. Dolores Dooley has very kindly sent me a photocopy of the text, for which I am immensely grateful. In this discussion I refer to the *Southern Reporter* letters because they are accessible to researchers and the newspaper contains extra material.

3

James Connolly's *Labour in Irish History*
Fintan Lane

Where O where is our James Connolly
Where O where is that gallant man?

Patrick Galvin, *Irish Songs of Resistance* (1955)

Introduction

James Connolly (1868–1916) – Marxist, trade unionist, historian, separatist rebel against British rule and national martyr – is embedded in Irish popular consciousness, and there are few on the island of Ireland who have not heard of him, even if their understanding of the historical figure is often somewhat hazy or coloured by misconceptions. In Dublin, the important Amiens Street train station is named after him, while his oversized statue (he was, physically, a relatively small man) stands purposefully, left foot forward, gazing manfully into the distance in nearby Beresford Place, where he regularly addressed street meetings at the end of the nineteenth century. Throughout the Republic of Ireland, several hospitals, bridges, streets and trade union halls carry his name, and popular folk ballads memorialise and mythologise a man who is simultaneously embraced as a forefather by the revolutionary left, the mild-mannered Labour Party and the neo-liberal Fianna Fáil party of government. Connolly is a cultural chattel of modern Ireland, a metonym for integrity and humanitarianism, but generally emptied of his subversive anti-bourgeois purpose.

Moreover, the southern Irish state officially reveres Connolly – a signatory of the 1916 Easter Proclamation – as one of its 'founding fathers', and respect for his memory is encouraged. Indeed, the elaborate statue in Dublin was ceremoniously unveiled in May 1996 by none other than Mary Robinson, the incumbent president of Ireland. Reverence is evident also in some quarters of the radical left to the extent that outrage was expressed by many leftists when on May Day in 2005 a group of young anarchists, part of a Reclaim the Streets demonstration, scrawled graffiti on the base of the statue at Beresford Place and – presumably to improve his revolutionary street cred – temporarily transformed Connolly into a Subcomandante Marcos look-alike by dressing him with a balaclava.[1] It is unlikely that much planning or theoretical discourse preceded the anarchist action, which seems to have been spontaneous, but it emblematically represented the disjunction between those political activists who live primarily in the moment, with a limited sense of the past, and those who lean heavily – sometimes to the point of dogmatic piety – on inspirational historical precedents and selected progenitors. In practice, of course, many leftist activists find a middle ground, where the past is drawn on to deepen one's understanding of the contemporary.

Connolly, from the outset, was firmly among those who saw history as an important political weapon, and throughout his life he referred to historical events in order to undermine political and class opponents; his approach to history-writing was instrumental and always that of an engagé. Born in Scotland to Catholic Irish parents, he had a strong sense of his Irish identity by his late teens at least, although, to his later embarrassment, his first visit to the country seems to have been as a soldier in the British army, which he joined as a 14-year-old and deserted in late 1888 (Nevin, 2005: 15–17).[2] In 1890, he married Lillie Reynolds, a working-class Irish Protestant he had met while serving in Ireland, and six years later moved to live in Dublin; Connolly underplayed his Scottish background and in fact deliberately misled friends and census takers by telling them that he was born in Ireland (Lane, 2000: 104).[3] It was a white lie, but one that accentuates his preoccupation with 'race', nationality and the components of a putatively authentic Irishness. This preoccupation almost certainly animated his public and familial adherence to Catholicism, despite private religious doubts, and his concealment of his years as a British soldier.

By the time he arrived in Dublin in 1896, he was an experienced social radical, profoundly influenced by Marxism, and determined to recast the tiny local socialist movement as a substantial player in Irish political life, but not as an 'anti-national' force: the name of organisation he established – the Irish Socialist Republican Party (ISRP) – contained the important words 'Irish' and 'republican', signifiers that alerted activists to its separatist intent. Connolly's interfusion of republicanism and Marxist class politics marked a sharp departure from the ideas articulated by Irish socialists during the 1880s and early 1890s when the national question was believed to be of little importance for the working class (Lane, 1997). Indeed, even the pro-home rule Independent Labour Party (ILP), which established Irish branches in the mid-1890s, was wary of entanglement with the nationalist movement, and its members in Dublin, Belfast and Waterford focused primarily on social issues (Lane, 1997: 192–209). Connolly, of course, in arguing for separatism was demanding something far more radical than the limited autonomy suggested by home rule: unlike the Irish home rulers and their supporters in the ILP, Connolly and his ISRP were advocating a complete break with the British Empire, and it is this – his anti-imperialism – that remained the dominant leitmotif of his political thought until his execution by a British firing squad in 1916.

The production of *Labour in Irish History*

Connolly's most significant and longest written work, *Labour in Irish History*, retains a central position in the canon of Irish socialist literature and was read assiduously by leftists until at least the 1980s; it became less important as a reference point for left-wing political activists in the 1990s and early twenty-first century, but is still treated widely with something approaching piety. A sociopolitical history of working-class radicalism in Ireland, with a pronounced emphasis on the eighteenth and nineteenth centuries, Connolly's book deployed the past to legitimate and naturalise his melding of socialism and Irish separatism – his 'hibernicisation of Marxism', as Bernard Ransom memorably termed it (Ransom, 1980: 7). As revolutionary literature and historiographical text, redolent of the possibilities of its time, it is treated very seriously by many socialists today when they engage in political analyses of the Irish past; moreover, the template it established greatly influenced later socialist historical polemics, most notably Peter Berresford Ellis's socialist-republican study, *A History of the Irish Working Class* (1972), explicitly described in its preface as 'no more than an attempt at expansion and updating' of Connolly's 'classic of Marxist literature' (Ellis, 1972: 9).[4] Indeed, it was Ellis's fidelity to Connolly's focus on working-class participation in a centuries-old national liberation struggle against British imperialism that ensured the popularity and wide circulation of his book among left-leaning Irish republicans in the 1970s and 1980s.

Although published in 1910, *Labour in Irish History* had its genesis in the late 1890s and its political kernel is consistent with positions that Connolly had articulated for many years. The genealogy of the book has been traced by Aindrias Ó Cathasaigh, who has highlighted its initial manifestation in 1898 as a series of articles in the *Workers' Republic* – the weekly newspaper of the ISRP – which was reprinted and added to intermittently in British, American and Irish socialist newspapers up to 1910; it seems that the bulk of the series was penned in the years 1898 and 1908–10 (Ó Cathasaigh, 2002: 103–5). According to Ó Cathasaigh, it is certain that, as early as 1898, Connolly 'envisaged the series becoming a book: only three weeks in, he is referring to "the preceding chapter" rather than the preceding article', an important point that impels the reader to consider the text as an integrated whole and not as a collection of disconnected newspaper articles (Ó Cathasaigh, 2002: 103). His efforts to have his work published as a book began in earnest in September 1909, while he was living in the United States and working as a national organiser for the Socialist Party of America; however, his correspondence at that time with his friend and comrade William O'Brien indicates that he was focused on the effect of the book in Ireland and was writing primarily for an Irish audience:

> The American publishers are ridiculously conservative, and will not touch that kind of book. I could get it published by Kerr & Co. of Chicago, but they would only reach the Socialist public, and another publisher who has

offered to handle it is only a new publisher and might not make good. My
desire is to get it published by some publisher who could reach the Irish
public in Ireland, and also in Great Britain.[5]

Connolly requested O'Brien, a leading figure in the recently formed Socialist
Party of Ireland, to persuade his fellow party member and writer Francis
Sheehy Skeffington to approach a suitable London publisher, partly because
it 'would be hopeless to expect an Irish publisher to handle it.'

> If he did, his introduction would go a long way to secure a reading and
> perhaps acceptance. Should the book be published on your side of the
> water, it would make a sensation, help to arouse attention on the Socialist
> position and also help to solve the economic problem for yours truly. If I
> cannot get it published there, I will get it published here but it will not be
> nearly as effective for propaganda purposes amongst our working class in
> Ireland as it would be if published in London. You can see that.
>
> It would be a great favour to me if you would do this *speedily*. Of course,
> tell our comrade that I do not ask him to endorse the book, but only to
> recommend it as a contribution to an unexploited side of Irish history and
> literature.[6]

What is most immediately striking about this letter is Connolly's political
purpose; his reference to the book as an intellectual achievement that breaks
new ground and explores 'an unexploited side of Irish history and literature'
is mostly in the context of a sales pitch to prospective publishers. Connolly
was not approaching Irish history as a disinterested scholar but as a political activist whose research was a probe for evidence of bourgeois perfidy
and who saw his book as one part of a campaign to draw large numbers of
people into the Irish socialist movement; the ambition of his vision is clear
from his desire to mainstream socialist ideas. In 1914, in a letter to the
prominent writer and artist George Russell ('AE'), he described his book
bluntly as 'a propagandist venture'.[7]

In the end, Connolly failed to secure a London publisher and, contrary
to his initial pessimism, it was in Dublin that the book was brought out.
Labour in Irish History appeared in early November 1910 under the imprint
of Maunsel & Co. of Middle Abbey Street, a firm that held the rights to
plays produced in the Abbey Theatre and published the work of several
leading figures of the Irish literary revival, including W. B. Yeats, George
Moore, Lady Augusta Gregory and John Millington Synge (Share, 2003:
701). Interestingly, at the time Connolly's book came out, Maunsel & Co.
– in the person of its managing director George Roberts – was engaged in
a now-famous dispute with the emergent writer James Joyce, which ended
rather badly. Joyce had sent them the manuscript of *Dubliners* in 1907,
but – following lengthy negotiations – Maunsel & Co. pulped the book
in 1912 prior to publication (Share, 2003: 701). Remarkably, as he was
happy to issue Connolly's social revolutionary tract, Roberts wrote to Joyce
in December 1910, a month after *Labour in Irish History* was published,
to object to negative depictions of the British king, Edward VII, and his

mother in the story 'Ivy Day': it was one thing to call for the overthrow of the Crown and quite another to fictively refer to the monarch's mother as a 'bloody old bitch' and claim Edward to be 'fond of his glass of grog and ... a bit of rake' (Ellmann, 1982: 310, 313–15).

Labour in Irish History was unimposing as a physical object: it was a small hardcover, pocket-sized book containing some 231 pages of text (including the foreword), bulked up through the use of thick paper – Fred Ryan, the proofreader, thought the volume 'particularly small and close packed'.[8] Ryan, aware that a book as cultural product is more than the words it contains, feared that its understated physicality could cause it to be taken less seriously than it deserved – a book is not simply a text; it has corporeal form that can limit or facilitate access to the words within. More importantly, only 200 copies were printed, which meant, of course, that it was not going to reach anything approaching a mass readership; in fact, most of the copies – at least 157 – were sold in advance, primarily to individuals already connected to the socialist movement.[9] Moreover, the relatively high price of two shillings and six pence ensured that few copies of the book would end up in the hands of unskilled workers.[10] This latter problem was not resolved until December 1914 when Maunsel & Co. issued a cheap one-shilling edition.[11]

Revising the past

The 'sensation' that Connolly had predicted his book would create failed to materialise and was scarcely likely from such a short print-run and narrow distribution. Indeed, the appearance of the book received little attention at the time, beyond the socialist and radical nationalist milieux. There were positive reviews in the mainstream *Irish Times* and *Freeman's Journal* and in the republican paper *Irish Freedom*, but it received a dismissive review in *Sinn Féin* (the organ of Arthur Griffith's Sinn Féin) (Nevin, 2005: 360). Nonetheless, within activist circles, Connolly's interpretation of Irish history provided a strong challenge to those who dissociated the problematics of national and social liberation. The political thrust of the book was twofold: it contained a vigorous assault on British imperialism, but, crucially, it also made difficult reading for the majority of nationalists because of its cold-eyed and hostile critique of the middle-class leadership of Irish nationalism, an elite that he harried and flayed through the decades, accusing them of betraying the Irish nation and, employing a biblical reference, of having 'bowed the knee to Baal' (Connolly, 1910: xiv). Connolly was claiming the leadership of the national movement for the working class.

The book has a conventional chronological structure, though episodic in approach, concentrating on key events and periods. Divided into sixteen short chapters, it opens, properly speaking, in the late seventeenth century, with Connolly arguing that modern Irish history began with 'the close of the Williamite Wars in the year 1691' and that the political and politico-religious divisions in Ireland in subsequent centuries must be traced back to the elite power struggle at that time between King James, a Catholic, and the successful Protestant claimant to his throne, William of Orange (Connolly, 1910: 9–10). In his attenuated description and analysis of the Irish Jacobites – the Catholics who supported King James – Connolly curtly dismisses the romanticised image that had been constructed in the nineteenth century by some nationalist propagandists and historians, in which Jacobite leaders, such as Patrick Sarsfield, had been cast as patriots and proto-nationalists. In Connolly's depiction, the Jacobite leaders are neither national heroes nor religious martyrs fighting the encroachments of foreign Protestantism but 'little better than traitors for their action in seducing the Irish people from their allegiance to the cause of their country's freedom to plunge them into a war on behalf of a foreign tyrant' (Connolly, 1910: 10–11); the fight to retain the throne for James was 'no earthly concern' of Irish Catholics, while the king himself is excoriated as 'one of the most worthless representatives of a worthless race that ever sat upon a throne' (Connolly, 1910: 10). Interestingly, however, Connolly is at pains to stress the bravery and 'undeniable patriotism' (Connolly, 1910: 12) of the rank-and-file, and this is a recurrent concept in the book: the honourable lower and working classes betrayed by the self-serving and traitorous middle and upper classes. For Irish nationalists, most of whom considered class divisions to be of little importance, Connolly's historical revisionism represented a serious challenge to their image of a people united, regardless of social differences, in pursuit of national liberation. 'Irish history', he wrote, 'has ever been written by the master class – in the interests of the master class', and his book was intended to present an alternative working-class perspective (Connolly, 1910: 2).

Nonetheless, in important ways, *Labour in Irish History* fits – albeit awkwardly – within the Irish nationalist historiographical tradition. This is most obvious in its privileging of moments and movements of resistance to British state power. Separatist and nationalist activities receive a great deal of attention and Irish history is presented as 800 years of intermittent revolt against foreign administration – 'the long drawn out struggle of Ireland' (Connolly, 1910: xiv) – while aspects of social life and class relations that were not linked directly to the national question are often absent. In fact, the chapters on the early socialist William Thompson and the Ralahine co-operative – though important – are exceptions to the general emphasis in the book, which did not aspire to be, as Connolly admitted, 'a history of labour in Ireland ... [but] rather a record of labour in Irish History', by which he meant a history of working-class involvement in political movements against British domination (Connolly, 1910: 197). Topics that receive particular attention include the Jacobites, the Volunteer movement of the 1780s, the United Irishmen, Robert Emmet, Daniel O'Connell, the Young Irelanders, Fenianism and, to a lesser extent, the Land League. In that sense, the book mirrors the concerns of nationalist narratives of the Irish past. However, in sharp contrast to those nationalist histories whose paradigm he adapted, Connolly emphatically highlighted class tensions within the nationalist tradition and, while positioning the working class as 'the incorruptible inheritors of the fight for freedom in Ireland', he condemned repeatedly the deleterious behaviour of the old Irish aristocracy and the middle class, who were characterised as either traitors to their 'race' and nation or compromisers who undermined the resolve of the national movement (Connolly, 1910: xiv). *Labour in Irish History* is heavily influenced by nationalist historiography but it is also a partial subversion of the genre.

Connolly directly contradicted many of the certitudes of nationalist historiography, especially those cherished by *constitutional* nationalists for whom he had little respect. Daniel O'Connell (1775–1847), the leader of the Catholic emancipation movement in the 1820s and, less consistently, of the Repeal campaign in the 1830s and 1840s, is a central figure in the pantheon of moderate Irish nationalism, an exemplar of fruitful non-violent, constitutional action, whose strategy has been counterposed frequently – though generally with little appreciation of its complexity – to the sometimes violent and often extra-legal activities of revolutionary nationalism; moreover, O'Connell has always been a favourite of those who linked Catholicism and nationalism in the Irish context. In *Labour in Irish History*, Connolly devoted a chapter to undermining O'Connell's reputation through a critical examination of his interaction with organised workers; never one to mince his words, he titled this section 'A Chapter of Horrors: Daniel O'Connell and the Working Class'. His method involved a mix of pathos and facts: he describes the dreadful conditions endured by British and Irish workers – including very young children – in the 1830s and, having roused the anger and empathy of the reader, then delineates O'Connell's behaviour at the time, which was to denounce trade unionism and oppose legislation aimed at improving the wages and conditions of ordinary workers. To prove his case, he referred to a debate in the British House of Commons in 1838 during which O'Connell refused to support a motion calling for the proper enforcement of a law 'forbidding the employment of *children under nine years of age* [Connolly's emphasis] in factories, except silk mills, and forbidding those under thirteen from working more than forty-eight hours a week' (Connolly, 1910: 155). According to Connolly:

> O'Connell opposed the motion, and attempted to justify the infringement of the law by the employers by stating that 'they (Parliament) had legislated against the nature of things, and against the right of industry.' 'Let them not,' he said, 'be guilty of the childish folly of regulating the labour of adults, and go about parading before the world *their ridiculous humanity*, which would end by converting their manufacturers into beggars' … O'Connell was not above using this clap-trap, as he … had not been above making the lying pretence that the enforcement of a *minimum* wage prevented the payment of *high* wages to any specially skilled artisan. (Connolly, 1910: 156)

The treatment of O'Connell is remarkably hostile and the campaign he led for the repeal of the Act of Union receives a very negative assessment; Connolly's explanation of mass working-class involvement in the O'Connellite Repeal movement is curious:

> At the outset of this agitation, the Irish working class, partly because they accepted O'Connell's explanation of the decay of Irish trade as due to the Union, and partly because they did not believe he was sincere in his professions of loyalty to the English monarchy, nor in his desire to limit his aims to repeal, enthusiastically endorsed and assisted his agitation. (Connolly, 1910: 149)

Workers are presented as a confection of guile and gullibility, whose primary motivation is economic but stoked up by O'Connell. In reality, working-class assumptions about the economic damage caused by the Act of Union pre-dated O'Connell's leadership of the Repeal movement, and it was less a case of O'Connell persuading the working class on the issue than an alliance of convenience, cemented by an elemental nationalism among urban workers that chimed with O'Connellite political rhetoric; the promotion of local manufactures and economic prosperity were central to O'Connell's Repeal campaign from at least the early 1830s (Cronin, 2000: 147–8). Moreover, working-class interest in Repeal was stronger at times than O'Connell's, and impatience with his leadership publicly manifested itself when he relegated the Repeal issue in 1834; it was a contingent relationship and O'Connell was not viewed as beyond criticism (e.g. Lane, 2001: 53–4). Connolly was aware of the complexity of the working-class interaction with O'Connell, but it is not clear that he understood that Irish urban workers – and tradesmen in particular – were already opposed to the Union on economic grounds and did not require much persuasion on the issue. In that sense, Connolly's image of workers overwhelmed by silver-tongued bourgeois nationalists is a misleading one.

Despite O'Connell's antagonistic attitude to organised labour, the popular memory of O'Connell among workers, and certainly among non-revolutionary nationalists, was largely a positive one. This was equally true of another national hero, William Smith O'Brien (1803–64), who had led the abortive nationalist rebellion of 1848 but whose political career was that of a social moderate; Connolly was dismissive of O'Brien's revolutionary credentials, describing him as an 'Irish Girondin'. In this regard, he deployed the historian Thomas Carlyle's definition of a Girondin as those 'who rebel, and urge [on] the lower classes' but who view the ordinary working people as 'only a raw material ... for blowing down Bastilles with' (Connolly, 1910: 159); in short, he accused O'Brien and the leading Young Irelanders of the 1840s of treating the working class as cannon fodder for a botched and half-hearted middle-class rebellion. Again, this was a direct attack on 'respectable' figures in the Irish nationalist tradition, men who would rather abort an insurrection than see it engender social conflict. Connolly was conscious of the consternation his treatment of O'Connell and O'Brien would provoke, commenting in a private letter to a friend in

1909 that those chapters were 'the most likely to arouse bitter comment, as they deal with O'Connell and his attitude to Labor, and with Smith O'Brien and the Girondin Young Irelanders, giving of course full credit to the real revolutionists of that period'.[12]

The 'real revolutionists' applauded in *Labour in Irish History* were also nationalists, but with a social programme that Connolly deemed progressive. He singled out James Fintan Lalor (1807–49) for particular praise; Lalor, a Young Irelander and agrarian radical, appealed to Connolly because his writings contained 'not only the best plan of campaign suited for the needs of a country seeking its freedom through insurrection against a dominant nation, but also held the seeds of the more perfect social peace of the future' (Connolly, 1910: 186). Describing Lalor as a 'peerless thinker', he accentuated his democratic values and progressive social policy (such as his opposition to the landlord system), contrasting him favourably with the elitist William Smith O'Brien. Connolly's admiration of Lalor was not new – one of the first pamphlets produced by the ISRP in 1897 was a collection of Lalor's writings and he was persistently recommended as a proto-socialist. Nonetheless, Lalor was certainly not a socialist and, while relatively progressive on agrarian issues, is best described as a radical democrat, who was much influenced by the democracy movement that swept across the European continent in the 1840s. Connolly, however, was keen to unearth socialist forebears within the Irish nationalist movement, and the chapter that deals with Lalor is pointedly titled 'Socialistic Teaching of Young Irelanders: the Thinkers and the Workers'.[13] Moreover, while the book embodied a powerful assault on the middle class as a whole, Connolly did differentiate the lower levels of that class from those who were very wealthy. In common with most Marxists, he believed that the lower middle class (or *petite bourgeoisie*) was capable of aligning itself with struggling workers, though such elements were generally a moderating influence, opposed to class conflict and untrustworthy:

> The lower middle class gave to the National cause in the past, many unselfish patriots, but, on the whole, while willing and ready enough to please their humble fellow-countrymen, and to compound with their own conscience by shouting louder than all others their untiring devotion to the cause of freedom, they, as a class, unceasingly strove to divert the public mind upon the lines of constitutional agitation for such reforms as might remove irritating and unnecessary officialism, while leaving untouched the basis of national and economic subjection. (Connolly, 1910: 8)

'The slavery of our race'

It is impossible to read *Labour in Irish History* without being struck by the author's desire to rewrite the history of Irish nationalism as a subaltern struggle against not just imperialism but the bourgeois enemy within: social and national liberation are inextricably linked and one cannot be achieved without the other. However, the uses of language and the modalities by which the author undermines the middle class are also interesting, especially his textual appeal to nationalist sensibilities. The working class is advanced as the true repository of revolutionary nationalism – the 'unconquered' fighters for Irish freedom (Connolly, 1910: xiv) – while the middle class consistently betrays the nation and is a contaminant within the Irish 'race'.

The deployment of racial language is worth noting, although common at the time. It is particularly striking in the twelve-page foreword in which Connolly set the scene, historically speaking, by describing the demise of the old Gaelic social order and the rise of capitalism in Ireland. In Connolly's version, the arrival of capitalism and bourgeois values was an act of cultural imperialism that necessitated the destruction of racial memory as well as social institutions. Capitalism is constructed as an entirely foreign imposition, with rapid cultural as well as economic implications, that ran contrary to the natural inclinations of the Irish people, who he claimed enjoyed a non-hierarchical, communistic clan-based society until as late as the seventeenth century, though it was under pressure from the time of Henry VIII and Elizabeth I: 'As the dispersion of the clans, consummated by [Oliver] Cromwell, finally completed the ruin of Gaelic Ireland, all the higher education of Irishmen thenceforward ran in this foreign groove, and was coloured with this foreign colouring' (Connolly, 1910: iv). For Connolly, the Irish race bore the cultural slave-marks of colonialism and a rejection of capitalism was an intrinsic element of authentic Irishness:

> One of these slave birth-marks is a belief in the capitalist system of society; the Irishman frees himself from such a mark of slavery when he realises the truth that the capitalist system is the most foreign thing in Ireland. (Connolly, 1910: x)

The words 'foreign', 'foreigner' and 'foreignism' appear seventeen times in the foreword and always with negative connotations; the Irish 'capitalist class' was judged guilty of 'apostate patriotism' and of being 'saturated with foreignism' (Connolly, 1910: xi). According to Connolly, the democratic traditions of the Irish race were abruptly destroyed by the foreign invader and a myth was carefully fostered that embedded in the popular consciousness an 'insidious lie about the aristocratic tendencies of the Irish' (Connolly, 1910: iv). The wealthy and middle-class Irish are denounced in *Labour in Irish History* as complicit in the demoralisation of the Irish people and were as much the enemy as the British imperialists: 'The Irish propertied classes became more English than the English, and so have continued to our day' (Connolly, 1910: xi). They are the Uncle Toms of the Irish people. Indeed, they made themselves outsiders to the Irish nation and could no longer be considered loyal to their race.

> The English slanderer lowered Irishmen in the eyes of the world, but his Irish middle-class teachers and writers lowered him in his own eyes by extolling as an Irish virtue every sycophantic vice begotten of generations of

slavery. Accordingly, as an Irishman, peasant, labourer, or artisan, banded together with his fellows to strike back at their oppressors in defence of their right to live in the land of their fathers, the 'respectable' classes who had imbibed the foreign ideas publicly deplored his act, and unctuously ascribed it to the 'evil effects of English misgovernment upon the Irish character', but when an occasional Irishman, abandoning all traditions of his race, climbed upon the backs of his fellows to wealth or position, his career was held up as a sample of what Irishmen could do under congenial or favourable circumstances. The seventeenth, eighteenth and nineteenth centuries were, indeed, the Via Dolorosa of the Irish race. In them the Irish Gael sank out of sight, and in his place the middle class politicians, capital-ists and ecclesiastics laboured to produce a hybrid Irishman, assimilating a foreign social system, a foreign speech, and a foreign character. In the effort to assimilate the first two the Irish were unhappily too successful, so successful that today the majority of the Irish do not know that their fathers ever knew another system of ownership, and the Irish Irelanders are painfully grappling with their mother tongue with the hesitating accent of a foreigner. (Connolly, 1910: ix–x)

Connolly's call for Irish racial solidarity against capitalism is clear, but it is also obvious that he is 'othering' the middle class and constructing them as traitors to their nation. In this, he followed closely the declamations of James Fintan Lalor, the nationalist and agrarian radical he so admired, who in 1848 had denied vehemently that the landlords were a part of the Irish nation:

I deny the claim. They form no class of the Irish people, or of any other people. Strangers they are in this land they call theirs – strangers here and strangers everywhere; owning no country and owned by none; reject-ing Ireland and rejected by England; tyrants to this island and slaves to another; here they stand, hating and hated – their hand ever against us as ours against them, an outcast and ruffianly horde, alone in the world and alone in its history, a class by themselves. They do not now, and never did, belong to this island at all. (Marlowe, 1918: 119)

However, Connolly's understanding of 'nation' and 'race' is not explicated in *Labour in Irish History*, and one is left wondering whether he is playing to the crowd, trying to win them to class politics by expropriating the lexicon of nationalism. Certainly, while Connolly was strongly anti-imperialist, he was not an insular racial nationalist or a xenophobe; he was proud of his Irishness but not dewy eyed about Ireland, and he was an internationalist with regard to working-class unity. Nonetheless, he did have a tendency to indulge in generalisations about nations and 'races', and was a believer in 'national characteristics', which he saw as the outcome of material condi-tions; for example, he famously declared – glumly and rather glibly – in *Labour in Irish History*: 'The Irish are not philosophers as a rule, they proceed too rapidly from thought to action' (Connolly, 1910: 109). More-over, as Ó Cathasaigh has highlighted, this remark was culled from a longer passage on national differences that appeared in the original 1909 article.

The passage continued:

> They are logical even in their errors, and consequently an Irishman who has been vouchsafed a new idea would have that idea translated into an accomplished fact whilst his German comrade would be still painfully thinking out all its logical possibilities and deductions before beginning to act. The impulsive Celt exhausts all the possibilities of error and arrives at the right course of action almost as quickly as the Teuton or the Saxon who must needs figure out all the possible mistakes to avoid before acting at all. (*Harp*, April 1909, quoted in Ó Cathasaigh, 2002: 107)

In terms of Ireland, Connolly's position on the cultural condition of the nation is analogous to that later adopted by, for example, 'Black nationalists' in the United States and the Gay Pride movement internationally; he supported the 'Gaelic revival' in an effort to promote 'Irish pride' and self-respect, a regeneration of the nation that was essential he believed if imperialism and capitalism were to be driven from the island. Criticising the depiction of Irishmen in English literature, he complained that the writers 'knew nothing of the free and independent Irishman of Gaelic Ireland, but they did know the conquered, robbed, slave-driven, brutalised, demoralised Irishman, the product of generations of landlord and capitalist rule, and him they seized upon, held up to the gaze of the world, and asked the nations to accept as the true Irish type' (Connolly, 1910: viii). In order to end what he called 'the slavery of our race' (Connolly, 1910: x), it was necessary for the 'incorruptible' and 'unconquered' – the working class – to rise from its knees. However, in October 1910, as Connolly was awaiting the publication of his book, he understood that this was more easily said than done; complaining to William O'Brien about his Dublin socialist comrades, he wrote acidly: 'Allow me also to say that I am convinced their work will be forever sterile and unfruitful unless they summon up courage to fight elections. I hate to say it of Irishmen, but that is what is lacking in Ireland today – *moral courage amongst Irish Socialists*. Their lack in that respect is a discredit to the race.'[14] No moral courage, no racial pride.

Afterlife

Connolly's book was not widely read prior to the 1916 insurrection and, despite a paperback edition becoming available in 1914, it failed to reach a significant working-class audience. In truth, Connolly's influence as a public intellectual increased immeasurably because of his execution; he was respected as a trade union leader before 1916 (he became Acting General Secretary of the Irish Transport and General Workers' Union in 1914), but was a minor public figure and unknown to many Irish people – that changed dramatically following his leadership role in the nationalist Easter Rising.

Connolly's central involvement in the 1916 rising, and more particularly his execution, transformed him into an icon for the resurgent separatist movement as it gathered pace and eventually displaced the constitutional nationalists between 1916 and 1918. From the outset, the nature of his legacy was strongly contested, with nationalists and socialists claiming him as their own (Woggon, 2005: 172–86). However, with a tiny socialist movement in Ireland at the time, the nationalists and republicans were easily the loudest voices in the debate on Connolly's politics, and most Irish people came to view him as a kind of left-wing labour-nationalist, a republican who was willing to put his social concerns to one side in order to join the fight for national liberation. This is clearly not how Connolly would have described his involvement in the separatist uprising, but there was more than enough in his writings that could be used to buttress the claim. Certainly, Connolly explicitly associated himself with the Gaelic Revival, conceding in *Labour in Irish History* that the book 'may justly be looked upon as part of the literature of the Gaelic Revival' (Connolly, 1910: xi). Moreover, from his arrival in Ireland in 1896, he consistently argued for socialists to position themselves within the revolutionary separatist tradition, while concomitantly eschewing the half-measure of home rule; however, after his death, Connolly's socialist-republicanism was often misinterpreted by left-wing nationalists as a form of bourgeois republicanism, albeit with a pronounced social conscience. Much of what he had written was ignored by those who considered themselves his followers in the century after *Labour in Irish History* was published; Connolly was a separatist, but the defining features of his politics were his Marxism and his belief in class struggle. In the book, he had warned against underplaying the importance of class interests: 'When questions of "class" interests are eliminated from public controversy, a victory is thereby gained for the possessing, conservative class, whose only hope of security lies in such elimination. Like a fraudulent trustee, the bourgeois dreads nothing so much as an impartial and rigid inquiry into the validity of his title deeds' (Connolly, 1910: 5). Ironically, the political parties of the Irish 'conservative class' – such as Fianna Fáil – did precisely that while simultaneously claiming Connolly as one of their political forefathers (Dunphy, 2005: 252; Allen, 1997: 15). Indeed, at the inaugural meeting of Fianna Fáil in 1926, the party's leader (and veteran of the 1916 rising) Eamon de Valera pointedly referred to Connolly and declared that he had come to 'sympathise fully with James Connolly's passionate protest' (Allen, 1997: 15). Even today, despite Fianna Fáil's eager embrace of neo-liberalism and its markedly conservative traditions, the party still views Connolly as an admirable figure with whom they are happy to be associated; in 2004, moreover, then Taoiseach and leader of Fianna Fáil Bertie Ahern ludicrously declared himself to be a socialist.[15]

While Connolly joined the pantheon of Irish national martyrs and was seen popularly and officially as one of the 'founders' of the independent Irish state, his writings were mostly ignored and forgotten by the state and mainstream political parties. Schoolchildren learned about his role in the famous 1913 Dublin lockout and were told of his central involvement in the 1916 rising, but they rarely had access to *Labour in Irish History*. In my own case, the book was available at home and I read it as a young teenager in the early 1980s, but mine was an uncommon experience: my father ran a leftist bookshop in Cork city and I came from a strongly left-republican family. By the age of 15, I was a political activist and *Labour in Irish History* was a key mobilising text in my life, but primarily as 'proof' that socialism historically had a place within the republican tradition: it existed as a vital counterpoint to those republicans who felt that 'social issues' were a dangerous distraction from the business of achieving national reunification and as evidence, in opposition to the hegemony of conservative politics, that socialist ideas had powerful and well-regarded advocates in the Irish past. As a text, those of us involved in republican activism read it uncritically as an account of Irish history, but, in the main, we treated it as a political instrument to be deployed in support of bolting a social dimension to the national liberation struggle; it was a guide to strategic practice only in the sense that its emphasis on a republican orientation towards the working class and distrust of middle-class nationalists informed the views of most left-republicans.

Labour in Irish History has remained consistently in print, but almost entirely because of the efforts of the trade union movement and small socialist groups.[16] The impact of the book on civil society has been negligible, and even among radical leftists it is now often seen as a relic of different times, though one that is revered. In truth, the various writings of Vladimir Lenin had much more influence than those of Connolly on the behaviour and organisational forms of the small Irish radical left from the 1920s onwards; Connolly's writings were read by Ireland's Marxists mostly to inform their views on the national question, but typically in conjunction with those of Lenin on national self-determination. The left-republicans, on the other hand, probably took Connolly more seriously as an inspirational figure, but generally their reading involved a demotion of his class politics and an accentuation of his separatism (Ó Broin, 2009). His standing within the Irish Labour Party was that of an icon, but his revolutionist class politics were seen as an embarrassment; the objective of a 'Workers' Republic' – first put forward by Connolly – was reduced to rhetoric within the mainstream labour movement (Puirséil, 2007).

In reality, no party or organisation – and certainly no significant social force – in Ireland relied heavily on *Labour in Irish History* for political guidance; this is scarcely surprising as Connolly had never intended it to be that type of book. However, the fact that it is still being read, one hundred years after its publication, is testament to its residual influence; it remains a compelling text for significant numbers of Irish leftists, especially those on the left of republicanism and some members of the various radical left groups. Connolly's general arguments for a linking of the struggles for national and social liberation were – and remain – influential in the Irish labour and republican movements, and also within the radical left, though perhaps less so since the ceasefire in Northern Ireland. In a peculiar way, the ending of the war in the north has made the national question a less urgent issue for many leftists on the island, and young socialists and anarchists, in particular, are now more likely to be tuned into global developments and found reading Noam Chomsky and Naomi Klein rather than James Connolly. Nonetheless, *Labour in Irish History* remains important for those leftist political activists who are anxious to identify themselves with a tradition of socialist resistance; it stands as a useful reminder that not all oppositional political thought on the island of Ireland has radiated from radical nationalism.

Notes

1 See www.indymedia.ie/article/69669 (accessed 10 November 2008).
2 Nevin's book is the most recent and largest biography of Connolly, but numerous studies of his life and politics have been published; the most valuable, aside from Nevin's, are Allen (1990), Anderson (1994), Greaves (1961) and Morgan (1988).
3 Connolly, in fact, was remarkably fickle with regard to his place of birth. In the (private) 1901 census, he listed himself as born in County Monaghan, but a year later he complained bitterly in a (private) letter when a New York socialist newspaper, the *Weekly People*, stated that he was Monaghan-born. It is clear that he varied his story and encouraged confusion on the matter. See James Connolly to Secretary ISRP, 7 August 1902, in Nevin (2007: 173–4). [Hereafter cited as *Connolly Letters.*]
4 Ellis's book, which was popular among leftists in both Britain and Ireland as well as with Irish republicans, was later updated and republished in 1985 by Pluto Press.
5 James Connolly to William O'Brien, 12 September 1909, in *Connolly Letters*, p. 408.
6 Ibid. There is some irony in Connolly soliciting Francis Sheehy Skeffington's help to promote his book, as the previous year he had written an assessment of Sheehy Skeffington's biography of Michael Davitt in which he pointedly criticised the subject; see *The Harp*, August 1908.
7 James Connolly to George Russell, 4 February 1914, in *Connolly Letters*, p. 508.
8 Fred Ryan to James Connolly, 7 October 1910, in ibid., p. 443.
9 Fred Ryan to James Connolly, 28 October 1910, in ibid., p. 446.
10 James Connolly to George Russell, 4 February 1914, in ibid., p. 508.
11 *The Worker*, 26 December 1914.
12 James Connolly to William O'Brien, 12 September 1909, in *Connolly Letters*, p. 408.
13 For an interesting critical discussion of the quality of Connolly's historiography in *Labour in Irish History*, see Howell (1986: 80–8).
14 James Connolly to William O'Brien, 11 October 1910, in *Connolly Letters*, p. 445.
15 *Irish Times*, 13 November 2004.
16 It was republished in early 1917 in a combined volume (with his *The Re-Conquest of Ireland* [1915]) under the title *Labour in Ireland* and this was reissued without change in 1922; both print-runs were paid for by the Irish Transport and General

Workers' Union (ITGWU). Donnelly Press in New York brought out a paperback edition of *Labour in Irish History* by itself in 1919; Maunsell & Co. in Dublin issued a paperback edition in parts in 1920. The ITGWU also published a paperback in 1934, and ten years later the union again financed the republication of the *Labour in Ireland* volume as part of a four-volume set of Connolly's writings. In 1956, New Books Publications, a communist publisher in Dublin, brought out a very cheap pamphlet-style edition of *Labour in Irish History*, which was reprinted several times thereafter. In fact, for many years, this unattractive and utilitarian Communist Party of Ireland edition was the only one available and remains the version that most people own today; the Socialist Workers' Party in Britain printed a slightly more elegant paperback edition in 1987, but that is rarely seen in Irish bookshops. In fact, in recent decades, copies of *Labour in Irish History* were hardly ever sold in mainstream bookshops and distribution occurred primarily through socialist groups and via the handful of left-wing bookshops on the island.

4

Robert Tressell's *The Ragged Trousered Philanthropists*

Rosie Meade

Introduction

With their much feted academic text *The New Spirit of Capitalism* Luc Boltanski and Eve Chiapello (2005a: 162) explore, with particular reference to contemporary France, what it is that 'justifies people's commitment to capitalism' and 'renders that commitment attractive' despite the obvious absurdity of the system itself. In the early years of the twentieth century the Irish born sign-writer Robert Noonan (1870–1911), using the pseudonym Robert Tressell, undertook a similar task. Posing as novelist rather than social researcher, he described and, crucially, *explained* the miserable circumstances and political acquiescence of tradesmen in Mugsborough or, as it is more commonly known, Hastings in southeast England. In this 'town of about eighty thousand inhabitants' of 'fair outward appearance', the majority 'existed in a state of perpetual poverty which in many cases bordered on destitution' (Tressell, 2004: 740–1).[1] Tragically, his was no tale of working-class heroism or defiance; instead we find a class of people so deluded and defeated that their real scorn is saved for the socialists in their midst. The abiding power of *The Ragged Trousered Philanthropists* lies in its explanation of why this was and continues to be so. It offers a peerless depiction of 'Hegemony' detailing how, in the home, the workplace and throughout this Edwardian society, oppression was sustained by the interaction of coercion and consent. Tressell's narrative also anticipated and illustrated what would later emerge as key themes in critical social theory during the twentieth and twenty-first centuries: the culture industry critique, false consciousness, the place of the intellectual in social struggle, and the meaning and political value of resistance.

In the following pages I try to explain why I regard *The Ragged Trousered Philanthropists (TRTP)* as a classic activist text, focusing on what I consider to be its most compelling themes. Doubtless, many readers will feel little connection to either the historical setting or the abject living conditions that it describes – in our time the anodyne phrase 'social exclusion' trumps 'poverty' in policy and public discourses. More problematically, *TRTP* can seem a demoralising read, perpetuating the kind of 'dead-end' analysis found in so much sociological writing; a litany of societal flaws or shortcomings is presented but too little is said about the political organisation and strategic thinking necessary to overcome them. Although the book ends with a rousing testament to the inevitable victory of socialism – 'from these ruins was surely growing the glorious fabric of the Co-operative Common-wealth. Mankind awakening from the long night of bondage and mourning' (Tressell, 2004: 738) – it seems at best a flight into fantasy as the content of preceding pages could only engender the opposite conclusion.

As a fan of *TRTP*, I cannot really pretend that it has had a profound influence over the ideas and positions adopted by Irish social movements since its publication in 1914. In Britain its political status is legendary, where by virtue of its popularity among Second World War soldiers and navy person-nel it is often claimed – somewhat extravagantly – that it 'won the '45 election for Labour' (Harker, 2003: 141). Its place in the public culture is also assured; cited as the 'favourite book' of Tony Benn, Ricky Tomlinson (alias Jim Royle) and the significant numbers of readers who voted it to Number 72 in the Big Read charts of 2003.[2] Unusually it has breached the artificial gap between the political and cultural spheres, and while certainly not a mass-market favourite it has won readers and listeners who might never voluntarily pick up Marx's *Das Kapital*. Noonan's singular contribution was to theorise through 'art' and to daringly presume that his kind of life and his kind of understandings might have broader resonance. Raymond Williams (1983: 251) describes the book as an enduring testament to the importance and utility of 'theory', demonstrating that 'experience alone will not teach us'. But cultural resources, be they novels, poems or songs, are also vital reservoirs of identity, hope and imagination, and *TRTP*, while never abandoning its commitment to story-telling, is ultimately a moral call to activism.

Robert and me

Although there is some uncertainty about his origins, it is likely that Robert Noonan was born in Dublin, the son of retired Royal Irish Constabulary man Samuel Croker and Mary/Maria Noone/Noonan (see Ball, 1979; Harker, 2003). During his late teens, Robert made his way to South Africa, via Liverpool, where he learned his trade as a painter decorator. During his time in South Africa he married and divorced Elizabeth Hartel and they had a daughter, Kathleen. He also developed the pro-Boer sympathies that may have led to his eventual deportation from the territory. Whether by choice or by force Robert and Kathleen arrived in London in 1901. It seems to have been an unhappy period in his life as the family experienced great finan-cial hardship and poverty. They later moved to Hastings, which, somewhat ironically, was famous as a 'health resort' (Harker, 2003; 11). Despite being renowned for his considerable skill and artistry, his employment record was chequered and he was afflicted by chronic ill health – possibly the early stages of tuberculosis. It is also probable, given his strong political opinions, that he found it difficult to ingratiate himself with local employers. Robert was active in Hastings' burgeoning socialist scene and the Social Democratic Federation, contributing leaflets, manifestoes and ideas on public relations strategy. His daughter Kathleen remembered him as a good-natured man, yet who was frequently demoralised by the backbiting ways and absent solidarity of his fellow tradesmen (Ball, 1979; Harker, 2003). *TRTP* draws extensively on his own work life and his encounters with employers and other workers. Noonan hoped to migrate with Kathleen to Canada and travelled to Liverpool to negotiate his passage in 1910. Sadly, he died prematurely in 1911, possibly from tuberculosis, and was buried in an unmarked 'workhouse' grave. His political engagement along with his efforts to analyse the material basis of the circumstances in which he, Kathleen and his workmates lived mark him out as a true organic intellectual.

I first read a version of *TRTP* as a teenager, and much as I would love to be able to exaggerate my 'socialist from cradle to grave' credentials, it was a sentimental rather than political encounter. While I was re-reading it on a Mayo-bound train in 1993 a man approached me exclaiming proudly, 'that's one of the most powerful books ever written' and we had a short chat about its message and Noonan's Irishness. Like my new friend, I knew little about Robert's life and his status as an 'authentic' voice of his class, but I was beginning to appreciate both the complexity and continuing relevance of his insights. Later I used the book as a teaching resource when interrogating concepts such as 'false consciousness', 'ideology' and 'oppression'. Now, as someone who considers herself a member of that pitifully small and dysfunctional family, otherwise known as the Irish left, I get a perverse consolation from the profound and disturbing questions that *TRTP* raises about the efficacy of socialist strategy. It lays bare our political failure, forcing us to confront the question 'what the hell are we doing wrong?' Why is it that despite having a compelling analysis and people's best interests at heart, the left seems bereft of imagination and allure (Duncombe, 2007b; Reed, 2000)? Or more crudely, why in 2010, when the Irish economic miracle has 'melted into air' and when the insanity of financial speculation has been exposed, are the Dublin and Cork Mayday marches still so marginal? Populist commentators breathlessly assure us that Ireland is ready for an alternative; tragically that alternative appears to be Fine Gael.

If I am bemused and disillusioned, *TRTP* reminds me that such feelings are a kind of inevitable socialist dividend. The book's central character, Owen, lurches between conviction and despair, between pity and contempt, as he struggles to convert his co-workers to socialism. It is difficult not to empathise, especially if you have ever been involved in campaigning in Ireland or even if you have just expressed a contrarian viewpoint to sceptical friends and colleagues. For me the electorate's ringing endorsement of the 2004 Citizenship Referendum was a particularly bruising encounter with democracy. Nor do the left's tendencies towards bickering and sectarian partyism – evident for example in wrangling about the character of the anti-war campaign – help to instil a strong sense of efficacy and relevance. But because *TRTP* presents such a powerful deconstruction of alienation and its consequences, it implicitly urges us to take matters of political strategy more seriously so that we search for some path through the impasse.

A working class novel in itself and for itself

Tressell (2004: 2) claimed that his 'main object was to write a readable story full of human interest and based on the happenings of everyday life, the subject of Socialism being treated incidentally'. Centred on the worsening financial circumstances and growing despair of Frank Owen and his family, *TRTP* is a richly populated text that provides fascinating ethnographic insights into family, community and political life in Edwardian Hastings. Shifting between humour, fury, sentimentality and gloom, it profiles a diverse cast of working-class characters; sweet-natured drinker Joe Philpot, loyal young apprentice Bert White, the oleaginous Christian, Slyme, and the ill-fated young married couple, the Eastons. Because this is a missive from and about the 'class war' (Sillitoe, 1991), Tressell also dissects the conduct and motives of the worst specimens of the managerial, employing and political classes. Some of those characterisations are drawn from Noonan's time in South Africa and England – aspects of Owen's biography mirror his own (Ball, 1979; Harker, 2003) – while others are deliberate caricatures, drawn to satirise the self-delusions, pretensions and hypocrisy of social elites. Contemporary readers might be turned off by Tressell's tendency to lay it on with a trowel, particularly when he details the immorality of Mugsborough's bourgeoisie. Apparently it was constituted by a collection of overfed sociopaths whose very names evoked their avarice and contempt for humanity, Sweater, Starvem, Didlum, Grinder and Sir Graball D'Encloseland. Clearly, there are tensions between Tressell's responsibilities as an 'artist' or 'novelist' and as a 'socialist intellectual'. Nuance is sacrificed in the name of political commitment (Miles, 1984; Nazareth, 1967) and the interior lives of the workers are more vividly realised than those of the privileged.

And hurrah for that! Although, I focus more on the book's political rather than its literary merits, it should be said that as a *socialist* and *working-class* story *TRTP* violated 'inherited assumptions of what it was to write a novel, and to write a good competent novel' (Williams, 1983: 242).[3] Its status as a 'Penguin Modern Classic' is attributable less to academic or literary judgements and more to its 'organic' popularity as a text that was passed from reader to reader, read collectively in workshops and performed by political theatre groups since the 1950s in Britain (Harker, 2003; Miles, 1984). It presents vivid descriptions of what people ate and drank and how they budgeted, of the atmosphere in the pub and at Sunday school, of racy dinner-break conversations and of brutish, pointless toil. Much of the action takes place in a house that is being renovated by the tradesmen – 'the Cave' – and we learn something about what it might have felt like to paint and scrub-down walls when hungry or frozen to the bone. Social historian Rebecca Yamin (2002) regards a passage in which the Owens anxiously calculate what Christmas gifts they can afford to buy their little son as an all too rare evocation of the status of toys and play in the lives of the poor. Brad Beaven (2005) also finds clues regarding working-class leisure pursuits, the popularity of music-hall songs and works' day-trips, all of which were essential diversions from drudgery.

Nowadays the parenting, recreational, eating and educational practices of working-class and poor communities are regularly served up as entertainment in the cultural sphere, most obviously in the genre of reality television. *Jamie's Ministry of Food, The Secret Millionaire, Pram Face (sic), The Jeremy Kyle Show* and a host of similar programmes invite viewers to ridicule, pity, judge and feign outrage at the inferior life choices and moral laxity of the so-called underclass. In stark contrast to the freakishness of those television narratives, Tressell's descriptions are underpinned by a political and economic analysis that allows readers to contextualise and problematise individual experience. Here is a discussion of the kind of mundane dilemma regularly faced by the Owens and, presumably, by Noonan and families of his class,

> Frankie's stockings were all broken and beyond mending, so it was positively necessary to buy him another pair for fivepence three-farthings. These stockings were not much good – a pair at double the price could have been much cheaper, for they would have lasted three or four times longer; but they could not afford to buy the dearer kind. It was just the same with the coal: if they had been able to afford it they could have bought a ton of the same class of coal for twenty-six shillings but buying it as they did, by the hundred weight, they had to pay at the rate of thirty-three shillings and fourpence a ton. It was just the same with nearly everything else. This is how the working classes are robbed. Although their incomes are the lowest, they are compelled to buy the most expensive articles – that is the lowest-priced articles. (Tressell, 2004: 366)

Furthermore, as Raymond Williams (1983)[4] reminds us, if working-class lives were not generally considered appropriate subjects for the literary form, real-life working-class people also made unlikely novelists. Condemned to spend the best part of their lives at labour, writers such as Noonan needed to be extraordinarily wilful and resourceful if their creative impulses were to find expression on the published page. *TRTP* was written by a 'worker fully engaged in his own work' who, for the purpose of mere survival, 'comes home from his job, writes, goes back to his job, writes, all under pressure' (Williams, 1983: 248). Kathleen Noonan, reckoned that the book took her father five years to write, during which time he was working 'a fifty-six and a half hour week' and maintaining his membership of the Social Democratic Federation (Ball, 1979: 140).

A social critique of capitalism

Noting that critiques of capitalism are as old as capitalism itself, Boltanski and Chiapello (2005b) distinguish two distinctive logics that have tended to frame oppositional discourses. *Social critique* focuses on the inequalities, poverty, 'misery, exploitation, and the selfishness of a world that stimulates individualism rather than solidarity', while the alternative critique highlights more existential or, as Boltanski and Chiapello (2005a: 175–6) term them, *artistic* concerns. These relate to capitalism's negation of 'individual autonomy, singularity and authenticity' (2005a: 176). Both forms of critique are central to the purpose and content of *TRTP*. They are articulated through the private thoughts and public arguments of Owen, and in the narrative commentary that overlays the story itself. Those critiques remain central to contemporary anti-capitalist discourses, although they are not always successfully fused into a coherent and strategically minded political position (Duncombe, 2007b; Frank, 2001; Reed 2000).

As a 'social' critique of capitalism, *TRTP* operates at a number of different levels. Most obviously, there is the emotional sway of a text that regularly moves the reader to tears and anger. Witness the diminishing fortunes of the once proud Linden family, its members variously rewarded with the workhouse, servitude and death. Bert White, based on a young friend and *protégé* of Noonan, is trapped in a pointless and exploitative apprenticeship where he learns little and is valued less. But viable critique needs to move beyond emotion if it is to have any long-term political impact. It requires a 'theoretical fulcrum and an argumentative rhetoric to give voice to individual suffering and translate it into terms that refer to the common good' (Boltanski and Chiapello, 2005b: 36). Tressell doesn't just want readers to sympathise with his characters, as Dickens was wont to do – indeed, most of the time his tone is sarcastic, impatient or goading. In the place of pity he offers the intellectual resources of anti-capitalism. Invoking an odd and deliberately jarring pedagogical device, reminiscent of Brecht's didactic method, the characters of Owen and later Barrington are quite literally given the floor to explain Marx's labour theory of value. In the chapters 'The Oblong' and 'The Great Oration' we learn that because workers are forced to sell their labour in the marketplace they are simultaneously robbed of their sense of entitlement to and ability to access the fruits of their own production (Williams, 1983).

> In return for their work they are given – Money, and the things they have made become the property of the people who do nothing. Then, as the money is of no use, the workers go to shops and give it away in exchange for some of the things they themselves have made. They spend – or give back – *All* their wages; but as the money they got as wages is not equal in value to the things they have produced they find that they are only able to buy back a *very small part*. So you see these little discs of metal – this Money – is a device for enabling those who do not work to rob the workers of the greater part of the fruits of their toil. (Tressell, 2004: 341–2, emphasis in original)

This is the fundamental injustice of capitalism; profit legitimises grand-scale theft from those who contribute most to society, reducing them to a perpetual state of misery and want. Through his alter-ego Owen, Tressell opposes those who genuinely contribute to wealth creation in society with those who merely monopolise or consume it. In one memorable and counter-intuitive stroke he dismisses 'Tramps, Beggars, Society People, the 'Aristocracy', Great Landowners, All those possessed of hereditary Wealth' as a common class of parasites undertaking nothing in the way of 'useful work' (Tressell, 2004: 330). Another category includes those whose work 'benefits themselves and harms other people. Employers – or rather Exploiters of Labour; Thieves, Swindlers, Pickpockets; profit seeking shareholders; burglars; Bishops; Financiers; Capitalists and those persons humorously called "Ministers" of religion' (Tressell, 2004: 331). Tressell thus upends the hierarchy of status and legitimacy that is normalised by capitalism, specifically as it applies in the town of Mugsborough, but more generally as it applies in our 'meritocratic' era. Interestingly one of the most dishonest yet convincing rhetorical tricks played by neo-liberalism's current apologists, one practised by Republicans in the 2008 US presidential elections, is to cast as 'elitists' those who argue for tighter regulation of business, higher taxes or universal welfare provision. What Frank (2001: 10) calls 'market populism' equates democracy with share holding, social security nets with serfdom and allows Warren Buffett and Bill Gates to pass as 'little guys'. Tressell reminds us that the primacy of capitalism rests in part upon such inversions of reality and the social critique must deal with ideology in a clear-headed way so that activists begin to posit alternatives to the accepted hierarchies of our times.

Even if new readers are emotionally stirred by *TRTP's* descriptions of absolute poverty, they might find its detours into Marxist theory somewhat removed from their own experiences of personal enrichment and consumption in a (now formerly) booming economy. However, rather than concentrate on the disparity between the earnings of skilled manual workers in the early 1900s and those of 'knowledge-workers' in twenty-first-century Ireland, consider instead the continuity of worker 'vulnerability', a key theme pursued by Tressell and one with particular relevance to these risky economic times. Kirby (2006: 636–40) argues that capitalist globalisation has generated new threats to human and social well being, while simultaneously eroding our 'coping mechanisms'. Volatile financial systems, insecure employment, credit enslavement, environmental hazards, social atomisation, withdrawal of the welfare net (Kirby, 2006) and other characteristics of our neo-liberal present not only condemn individuals to life on the perpetual brink but also mean that if and when their fortunes decline they are less able to obviate the consequences. Concepts of globalisation or neo-liberalism were not common currency in Tressell's day, but his workers were ever cognisant of the precariousness of their 'situations' and the constant threat of being laid off:

terror of the impending slaughter pervaded the house. Even those who were confident of being spared and kept on till the job was finished shared the general depression, not only out of sympathy for the doomed, but because they knew that a similar fate awaited themselves. (Tressell, 2004: 263)

Having catalogued the shaky home and work circumstances of the 'Philanthropists', their constant and often counter-productive struggles to make and stretch their pathetic incomes, Tressell makes few concessions in terms of a happy ending. There are some glimmers of hope. Owen helps reconcile Easton and his wife Ruth, whose marriage is being sabotaged by a combination of shared poverty, Easton's boozing and the lecherous presence of their lodger Slyme. Owen confronts the employer Rushton about his scandalous treatment of young Bert White; 'I give you fair warning – I know – enough – about you – to put you – where you deserve to be – if you don't treat him better – I'll have you punished – I'll show you up' (Tressell, 2004: 710, pauses signifying Owen's rage and ongoing battle with tuberculosis). Barrington, who comes from a prosperous family, makes a financial gift to Owen that could lift his family temporarily out of financial ruin. But these ephemeral moments of possibility actually serve to underline the working class's more general enslavement to material relations. Worst of all is their vulnerability to needless and otherwise avoidable death, whether in the form of 'industrial accidents' of the kind that befalls Joe Philpot, or the tuberculosis that is certain to kill Owen, or 'that most unnatural act of all, suicide' (Hunt, 2004: xiii).

An artistic critique

Tristram Hunt (2004: xviii) notes that Tressell was influenced by competing 'traditions within the socialist canon' and integrated 'both ethical and economic schools of thought'. He recognises the puritanism that fuels the book's regular attacks on the cultural lives and entertainments of the workers; their fondness for the pub, sporting events, music hall songs and newspapers like the *Daily Chloroform*. Here Tressell anticipates critiques of commodified mass culture, such as those by Horkheimer and Adorno (1973) that would emphasise cultural consumption's role in dulling the political sensibilities of the working class, accommodating them to the discipline of capitalist production and eroding their capacities for critical thinking. Unfortunately, as an intellectual, Owen is a regular source of bemusement to his workmates, marked out as different not only for the nature and fervour of his political conviction but also for his atheism, precise use of grammar, gravitas and tee-total ways (see Hunt, 2004). Problematically for those of us less ascetic in our habits, Owen's restraint and rational arguments contrast too sharply with the workers' hedonism and emotional understandings. He cannot or will not appeal to their dreams, fantasies or hunger for escapism. With this juxtaposition of opposites Tressell exposes an important dimension of the left's continued estrangement from the broader population; the lapses in empathy that make socialists condescend to those around us, proscribing behaviour, invoking taboos and ridiculing or demonising 'popular desire' (Duncombe, 2007b: 37). All of this is of course symptomatic of Owen's (and our) more general failure to establish real lines of communication with putative 'comrades'.

But Owen is not just the archetypal socialist kill-joy. If he is frustrated by the degraded cultural and productive lives of his colleagues, unlike them he actually believes that the working class should have more of the finer things in life and he clings to a romantic vision of work as personally fulfilling, socially useful and aesthetically rewarding. Tressell echoes the philosophical concerns of the Victorian socialist poet and artist, William Morris (Hunt, 2004) and his understanding of work's purpose:

> It is threefold, I think – hope of rest, hope of product, hope of pleasure in the work itself; and hope of these also in some abundance of good quality; rest enough and good enough to be worth having; product worth having by one who is neither a fool nor an ascetic; pleasure enough for all of us to be conscious of it while we are at work. (Morris, 1944: 604)

Morris (1944) envisaged a world of work that nurtures both the mind and the soul, one that can validate skill and release imagination. Likewise, Tressell believes that workers, when encouraged to experiment or practise creativity, can prefigure the experience of personal liberation by making and doing. Owen secures a commission to decorate a room according to his own artistic vision, a job that preoccupies and excites him. He researches 'Moorish design', meticulously plans every detail of his project and, gallingly for his boss, demands decent materials. As Owen loses himself in these tasks he becomes detached from the ongoing misery of his situation and experiences a genuine harmony with his labour, all the more precious because it is so rare and unexpected.

Acutely conscious of the real-world disjuncture between time spent at production and consumption, how those who sacrifice most to the former do least of the latter, Morris (1944) and Tressell also recognised that too much time and energy are diverted into the manufacture of cheap, substandard and unnecessary goods. If Tressell hoped that work might bring its own intrinsic rewards, he also understood the impossibility of such ambition under the corrupting influence of capitalism. Witness the employer Rushton, and his enforcer Hunter, cutting corners on costs; employing men at lower rates, overpricing jobs, advocating the lowest grade materials and the most slapdash of methods.

> According to the specification, all the outside woodwork was supposed to have three coats, and the guttering, rain-pipes and the other ironwork two coats, but Crass and Hunter had arranged to make two coats do for most of the windows and woodwork and all the ironwork was to be made do with one coat only. (Tressell, 2004: 307)

The workers, unsurprisingly, respond with cynicism – 'none of them took any pride in their work; they did not 'love' it. They had no conception of that lofty ideal of 'work for work's sake', which is so popular with the people who do nothing' (Tressell, 2004: 101) – and consequently the workplace culture is characterised by insincerity and alienation.

Paulo Freire (1972; 32) observed that as 'oppressors dehumanize others and violate their rights, they themselves also become dehumanized'. The reader is embarrassed by Hunter's surveillance of the workers and his misplaced loyalty to his employers. His obsessive desire to 'catch out' the others drives him to ludicrous extremes and he creeps up ladders, struggles through windows and tiptoes about to spy undetected. A mere employee he identifies upwards in the hierarchy not downwards: therefore he is hated by the workers and patronised by the bosses. In one scene where Rushton and Sweater, owner of the *Cave*, survey the renovations, Hunter, or Nimrod as he is nicknamed, waits eagerly to do their bidding. When finally called by Rushton, 'Nimrod ran to him like a dog taken notice of by his master: if he had possessed a tail, it is probable that he would have wagged it' (Tressell, 2004; 126). While this is a comical image, there is cold comfort in the realisation that the other workers would have behaved similarly if roles had been reversed. In the face of arbitrary sackings and a general culture of fear, employees do the needful to curry favour with Hunter or anyone else with leverage. Crass, a man devoid of charm and talent who has secured the role of foreman, dedicates his working week to 'cringing, fawning, abject servility' (Tressell, 2004: 351). Appreciating the marginal power that this affords him, the others ply Crass with alcohol they cannot afford and publicly defer to his opinions while privately detesting him.

Will twenty-first-century employees be surprised to learn that workplaces destroy initiative, reward arse-licking and perpetuate rivalry? Possibly not, but because those tendencies now get dressed up in the language of Human Relations, it is often difficult to trace the power dynamics involved. In the years since publication of *TRTP* capitalism has learned to embrace some of the elements of the 'artistic critique'. One of neo-liberalism's ideological innovations (Boltanski and Chiapello, 2005a; Frank, 2001; Klein, 2000) has been to colonise the counter-cultural tropes of freedom, creativity and dynamism. As the 'public sector' becomes semantically associated with torpor and bureaucracy, the free-wheeling skateboarding CEO epitomises the vibrancy of private enterprise. We occupy a time intellectually and politically when rigid and polarised thinking is widely distrusted, especially when it comes to matters of social class. Theoretically, social scientists are indebted to analyses of power that highlight its diffusion rather than its monopolisation and we imagine that in many workplaces, maybe even our own, there is scope for communication and negotiation across the employer/ employee axis. We hear, for example, that at Google, the 'laid-back ambience is credited as a key part of its success. Free perks for staff include three healthy meals a day, massages and laundry services as well as an on-site gym and swimming pool' (Smith, 2008).

Superficially, we experience a more humane version of capitalism, one that treats workers like people too. But as Jacques Donzelot (1991: 251) correctly observes, '[F]lexible hours, job enrichment, self-managed work teams, continued retraining', cannot be 'regarded as serious efforts to modify the capitalist regime'. After all, the Irish Small Firms Association can square its demand for a reduction in the already paltry minimum wage (Small Firms Association, 2008b) with its promotion of 'Work–Life Balance' (www.sfa. ie). Detached from its social conscience, the artistic critique can and is being adapted in service of capitalism's bottom line, the profit-motive. Workplaces are being humanised in order to minimise resistance and mobilise workers towards fuller participation in the dominant 'logic of production' (Donzelot, 1991: 279). Although he could never have anticipated the form and content of these new management approaches, Tressell would have seen through the artifice. He understood that alienation encompasses *both* artistic and social dimensions; that a 'work–life balance' is impossible when worker vulnerability and material inequality grow ever more pronounced.

Acquiescence, consent and sporadic resistance

That capitalism is founded upon and is sustained by violence has been a significant theme in theoretical and popularising analyses of neo-liberalism over the last decade (Klein, 2007; Negri, 1999). Naomi Klein (2007) has highlighted the shock tactics and 'therapies' practised in Chile, South Africa, and post-Katrina New Orleans; where ideologues, opportunistic corporations and political elites have actively cultivated and exploited instances of war, terror and social disintegration in order to establish the primacy of the market. Antonio Negri (1999), borrowing from Marx, maintains that violence has been a 'constant' in capitalism, although its form and substance have changed over time. Earlier processes of accumulation were supported by the overt brutality of theft, enclosure, slavery and imperial conquest, but as the capitalist system developed, the 'silent coercion of economic relations' became fundamental to its survival and identity (Negri, 1999: 250–67).

Tressell evokes both the silent and more vulgar forms of coercion as he describes the symbiotic relationship between violence and capitalism in *TRTP*. As the tradesmen renovate the Cave, their workdays are punctuated by episodes of bullying, summary dismissal and Hunter's creeping surveillance.

> Get the work done! Or if you don't want to I'll very soon find someone who does! I've been noticing your style of doing things for some time past and I want you to understand that you can't play the fool with me. There's plenty of better men than you walking about. (Tressell, 2004: 35)

It is a 'reign of terror – the terror of the sack' (Tressell, 2004: 493). Even the most intimate personal relationships are contaminated by 'jealousy and ill-feeling' (Tressell, 2004: 404) as the workers vie for petty privileges or the simple honour of being kept on. Their family lives also suffer. Although obviously underpaid Easton turns his resentments on his wife, blaming her for their financial hardship; 'It seems to me ... that you don't manage things as well as you might' (Tressell, 2004: 52). The childhoods of Mugsborough's youngsters are devastated by poverty and want, what Owen regards as another kind of violence, and he despairs that parents are 'willing and content that their children should be made into beasts of burden for the benefit of other people' (Tressell, 2004: 280).

Claims of 'coercion' or 'force' do not fully explain why so many workers then and now are impervious to solidarity and socialist argument. Undeniably violence of the kind described above is a disincentive to collective organisation, but Tressell, like Gramsci, also recognised the deeper problem of consent. Mugsborough is a 'perfect' example of Hegemony, a place 'where dominated groups are unable to distinguish between their own interests and attitudes and those of dominant groups' (Van Dijk, 1998: 102). The workers believe themselves to have informed political opinions – affecting Tory or Liberal allegiances – and demand that those viewpoints be respected by the ever-contemptuous Owen. Paradoxically, they seem equally convinced that they cannot or should not leave any discernible mark on the world around them. They regularly interrupt debates about politics – farting, wisecracking or digressing – and proudly claim disinterest in life's bigger philosophical questions. This culture of self-satisfaction, ignorance and apathy is reinforced by Mugsborough's 'ideological state apparatus' (Althusser, 2008); its Sunday schools, churches, politicians and popular entertainments. In some of its most powerful paragraphs, *TRTP* explains how those institutions distort and obscure social reality and further infantilise an all too receptive working class. 'From their infancy they had been trained to distrust their own intelligence, and to leave the management of the affairs of the world – and for that matter the next world too – to their betters' (Tressell, 2004: 247). In the place of social policy there is the Organised Benevolence Society, providing charity that 'humiliated, degraded and pauperized' its victims 'and prevented the problem being dealt with in a sane and practical manner' (Tressell, 2004: 428).

Despite living with and managing poverty on a daily basis the workers present the most facile explanations of its causes:

> 'The greatest cause of poverty is hover-population' remarked Harlow.
> 'Drink is the cause of most of the poverty' said Slyme.
> 'Yes' said Crass agreeing with Slyme, 'an thers plenty of 'em wot's too lazy to work when they can get it'. (Tressell, 2004: 17)

This from men who were acutely aware of how few decent opportunities existed locally and lived in constant dread of being laid off! Much of their chatter fixates on the inevitability of things as they are and demonstrates their resignation towards their fate, while also recording a disturbing lack of empathy towards each other. They distance themselves from the shame of their own unacknowledged poverty by demonising and scapegoating anyone lower down the pecking order, whether women, foreigners or the unemployed.

TRTP is torn between what James Scott (1990) calls 'thick' and 'thin' theories of ideology. The former refers to a highly deterministic analysis of capitalism as the *Great System* that structures and routinises the attitudes and behaviours of all social classes; 'the present system compels selfishness. One must either trample upon others or be trampled upon oneself' (Tressell, 2004: 246). The 'thin theory' is a based on the (marginally) more actor-oriented assumption that workers pragmatically resign themselves to the impossibility of change:

> 'I begin to think that a great deal of what Owen says is true. But for my part I can't see 'ow it's ever goin' to be altered, can you?'
> 'Blowed if I know mate. But whether it can be altered or not, there's one thing very certain, it won't be done in *our* time.' (Tressell, 2004: 264)

Admittedly, in this day and age it is a barbed compliment to describe a book as offering great insights into the workings of ideology. Neo-liberalism assumes that we are rational actors propelled onward by our self-interest; sussed and savvy consumers empowered by our autonomous market choices. To speak about false consciousness is a kind of heresy, and even among socialists it is difficult to sustain the argument that the masses are duped by the seamless operation of ideology. It is an insult to democracy or cultural pluralism, leaves us open to the inevitable charge of elitism and raises uncomfortable questions about the possibility and desirability of popular activism. When Tressell presents the workers as deluded foils to Owen's intellectualism it is a risky strategy for anyone seeking political allies, and one I find difficult to endorse. Optimistically perhaps, I choose to believe that something more interesting might be going on in the text. Although the book draws on real acquaintances of Noonan, it is less a commentary on the health of their consciousness than an attempt to activate the consciousness of the readership. As Roland Barthes (1993: 40) has observed, '[T]o see someone who does not see is the best way to be intensely aware of *what* he does not see'. If the workers cannot see through capitalism's mystifications, Owen cannot see the limitations of his own style of communication. By revealing this disconnect between Owen's theory and the workers' ideology, Tressell calls on us to fill the intellectual space between; so that we name and clarify our political analysis, recognise the challenges implicit in collective organisation and begin to construct convincing counter-hegemonic arguments.

Even when subordinates appear to acquiesce in the face of domination, their behaviour 'offstage' in privatised or sequestered social spaces may suggest critical attitudes that are otherwise imperceptible from their formal encounters with elites (Scott, 1990). Although, Tressell is deeply frustrated by the workers' collusion with oppression, it is not the only story he tells us about their political awareness. He records various acts of subversion and resistance, what Scott (1990) calls 'hidden transcripts', all reflecting an underlying sense of grievance and dispossession. These transcripts include disparaging nicknames, 'Nimrod', 'Misery' or 'Pontius Pilate' for their overlord, Hunter. Instances of theft are framed as acts of vengeance. When Joe Philpot steals turpentine to rub into his aching legs and shoulders, he mutters '[T]his is where we gets some of our own back' (Tressell, 2004: 351). Even pious young Slyme, repeating the sentiment 'we must get our own back somehow' (Tressell, 2004: 250), engages in industrial sabotage, destroying perfectly good wallpaper so he can feign greater productivity. Furtive cigarettes, Joe Philpot's illicit excursions to buy beer for his mates and their occasional outbursts into song all suggest that the workers appreciate the awfulness of their conditions and they try to claw back dignity and autonomy whenever they can.

Robin Kelley's (1996) *Race Rebels* traces the hidden history of Black working-class resistance in the USA. Much of this resistance was and is expressed outside formal political channels; rarely claiming an *a priori* philosophical vision or status, more typically focused on issues of 'identity, dignity and fun' (Kelley, 1996; 3) in work, cultural or public spaces. Kelley also foresees the dangers in romanticising this conduct, whether by over-stating its political impact or by assuming that it is a substitute for organisation (Duncombe 2007a; Reed, 2000). Although he does not invoke the now fashionable discourse of resistance, Tressell recognises its limitations and ostensibly treats such survival strategies as expressions of 'apolitical' as opposed to 'political' consciousness. Interestingly, Joe Philpot, who is perhaps the greatest workplace resister of them all, is also one of Owen's few converts to Socialism. It is a pity then that *TRTP* does not go further with this theme, that it does not explore if and how Owen and Barrington might have built upon the sublimated anger of their colleagues in order to win lasting concessions from the bosses. But again this is not just Tressell's failure, it is ours. The Irish left still finds it difficult to harness those sporadic outbursts of dissent – rejected EU referenda or complaints to Liveline – that suggest that capitalism's ideological supremacy is less secure than we would otherwise imagine.

The legacy – a how 'not to' of socialism?

At the risk of alienating prospective readers, particularly those already committed to the left, I admit that *TRTP* is a deeply ambivalent appraisal of socialist consciousness and its ability to thrive when and where it is most needed. Tressell suggests that even when such consciousness does emerge it is easily corrupted by hopelessness – Frank Owen's despairing lurches into suicidal fantasy – and cynicism – the renegade socialist who believes that people 'are being beaten with whips of their own choosing' (Tressell, 2004: 721). When a motley crew of activists finally mobilises in Mugsborough they are attacked by a mob. Unsurprisingly, Tressell's pessimism is much criticised by socialist writers. Dave Harker (2003) correctly problematises the mismatch between *TRTP's* obvious engagement with theory and critique and its limited acknowledgement of really existing socialist organisations. References to the labour movement are oblique and Tressell never really considers what role unions might play in confronting ritualised exploitation in the Cave. Noonan's biographer, F. C. Ball (1979; 120), observes how Owen stumbled over his 'arguments upon fundamentals, which the men neither understood nor related to their own experience' when he might have fared better if he had identified a practical issue around which they could coalesce. James D. Young (1985: 292) is more scathing still, finding Tressell guilty of a kind of revolutionary bad faith;

> Robert Tressell's explicit rejection of the classical Marxist argument that the emancipation of the working class could only be accomplished by the working class themselves permeates his socialist concepts and colours his portrayal of the English working class. Though he was critical of 'thieves, swindlers, pickpockets, burglars, financiers bishops and ministers of religion', he reserved his most bitter criticism for the 'real enemy' – the English working class.

However, I think that one of the greatest achievements of *TRTP* is to evoke the frustration that is engendered when socialist consciousness is abstracted from the practical politics of doing. Owen uses his lunch breaks to lecture the others on theory, but does not speak directly to the indignities they suffer on a daily basis. Tressell knows that Owen fails to make socialism relevant, but *TRTP* cannot (or will not) provide the blueprint for a better society. Instead he uses Owen to explore the personal isolation that many activists experience when they find themselves out of step with the general mood – the loneliness of the long-distance socialist. Isolation is exacerbated by a recurring contradiction; socialism privileges the working class as revolutionary subjects, yet socialists are often unable to establish real lines of communication with that broader constituency. Most obviously, *TRTP* explores how a combination of ideological forces and ritual humiliations fracture and erode worker solidarity. More subtle, however, is its reminder that political conviction and theoretical clarity offer little protection against the disappointment of not making an impact.

If *TRTP* exposes the left's problem with relevance it also suggests that we suffer a deficit of imagination. In the course of the novel, Tressell keeps a certain analytical distance from Owen, often extending, sometimes challenging the conclusions drawn by his lead character. Noonan's daughter Kathleen believed that Noonan saw himself as a composite of the temperaments of Owen and Barrington, the latter a high-born, slightly shadowy figure who does not need to labour but chooses to do so in order to understand the lives of the workers (Harker, 2003; 68). While Owen debates the issues of the day with his colleagues, scorning their judgementalism, their nationalism and their rudimentary take on economics, he, like so many of us, is unable to explain what form really existing socialism might take. At best and somewhat unconvincingly, he can only suggest what socialism is not. Like his colleagues he too is ultimately tied to a vision of things as they are.

Barrington, probably dredging his personal history of advantage, is better able to imagine and explain what a socialist society might actually entail. The chapter 'The Great Oration' is a rare opportunity for him to take the workplace lectern and flesh out that vision;

> PUBLIC OWNERSHIP and cultivation of the land, the PUBLIC OWNERSHIP of the mines, railways, canals, ships. Factories and all the other means of production, and the establishment of an Industrial Civil Service – a National Army of Industry – for the purpose of producing the necessaries, comforts and refinements of life in that abundance which has been made possible by science and machinery – for the use and benefit of the *whole of the people*. (Tressell, 2004: 598, emphasis in original)

Towards its end *TRTP* shifts focus slightly from Owen to Barrington, perhaps implying that the latter is better resourced to sustain his socialist convictions into the long-term. Predictably, some writers attribute this to Tressell's innate conservatism, his implicit advocacy of 'socialism-from-above' (Young, 1985; 296) and his belief that real-life workers, including Owen, will never make it without bourgeois paternalism and direction. I think that Young's commentary lacks generosity and is too fixated upon the wearying factionalism of the left where tendency battles counter tendency to 'authenticate' and own the movement. *TRTP*'s message is more nuanced and more honourable. Tressell recognises that for all who participate in struggle, our greatest strengths may be our greatest weaknesses. The workers are practical and attuned to the obstacles in their lives, but are too wedded to the here and now to embrace new possibilities. Owen's analysis of his class position is acute, but it distances him from his workmates and denies him vital forms of community and personal solidarity. Barrington's privilege protects him from deprivation and reprisal, but he will never truly know the daily grind of oppression. Together all of these characters bring something valuable and useful to the left, but separately their vision is partial and their reach is limited.

TRTP is not necessarily the best book written about socialism, but it is one of the most insightful stories ever written about the left. As a 'problem posing' text in the Freirean sense, it avoids easy solutions and alerts us to the tensions that beset activism. It does not and cannot resolve the left's problem with broader political strategy or our failure to connect with the majority of people's hopes and dreams, but it recognises the costs associated with that failure. Perhaps that doesn't sound like much of an achievement, but I think we need constant reminding of how and why it is important. And as long as we indulge ourselves with sectarianism and recrimination, Tressell's work will sound a righteous note of disapproval.

Notes

1 Working-class people are in Tressell's view society's real philanthropists – hence the book's title – because they abandon their social, economic and political rights without due consideration of their real interests.

2 In 2008 BBC Radio 4 ran a three-part serialisation of *TRTP*, starring Johnny Vegas and, bizarrely, John Prescott, MP.

3 Following his death, Kathleen took possession of her father's manuscript and later showed it to the children's writer Jessie Pope, who brought it to the attention of Thomas Franklin Grant Richards of Richards Press. Although impressed by the manuscript (Harker, 2003: 74), he considered it somewhat rambling and it was abridged for publication. Significant editorial changes were made to the texture, tone and content of the book, pulling its political punch somewhat. The full edition was first published in paperback by Paladin in 1991 with Alan Sillitoe's introduction (Ball, 1979; Harker; 2003).

4 Like Williams (1983), I prefer the book's original title '*The Ragged Arsed Philanthropists*'.

5

Simone de Beauvoir's *The Second Sex*
Fiona Dukelow

Introduction

Written in the late 1940s, *The Second Sex* is acclaimed as one of the major wells of inspiration for subsequent feminist thinking and action in the 1960s and 1970s. For writing it, Simone de Beauvoir (1908–86) is hailed as a pioneer, a beacon, the 'mother of us all',[1] the woman to whom we 'owe everything',[2] or, as Beauvoir herself dryly observed, 'this "sacred relic"' (Beauvoir, 1983 in Bair, 1990: 604). Yet, while Beauvoir and her book may have attained iconic status within feminist historiography, and she still commands widespread popular recognition, it is rare now for the book to be read. The book is limited to its famous reputation and a few of its well-known sentences, most notably, 'one is not born, but rather, becomes a woman' (Beauvoir, 1997: 295). The truth of that statement proved revelatory for second-wave feminist activists across many countries and provided the starting point for much subsequent feminist theorising. Since then feminist ideas and debates have proliferated in multiple, diverse ways which seem to have the effect of rendering Beauvoir's arguments and perspective obsolete and of historical significance only. While the text, or portions of it, appear as canonical reading within feminist literature, it is used mostly to demonstrate a stage in the progression of feminist ideas and arguments, so that, as Nancy Bauer (2004: 116) puts it, reading Beauvoir is equivalent 'to genuflecting on your way into the family pew'.

However, reading Beauvoir should not be so readily dismissed or relegated to feminist annals, especially in a context where feminist politics has to grapple with the implications of post-feminist culture, which posits feminism as a movement of the past, and acknowledges only ahistorical and apolitical expressions of feminism (McRobbie, 2004). Returning to *The Second Sex* reminds us that, while certainly the condition of many women's lives have in many ways improved considerably since the book was written, some of the most vexed issues, such as equality between women and men at work, women as mothers, and, in the Irish context in particular, freedom of choice regarding abortion, remain the same. This reflects the continuing effect of patriarchal oppression on women's freedom, which was central to the analysis of the book. Furthermore, the text should not be considered a static work with a fixed interpretation. It could be said that *The Second Sex* only became a feminist text in the way that it was read by women in the 1960s and 1970s. In other words, it was not a ready-made feminist text but became a feminist text through women's reading of it in the context of second-wave feminism. Following a subsequent turn against the kinds of feminist thinking read into the text, in the last decade or so the text has been 're-opened' and read in new ways. Broadly speaking these new readings appreciate both its philosophical style and development of concepts, and consider Beauvoir's potential as 'a feminist thinker for our times' (Vintges, 1999), especially regarding questions of identity and the notion of reciprocity. In this sense *The Second Sex* may be read not just as an audit noting resonances between the past and the present but as a book open to continual re-readings which reveal ways in which Beauvoir's words and ideas retain their power to inspire.

Encountering *The Second Sex*

Given the cultural ubiquity of French existentialism, and the lives, or perhaps mythology of the relationship between Simone de Beauvoir and Jean-Paul Sartre at the heart of that, I can't remember when I first became aware of the life and work of Simone de Beauvoir. Like many other women I was primarily interested in her life and how she lived her ideal of independence as a woman. She recorded her life in four volumes of autobiography and she developed her philosophy in her fictional writing, in particular *She Came to Stay* and *The Mandarins*, probably the best known of her novels. I came to read her work more closely during a summer of the late 1990s. At that time, debates about the relationship between feminism and postmodernism were in full flight, with postmodern theory calling into question many of the foundations on which feminist knowledge, agency and political praxis were built. During the same period the notion of post-feminism also undermined feminist thinking by suggesting that the need for sustained feminist thought and action was over. Popular feminist books of the time, such as Natasha Walter's (1998) *The New Feminism*, seemed to me to offer a very shallow version of what it meant to be a feminist and of what contemporary feminism was, all in an attempt to show how women could be considered feminist without explicitly claiming a feminist identity. To me it seemed that feminist ideas and debate were caught between an abstract theorising which had little tangible connection with the everyday world and accounts of 'new'- or post-feminism which might have something to say about the everyday world but offered an individualised and uncritical expression of feminism within contemporary capitalist culture.

Deciding to return to some earlier feminists and their writing for inspiration, I read some of Beauvoir's novels and her autobiographical writings, as well as *The Second Sex*. Spending a summer in London, I bought an already well worn copy of the second volume of *The Second Sex*, published by the New English Library in 1969, in one of the second-hand bookshops in Greenwich.[3] On the cover, rather bizarrely, was a photograph which reinforced the sexual objectification of women, contrary to Beauvoir's analysis within the book. The image is of a naked woman with her back and right side oriented towards the camera, and her right arm over her head, partly shielding her face, which looks downwards. Underneath is a quotation from *Truth* magazine: 'the best book on women ever written'. If you didn't know it was a feminist book, the cover would have you wondering what lay in store on the pages inside. The cover image added to something of the notorious reputation of the book when read in the 1950s and 1960s. For example, Kate Millet, who became a friend of Beauvoir and credits her influence in writing *Sexual Politics*, recalls, 'When I read *The Second Sex* I was at Oxford; I read it shortly after it came out. It was a very disturbing book ... Apparently it was so subversive that it got mixed up with being a little sexy too. You were a real firebrand if you read that book, and if you paid any attention to it, you were – you know, all the awful things you tried so hard not to be: a castrating bitch or not satisfied with your fate or in need of a therapist or something' (Millet, 1989: 20). In effect, it seemed that readers, on reading the book, got the same kind of treatment as Beauvoir did after her book was published. Beauvoir was much maligned: 'The critics went wild ... I was a poor neurotic girl, repressed, frustrated, cheated by life, a virago, a woman who'd never been made love to properly, envious, embittered and bursting with inferiority complexes with regard to men, while with regard to women I was eaten to the bone by resentment' (Beauvoir, 1968: 198).

With the book freed of those connotations now, on the day I bought it I went to sit in Greenwich Park and began to read it. I did not get very far on the first day. It is a long and complex book and unlike other classic texts typically associated with second second-wave feminism such as Germaine Greer's (1970) *Female Eunuch* and Shulamith Firestone's (1970) *The Dialectic of Sex*. Texts such as these were written with what Beauvoir called 'the eye-that-looks, as subject, consciousness, freedom' (Beauvoir, 1968: 203). That is to say, they were written by women who had gained from the emerging feminist movement and who were able to write with more direct voices without the need to minutely defend everything they articulated. Some, such as Germaine Greer, were also mindful of the time restrictions many women had for reading and tended to be much more concise. This is not the case with Beauvoir's book. It is a vast groundwork spanning analysis of science, psychoanalysis, political economy, history, anthropology, and literature regarding the 'myths of femininity', followed by an extremely detailed account of the 'situation' or lives of women prevailing in the early to mid-twentieth century. When originally published in French in 1949 the work was produced as two volumes which together amounted to about one thousand pages. In the English translation, published in 1953, between ten and fifteen per cent of the original text was omitted and the remainder squashed into more than seven hundred pages of relatively dense text.[4] As well as its length, one of the other initial impressions I got from the book was how often it veered, in the space of a paragraph or two, from concerns that seemed very quaint to ones that still very much mattered, despite the fact that the text was by then about fifty years old. Working women, for example, are no longer so bothered by the fact that 'stockings get runs, shoes get down at heel, light-coloured blouses and frocks get soiled, pleats get unpleated' (Beauvoir, 1997: 693). Yet, given the continuing situation that women have equal pay in theory but not in fact, that the gendered division of labour remains very much intact, and that women face a much greater share of household labour and caring duties, it still remains the case that 'working, today, is not liberty. The social structure has not been much modified by the changes in woman's condition; this world, always belonging to man, still retains the form they have given it' (Beauvoir, 1997: 599).

Beauvoir, feminism and writing *The Second Sex*

By the time she came to write *The Second Sex*, Beauvoir already had a well-established reputation in France as a writer, and she and Sartre were two of the most prominent public intellectuals in France, known for their existentialist writing and their lifestyle; though they were committed to each other as couple, they neither lived together nor had a monogamous relationship. Simone de Beauvoir had grown up in a conservative, bourgeois Catholic family in Paris; however, her intellectual ability allowed her to escape the confines of that upbringing, whose values she rejected. In 1929, at the age of twenty-one, she gained the distinction of being the youngest person ever in France to pass the philosophy *aggrégation*, a postgraduate qualification enabling its holders to teach philosophy at second-level schools, an opportunity which at the time had not long been open to women (Imbert, 2004). She gained the second highest mark in her year, surpassed only by Sartre, who was making his second attempt at passing the exam. While preparing for the exam, she became acquainted not only with Sartre but also with a number of other intellectuals who influenced her writing and ideas, including the anthropologist Claude Lévi-Strauss and the philosopher Maurice Merleau-Ponty. In her early adulthood, Beauvoir made a living as a teacher of philosophy and literature and was not politically minded. The fulfilment of her ambition to become a writer did not come easily to her. After some unsuccessful attempts at writing she completed a book of short stories, drawing on some of her experiences as a young woman, but this was rejected for publication and did not appear in print until 1979 as *When Things of the Spirit Come First*.[5] By the early 1940s, however, she had begun to write full time, and her first novel, *She Came to Stay* ([1941] 1943), gained her widespread recognition as a novelist. As well as writing another novel, and a play, and co-founding the left-wing journal *Les Temps Modernes* prior to embarking on *The Second Sex*, Beauvoir also completed two philosophical essays, *Pyrrhus et Cinéas* (1944) and *The Ethics of Ambiguity* ([1947] 1967), both of which are significant in recent interpretations of the philosophical framework underpinning *The Second Sex*.

Beauvoir did not regard herself as a feminist when she wrote *The Second Sex*. The years in which she wrote the book were dominated by the aftermath of the Second World War, and issues affecting women's lives were not high on any political agenda. What would later be identified as first-wave feminism had faded away (although in France women achieved the right to vote only in 1944) and within mainstream sensibility there seemed to be an assumption that, by granting women the right to vote, the most emblematic mobilising issue of first-wave feminism had been addressed and feminist issues were no longer relevant. Beauvoir did not identify with the feminist thinking and politics of the first wave, regarding it as 'reformist and legalistic' (Okely, 1986), and she did not regard feminist politics as a source of solutions to the problems she discussed in the book. At the same time, it is clear that Beauvoir was aware of the possibilities opened up for women by first-wave gains, and that she considered women to be in a state of transition or of becoming, edging towards independence but not yet achieving it. In a way, in the introduction to the book Beauvoir seems to be defending her decision to write about women against her time's version of post-feminism: 'for a long time I have hesitated to write a book on woman. The subject is irritating, especially to women; and it is not new. Enough ink has been spilled in quarrelling over feminism, and perhaps we should say no more about it' (Beauvoir, 1997: 13). The book, as Felstiner (1980: 250) notes, 'bears the marks of isolation and defensiveness'; while first-wave feminism had waned, Beauvoir also wrote without the benefit of any harbingers of the emergence of second-wave feminism, and for this reason alone the book would earn its status as a highly original and groundbreaking text, even prior to becoming a key resource for second-wave feminism.

It was only by the 1960s that Beauvoir began to more strongly identify with feminism and feminist politics, and not until the 1970s that she explicitly claimed to be a feminist. This is something she reflects on in the closing pages of the final instalment of her autobiography *All Said and Done* ([1972] 1974). Until this time, Beauvoir's politics are primarily socialist in outlook, and she believed that 'the state of women and society would evolve together' (Beauvoir, 1974: 455). By the 1970s the eruption of the women's movements across many countries taught her that 'socialism and the left-wing movements have not solved ... [women's] problems. Changing relationships in production is not enough to change the relationships between individuals' (Beauvoir, 1974: 454). While still believing that 'a feminist, whether she calls herself a leftist or not, is leftist by definition' because of her struggle for equality (Beauvoir in Gerassi, 1976: 81), Beauvoir begins to recognise more clearly the need for feminist politics in its own right and writes of feminist activists' refusal 'to trust in the future; they want to tackle their problems, to take their fate in hand, here and now'. She continues: 'This is the point upon which I have changed: I think they are right' (Beauvoir, 1974: 455). For her part Beauvoir also became involved with the feminist movement in France and, amongst other things, signed the *Manifeste des 343* organised by the Mouvement de Libération des Femmes. This was a list of 343 women who had had abortions, published in an effort to campaign for free access to contraceptives and demand freedom of abortion, contrary to a bill coming before parliament which proposed to legalise it in restricted circumstances. Until her death in 1986 she remained active in various ways within the feminist movement in France. She supported feminist causes in other countries as well, including Ireland when, for example, she wrote to Senator David Norris in order to support the legalisation of contraceptives and the de-criminalisation of homosexuality (Bair, 1990). However, her position was often more as a figurehead for campaigns and debates that were informed by very different theoretical underpinnings to the philosophy Beauvoir developed in *The Second Sex*, from which she never wavered.

Reading and re-reading *The Second Sex*

Beauvoir came to writing *The Second Sex* via plans to write something auto-biographical. She recounts the origins of the idea for *The Second Sex* in a later volume of autobiography, *Force of Circumstance* ([1963] 1968).

> I wanted to write about myself ... I realized that the first question to come up was: What has it meant to me to be a woman? At first I thought I could dispose of that pretty quickly. I had never had any feeling of inferiority, no one had ever said to me: 'You think that way because you're a woman'; my femininity had never been irksome to me in any way. 'For me', I said to Sartre, 'you might almost say it just hasn't counted'. 'All the same, you weren't brought up in the same way as a boy would have been; you should look into it further'. I looked and it was a revelation: this world was a masculine world, my childhood had been nourished by myths forged by men, and I hadn't reacted to them in at all the same way I should have done if had been a boy. I was so interested in this discovery that I abandoned my project for a personal confession in order to give all my attention to finding out about the conditions of woman in its broadest terms. I went to the Bibliothèque Nationale to do some reading, and what I studied were the myths of femininity. (Beauvoir, 1968: 103)

From these personal origins, the text and its relevance may be read on at least two planes. At one level the book is significant as a philosophical treatise. Reading *The Second Sex* as a work of feminist philosophy, it is clear that Beauvoir made a pioneering contribution to feminist theory, as the book preceded and paved the way for the burgeoning feminist thinking from the 1970s on. Moreover, as more recently recognised in re-readings of *The Second Sex*, the way Beauvoir 'does' philosophy is in itself significant, especially considering that the question of whether women can be intel-lectuals still needs to be addressed (Evans, 2009). Beauvoir's approach set her apart from the male-dominated norms and conventions of philosophy of her time, and which still dominate the production of ideas. Unlike her male contemporaries, she practised philosophy across a variety of genres outside of the academic discipline of philosophy, and turned away from historical problems within philosophy towards treating 'the present, real world philosophically' (Imbert, 2004: 10), starting with herself. Furthermore, her writing about women was not done from the point of view of theory building, or by claiming to create original concepts, but from a particular ethical standpoint. Yet Beauvoir has been accused, both from within feminism and without, of being a derivative and muddled thinker, 'out of her depth and inferior as a writer' (Marks, 1987:2 in Moi, 2008: 94), who absorbed the misogynistic and masculinist bias of the (mainly Sartrean) ideas she worked with. Contrary to this mix of hostile and condescending views, Secomb (1999: 97), for example, suggests that Beauvoir created 'nascent concepts within a pastiche plane of thought constructed from her colleagues' and precursors' philosophies' and by so doing she overturned 'the philosophical pretensions of originality and single authorship'. Beauvoir did not spend time refining her philosophical ideas, neither did she do 'philosophical hand holding', as Bauer (2004: 121) puts it. Instead she matter-of-factly embedded the abstract concepts she used in a descriptively rich account of the feminine myths which have shaped women's existence through time, and of women's experience and the reality of their lives from birth onwards as prevailed in the early to mid-twentieth century.

The connection the book made with women's experience and the way in which it inspired action to change that experience constitute the second plane on which the book may be read. The book crossed the boundaries of philosophy and inspired affinity and action in a way that conventional philosophical texts do not. As previously noted, women, by their reading of the text, brought its feminist potential into being. As Beauvoir put it, 'if my book has helped women, it is because it expressed them, and they in turn gave it its truth' (Beauvoir, 1968: 203). For this reason, Moira Gatens (Gatens, 1996 in Bulbeck, 1999: 10) describes the text as an 'atopian text', which is 'a text which has no place, a text which is bizarre or extravagant and therefore does not offer a single meaning to its reader. The atopian text is not written to a circle of witnesses or a readymade public. It requires mediation'. Read as an activist text, it offered a way of interpreting women's experience which cut through myths and conditions, most controversially myths associated with biology and conditions associated with motherhood, that relegated women to the status of the second sex and denied them liberty and independence. In this way the book was, or could be, read and used without necessarily taking on board its philosophical language and perspective. Clearly women did not take to the streets with placards damning immanence and demanding transcendence, which were two of the concepts Beauvoir used repeatedly in the book to describe the gulf between women's subordination and men's freedom. However, the book's key claim that 'one is not born, but rather, becomes a woman' became its central mobilising message. If there was nothing fixed or natural about women's identity and experiences, as Beauvoir substantiated at length in the book, then it was possible to resist the societal constraints and become women in different ways.

'She is the Other'

Looking first in some more detail at the philosophical underpinnings of the book, the central claim or concept that Beauvoir offers is the notion of woman as 'other'. Her use of the concept 'other' is couched in existentialist terms. In the opening pages Beauvoir claims her stance as one of 'existential ethics' (Beauvoir, 1997: 28). Her way of understanding individuals in the world is therefore informed by the value of liberty, and what is most important to her is that women are free and independent. Her guiding question is 'what is a woman?' and her response, in short, is that woman is the 'other', she 'is defined and differentiated with reference to man and not he with reference to her; she is the incidental, the inessential as opposed to the essential. He is the Subject, he is the Absolute – she is the Other' (Beauvoir, 1997: 16).

This argument draws on a number of tenets of existentialist philosophy, but throughout the book Beauvoir refracts them through the particular experiences of women in order to understand their subordination. A major point of existentialist philosophy is that individuals (or at least men) are to be understood as free subjects, free to make choices regarding their existence or their projects in the world, and free to attribute particular meanings to those projects. Within an existentialist worldview, therefore, individuals have responsibility for and 'author' their own lives, and in cases where individuals live in situations that are not shaped by freedom and independence these are at root a matter of bad faith.

However, for Beauvoir, for the most part, this cannot be held true in the case of women as they are compelled by men to live in situations where they are not the authors of their own lives. This denies them their freedom and autonomy as human beings and consigns them to a life of stagnation, frustration and oppression. By looking at the position of women in this way, Beauvoir significantly modified some of the arguments in Sartre's previously published 'bible' of existentialism, *Being and Nothingness* (1943), and in the process probably produced a more enduring version of existentialism than Sartre's. However, in *The Second Sex* Beauvoir simply states her existentialist position without explicating or defending it, and she does not draw attention to the ways in which she departs from Sartre's existentialism or to the particular ways in which she draws on the work of others from within the phenomenological tradition, such as Husserl and Merleau-Ponty, as well as Hegel, Marx and Heidegger.

Beauvoir draws on Sartre's use of 'the look' to explain the relationship between men as subjects and women as objects or the 'other'. Sartre argued that individuals are aware of people as free subjects, and that we become aware of this when we experience the look of another. The particular instance Sartre used to explain this is the case of a man who, for whatever reason, is spying through a keyhole and becomes aware of another person looking at him doing this. The person spying becomes conscious of being seen as a physical object and realises that in the eyes of the looker he may be seen as a snoop, a voyeur, or that, in other words, his project is transformed into a fixed set of objective properties. Living in a world full of people, this experience of being looked at occurs constantly, which from an existentialist view constitutes a threat to individual freedom because it objectifies us, transforms us from a subject to an object, from one who is self-defined to other-defined. But this does not occur because, as subjects, we don't passively accept how another defines us; we turn it around and 'set up a reciprocal claim' (Beauvoir, 1997: 17) – that is, we stake our claim as a subject and thus render the other person an object.

In the case of relations between women and men, Beauvoir claims that this has not happened, 'this reciprocity has not been recognized between the sexes, ... one of the contrasting terms is set up as the sole essential denying any relativity in regard to its correlative and defining the latter as pure otherness' (Beauvoir, 1997: 17–18). Here Beauvoir contrasts the experience of women with other oppressed groups, such as Black people, Jews and the proletariat, who have not submitted to the status of an absolute other and have claimed a subjective identity for themselves. Women

> lack concrete means for organizing themselves into a unit which can stand face to face with the correlative unit. They have no past, no history, no religion of their own; and they have no such solidarity of work and interest as that of the proletariat ... They live dispersed among the males, attached through residence, housework, economic condition, and social standing to certain men – fathers or husbands – more firmly than they are to other women ... woman cannot even dream of exterminating the males. The bond that unites her to her oppressors is not comparable to any other. (Beauvoir, 1997: 19)

Women's submission to male sovereignty is, in Beauvoir's view, something which has always been the case, which gives it the appearance of being an absolute, a pure or natural condition. However, with its emphasis on freedom, an existentialist perspective rejects the notion of fixed natures or essences. Thus women's condition is not 'immutably given' (Ibid.), but the reason that it appears to remain so is because women have not changed it. Women lack a sense of themselves as subjects: 'they do not authentically assume a subjective attitude' (Ibid.). Women have absorbed and internalised the male view of women or the male look, the idea of natural feminine traits and feminine destiny. Living by the myths of femininity, women live as beings *en-soi*, living in themselves, in a state of immanence which is 'the brutish life of subjection to given conditions – and of liberty into constraint and contingency' (Beauvoir, 1997: 29). Men by contrast live as beings *pour-soi*,

living for themselves, in a state of transcendence which is a state of freedom
and action in the world, and life with an open future. While at some points
in the book Beauvoir touches on the notion of women's complicity with this
situation and their choice to remain in a state of immanence, for the most
part she reinforces the point that

> what peculiarly signalizes the situation of woman is that she – a free and
> autonomous being like all human creatures – nevertheless finds herself
> living in a world where men compel her to assume the status of the Other.
> They propose to stablilize her as object and to doom her to immanence
> since her transcendence is to be overshadowed and for ever transcended
> by another ego (conscience) which is essential and sovereign. (Beauvoir,
> 1997: 29)

'One is not born, but rather, becomes a woman'

The book, in fact, spends little time theoretically discussing the concept
of woman as other as outlined above. The pages are filled with discussion
and demonstration of how woman actually becomes the other, or how, in
other words, 'one is not born, but rather, becomes a woman'. In practical terms, for Beauvoir, woman is defined by the myths of femininity. She
demonstrates the myths of femininity from the point of view of scientific
and theoretical systems which try to generate explanations for why women
should be considered other, from the perspective of man's view of woman,
and from the point of view of women's experience, including childhood,
sexuality, marriage, motherhood and old age. The final part of the book
outlines Beauvoir's assessment of how women could become liberated, and
were beginning to, in her time.

Some of the most striking chapters in the book include the first chapter,
'The Data of Biology', and a later chapter on 'The Mother'. A more detailed
examination of these reveals some of the ways in which Beauvoir discussed
and deconstructed the myths of femininity. Beauvoir discusses the data or
facts of biology in order to dispel the myths about men and women related
to biology. She suggests that biology is described, both scientifically and otherwise, to denote the passivity of woman and her enslavement to her sex, in
contrast to the active part played by the male, who views the female sex in a
number of derogatory ways: 'females sluggish, eager, artful, stupid, callous,
lustful, ferocious, abased – man projects them all at once upon woman'
(Beauvoir, 1997: 35). However, for Beauvoir, woman's biological status is
not inherently natural; rather, it is how biology is interpreted by society that
matters: 'the individuals that compose the society are never abandoned to
the dictates of their nature; they are subject rather to that second nature
which is custom and in which are reflected the desires and the fears that
express their essential nature … [I]t is not upon physiology that values can
be based; rather, the facts of biology take on the values that the existent
bestows upon them' (Beauvoir, 1997: 68–9). Even though Beauvoir clearly

states that issues such as biology are to be understood primarily in terms of how they are mythologised, it is difficult not to read into her writing profound dislike of the female body on her part with regard to experiences such as menstruation, childbirth and breastfeeding. Similar derogatory attitudes on Beauvoir's part seem evident later in the book when she discusses female sexuality and, most particularly, motherhood. She likens feminine sexual desire, for example, to 'the soft throbbing of a mollusc' (Beauvoir, 1997: 407), while she describes maternity as 'usually a strange mixture of narcissism, altruism, idle day-dreaming, sincerity, bad faith, devotion and cynicism' (Beauvoir, 1997: 528). Her overall argument here again, however, is to dispel the myths associated with maternity, in particular the myth of maternal instinct and the conception that mothers are 'natural' or, conversely, the idea that there are 'unnatural' or bad mothers.

On the whole, Beauvoir dismisses the notion that fixed essences exist with regard to any aspect of a woman's life. However, they are doomed to live as if they embody the eternal feminine, in ways in which they cannot be held responsible for doing so:

> as against the dispersed, contingent and multiple existences of actual women, mythical thought opposes the Eternal Feminine, unique and changeless. If the definition provided for this concept is contradicted by the behaviour of flesh-and-blood women, it is the latter who are wrong: we are not told that Femininity is a false entity, but that the women concerned are not feminine. The contrary facts of experience are impotent against the myth. (Beauvoir, 1997: 283)

In 'Towards Liberation,' the final part of *The Second Sex*, Beauvoir puts forward a brief outline of the emancipated woman which clearly ties in with the progression towards a socialist society. However, as already noted, she did not focus on the need for collective feminist action to make this a reality; she seemed to think that women's liberation would coincide with the realisation of socialist goals. At the heart of her vision is work as the route to transcendence for women:

> it is through gainful employment that women has traversed most of the distance that separated her from the male; and nothing else can guarantee her liberty in practice ... When she is productive, active, she regains her transcendence; in her projects she concretely affirms her status as subject; in connection with the aims she pursues, with the money and the rights she takes possession of, she makes trial of and senses her responsibility. (Beauvoir, 1997: 599)

Alongside this Beauvoir also argued that 'in a properly organized society, where children would be largely taken in charge by the community and the mother cared for and helped, maternity would not be wholly incompatible with career for women' (Beauvoir, 1997: 540). The need for free and legal access to contraception and abortion were also central to her view of a liberated society. Arguments for these elements of a liberated society, the right to work, to equal pay, to contraception and abortion, and so on, became, in various ways, central demands of the women's movement of the 1960s and 1970s, and in the process women aimed to resist the constraints and dependencies associated with the myths of femininity.

Beauvoirian feminism as 'phallic feminism'?

As early as the 1970s the Beauvoirian basis for feminist thinking and politics was rejected for being theoretically *passé*. Beauvoir was criticised for 're-heating' Sartre by reflecting his male-centred and misogynistic views and for privileging male values and male sexuality; this became known as a phallocentric viewpoint, and Beauvoir's feminism as 'phallic feminism'. The most strident critique of Beauvoir in this vein came from a group called *Psychanalyse et Politique*, or 'Psych et Po', with whom the psychoanalytic feminist Hélène Cixous was associated. The group's journal, *des femmes hebdo,* published a satirical piece on Beauvoir and the feminism she represented to coincide with a colloquium held in New York in 1979 marking the twenty-fifth anniversary of the publication of *The Second Sex*. Beauvoir is depicted as the Big Bad Wolf, and a feminist Little Riding Hood declares to her 'O Grandmother, what fine concepts you have!', to which she replies, 'The better to retard you with, my child!' (*des femmes hebdo* 1, 1979: 11–12 in Kaufmann, 1986: 123).

The roots of this rejection of Beauvoirian feminism can be found in French philosophy's turn away from existentialism and phenomenology, and towards poststructuralism, in the 1960s and 1970s. Poststructuralism aimed, in Foucault's (1980: 117) words, to 'get rid of the subject', seeing the subject not as the author of a life, nor as transcendent or as a being for itself, but instead as an effect of particular discourses, and constituted through discourse. Some influential strands of French feminist thinking also steered in that direction and moved focus from patriarchal oppression mediated through societal institutions, to discourse as it constitutes reality and subjectivity. 'Psych et Po', for example, did not get involved in campaigns for the legalisation of abortion, considering them 'a reactionary petit bourgeois affair' (Tristan and de Pisan, 1987: 53 in Stavro, 1999: 265). In the emerging work of writers such as Hélène Cixous and Luce Irigaray, the problem was not so much that patriarchal institutions obstructed women's potential to become fully human, but that the phallocentrism of dominant discourses repressed woman's difference, which is the source of her liberation. Real revolution lay in challenging and changing the status of the feminine in language and culture, not in intervening in male-dominated political structures which have the effect of aligning women with male interests. This shifted the focus of thinking about women from equality with men to their difference from men, specifically their feminine difference. Irigaray, for example, argued that 'women simply equal to men would be like them and therefore not women. Once more, the differences of the sexes would thus be annulled, unrecognised, covered up' (Irigaray, 1977:150 in Kaufmann, 1986: 122). For writers such as Cixous, recognition of such differences is to be realised through *feminine écriture*, valuing women's writing and the search for the feminine in writing. For Cixous 'there is no "writing" (*écriture*) in *The Second Sex*' (Cixous, in Rodgers, 1998: 79). Irigaray wrote of building a feminine culture, of valuing, for example, female sexuality, the female body, pregnancy and so on, which clearly contrasted with Beauvoir's efforts to dismantle, what was for her, the oppressive mythology of femininity associated with these. As this kind of thinking began to have a wider effect outside of France, early second-wave feminism became labelled as 'equality feminism', to be distinguished from the concept of 'difference feminism' generated by this theoretical turn.

While important in highlighting representations of women in the cultural and symbolic order, problems with these forms of feminist thinking became increasingly apparent. The ideas seemed to lead to theoretical and political cul-de-sacs, as mentioned at the beginning of this chapter, in relation to debates between postmodernism (which was often conflated with poststructuralism) and feminism. The gulf between concepts of difference and equality seemed irreconcilable, as did the gulf between theory and women's struggles in actual or concrete reality (which theoretically speaking seemed to be said not to exist). It is in this context that *The Second Sex* has come back into view (Kruks, 2005; Tidd, 2008) and is being re-read with an appreciation of how Beauvoir's thinking differed from Sartre's and was much more influenced by a phenomenological view of the subject as 'situated' or 'embodied' or having a 'lived body' as opposed to a separate body and mind (Kruks, 1992; Vintges, 1999). This line of thinking and re-reading has many implications. One of them is that it is a mistake to interpret Beauvoir as conceiving of equality between men and women as 'raising' women to a transcendent state, and therefore to male standards and experiences in the world. Instead, drawing on her essay *The Ethics of Ambiguity*, it is argued that Beauvoir believes that all human beings live lives which are a mix of transcendence and immanence, contrary to the consigning of women to immanence and men to transcendence. This kind of analysis has the potential, perhaps, to surpass the irreconcilability between equality and difference feminism, between essentialising identity and the notion that identity can only be discursively constructed. In the process, it offers a freer and less conflictual vision of reciprocity between women and men that Beauvoir seemed to have in mind in the final pages of *The Second Sex*.

Reading *The Second Sex* in Ireland

While working on *The Second Sex*, Beauvoir also wrote a travel journal, *America Day by Day* (1948), recording her time in America in 1947 on one of her visits to the novelist Nelson Algren, with whom she had a relationship. This visit gave rise to one of her few encounters with Ireland. One of the engines of the plane she travelled on to the USA failed and the plane had to return to Shannon. While waiting for the flight to resume Beauvoir spent two days in County Clare. In *Force of Circumstance* she gives the impression of Ireland as quite an alien place to her:

> a bus took us a long way away, to the edge of a fjord where there was a mock village that belonged to the airport; everyone had a little house to himself with a peat fire burning in it. I stayed there two days, dragging myself along roads whose signposts and notices bore indecipherable words, I sat on the soft slopes of ash-green meadows laced with low walls of grey stones. In the bar I drank Irish whisky while I read Algren's first novel which told me all about his childhood. (Beauvoir, 1968: 145)

If Ireland seemed alien to Beauvoir, Beauvoir's writing was certainly seen as an alien and corrupt influence by official Ireland. *The Second Sex* suffered the same fate in Ireland as Beauvoir's previously published novel, *She Came to Stay*, which was banned in 1949 and remained so until censorship legislation was amended in 1967. The 1967 amendment set a twelve-year limit on the censorship of books listed under Part I of the Register of Prohibited Publications for being obscene and indecent literature. After that period the ban is automatically revoked but can be re-imposed if the censorship board so chooses, or if a complaint is made by a particular individual or group (Ní Chuilleanáin, 1988). *The Second Sex* was banned on 18 December 1953 for being indecent and obscene, and for advocating methods which prevented or terminated pregnancy. This meant that it was listed under Part II of the Register of Prohibited Publications, which includes books with no time limit on their banning, though their prohibition can be revoked on appeal. The regulations regarding Part II books were not amended in 1967 and *The Second Sex* remained officially banned until the year 2000. At that point the Labour Party successfully appealed against the banning of several books, including *The Second Sex*, on the grounds that legislative changes regarding contraception and the provision of information on abortion invalidated their censorship. By then the ban on *The Second Sex* was more or less a technicality, and the book was widely for sale, and used extensively on courses regarding feminism and women's studies.

In earlier years, prior to the growth of second-wave feminism in Ireland, it is unlikely that the book was read by many women. The ban was actively implemented. Judith Okely (1986), for example, records that a copy she posted to her sister in Dublin in 1962 was confiscated by customs officials. Students had restricted access to the text in universities, where it had to be read 'under supervision' (Murtagh, 1980). By the mid-1970s, however, it was openly for sale in bookshops (Keating, 1977). That it was read and identified with by women is evident, for example, from pieces of feminist journalism during the 1970s and beyond which quoted Beauvoir on issues such as women submitting to the idea that it is 'a man's world', on the dangers marriage and motherhood posed to women's independence, and the Beauvoir-inspired ideal of the modern woman as someone who was professionally fulfilled and neither financially nor sexually dependent on any man.

On the whole, however, it seems there is little direct mention of Beauvoir within second-wave feminist thinking in Ireland. Much remains to be documented and understood from that time. Fuller accounts of the period are emerging through archival work, as mentioned in more detail in Chapter 10 by Tina O'Toole. Accounts of particular groups, such as *Monday at Gaj's: The Story of the Irish Women's Liberation Movement* by Anne Stopper (2006), and feminist autobiographies, such as *Sisters* by June Levine (1982) and, more recently, Nell McCafferty's (2004) autobiography *Nell*, also help to fill in some of the detail of the time. But generally, within accounts such as these, only passing mention is made to influences particular feminist texts might have had on particular individuals or feminist groups. For the most part references are made to the influence of feminist texts by authors who could be considered the 'first daughters' of Beauvoir, such as Kate Millet, Germaine Greer, or Betty Friedan, the most detailed perhaps being June Levine's (1982) account of the effect on her of reading Friedan's *The Feminine Mystique*.

Regarding Irish feminist campaigns of the 1970s, members of various groups, including the Irish Women's Liberation Movement and Irish Women United (IWU), reflected a range of views and influences, including socialism, liberalism and republicanism. However, the concepts and mobilising issues generated by texts such as *The Second Sex* resonate in particular with the analysis and the vision of the charter of the IWU written in 1975, which states:

> At this time, the women of Ireland are beginning to see the need for, and are fighting for liberation. This is an inevitable step in the course of full human liberation ... We pledge ourselves to challenge and fight sexism in all forms and oppose all forms of exploitation of women which keep them oppressed. (from the 'Irishwomen United Charter' published in each edition of *Banshee*, the journal of IWU in Connolly and O'Toole, 2005: 32)

The charter goes on to make seven main demands, including 'the removal of all legal and bureaucratic obstacles to equality'; 'free legal contraception, state financed birth control clinics and the right to a free, legal and safe abortion'; 'the recognition of motherhood and parenthood as a social function with special provision for state support for programmes implementing the socialisation of housework, i.e. community laundries, kitchens, eating places etc, ... and the provision of local authority, free of charge, twenty-four-hour nurseries'; 'equality in education – state-financed, secular, co-educational schools with full community control at all levels' (Ibid.). Reading the charter now, it is remarkable to consider how many of these demands and issues remain contentious and unresolved for women thirty-five years later. Furthermore, in the context of the current crisis in capitalism, the fragility of some of the gains made regarding equal rights and financial supports to raise children is clearly evident.[6] These are sobering thoughts against the idea that feminism is a movement of the past and we can all be post-feminist now.

Ideas from *The Second Sex* also filtered through (somewhat ironically given the illegal status of the text) into Dáil and Seanad debates. These include debates about discrimination against women in the context of debate about the Employment Equality Bill 1975 (Seanad Éireann, 1977), while Senator John Robb referred to the existentialism of Beauvoir and Sartre to argue that the use of contraception was simply a reality of life, and to support what he regarded as the still relatively modest proposals in the Health (Family Planning) (Amendment) Bill 1985 (Seanad Éireann, 1985). In 1983, during a debate on the second stage of the Eighth Amendment of the Constitution Bill, 1982, Nuala Fennell, then Minister of State with responsibility for Women's Affairs and Family Law, who was actually opposed to abortion, chose to quote a relatively lengthy paragraph from Beauvoir's description of the experience of women who have no option but to pursue an illegal abortion, and the distress that having an abortion could cause (Beauvoir, 1997: 507–9), in order to provide some insight into situations faced by Irish women seeking abortions abroad at that time (Dáil Éireann, 1983). However, she left aside the fact that Beauvoir unequivocally supported the right to abortion.

More broadly, then and now, the word 'Irish' could easily be substituted for the word 'bourgeois' in Beauvoir's view that 'there are few subjects on which bourgeois society displays greater hypocrisy; abortion is considered a revolting crime to which it is indecent even to refer' (Beauvoir, 1997: 502). Though Beauvoir made light of the fact that she signed *Manifeste des 343* in 1971, and argued that 'it was up to women like me to take the risk on behalf of those who could not, because we could afford to do it' (Beauvoir in Bair, 1990: 547), in Ireland a similar attempt to highlight the issue of abortion, and normalise it, failed against the strength of the culture of secrecy and shame regarding abortion that still persists. As June Levine (1982: 95) recalls, an attempt by Mary Holland to compile and publish a list of women who had abortions, beginning with herself, was 'greeted with silence'. Since then only a very small number of women have publicly stated they have had abortions, while some women's stories have also been published anonymously (Irish Family Planning Association, 2000; Rossiter, 2009). However, perhaps the almost identical fit between Beauvoir's writing on abortion in the late 1940s and contemporary Ireland may be starting to come apart. A video posted on YouTube by Ireland's Safe and Legal Campaign as part of a series entitled *Stop the Silence, End the Stigma* was, in mid-2008, the second most watched by YouTube users in Ireland[7] (McAvoy, 2008). The video contained clips of Irish women and men talking about the difficulties encountered accessing abortions abroad, the stigma felt in Ireland, and politicians' avoidance of the issue. The issues may not have fundamentally changed, but perhaps there are greater cracks in the culture of silence and hypocritical attitudes. Reading texts such as *The Second Sex* for insights into the present as well as the past may eventually become redundant, but not, it would seem, anytime soon.

Notes

1 From an article by Carol Ascher on Simone de Beauvoir, written shortly after her death. First published in *New Directions for Women*, September/October (1986) and re-printed as Ascher (1987).

2 The phrase 'Women, you owe everything to her' is attributed to Elisabeth Badinter, on the occasion of Simone de Beauvoir's funeral (Bair, 1990).

3 The edition of *The Second Sex* used in this chapter was published by Vintage in 1997.

4 There are several difficulties with the 1953 English translation of the text. These include the mistranslation of key philosophical terms, the exclusion of several significant women in history and writings by such women, the exclusion of many of Beauvoir's own personal anecdotes, the deletion of much of her discussion of Marxism, and some basic errors in translation which quite seriously distort some of Beauvoir's arguments. See, for example, Margaret Simons (1983), Moi (2004) and Glazer (2007). After some lobbying for a re-translation, Jonathan Cape published a new translation in November 2009 (S. de Beauvoir, *The Second Sex*, trans. C. Borde and S. Malovany-Chevaillier, London: Jonathan Cape, 2009), which was after this chapter was written.

5 References cite the date of original publication in French first and the date of publication in English second.

6 See, for example, the Equality and Rights Alliance 'Wake Up' campaign at www. eracampaign.org.

7 Video available at www.youtube.com/profile_videos?user=SafeAndLegalIreland &p=d.

Thomas Szasz's
The Myth of Mental Illness
Orla McDonnell

Introduction

Thomas Szasz's *The Myth of Mental Illness: Foundations of a Theory of Personal Conduct*, first published in 1961, is a classical radical work that challenges orthodox psychiatry and the core assumptions behind the belief that what we have come to understand as mental illness belongs to the medical realm. My main motivation for rekindling an intellectual and political engagement with Szasz's original thesis is threefold. First, in the current context of mental health policy and service reform in Ireland, both the Mental Health Commission (established under the Mental Health Act, 2001) and the Expert Group on Mental Health, which was responsible for the new policy framework *A Vision for Change* (Department of Health and Children, 2006), have mobilised expectations of a 'paradigm shift'. Second, we are seeing the first wave of social change mobilisation in the area of psychiatry and mental health services in Ireland. To speak of a social movement proper is premature, although we can talk about an emergent movement – a growing sense of collectivity and politicisation among those dissatisfied with or disaffected by psychiatry and the mental health services, which has coincided with a policy-reforming agenda. Finally, my motivation was prompted by the absence of a tradition of intellectual radical thinking within Irish psychiatry and the Irish social sciences about the philosophy of psychiatry. The presence of Professor Szasz at the 2007 Health4Life mental health conference in Dublin brought this point home to me. My own personal interest in Szasz stems from trying to making sense of my own experiences as a carer, which began early in my childhood. The language of biology has provided me with no insights whatsoever into the suffering that has irrevocably become etched into my own biography. When I lecture to health students on the sociology of mental health, I am struck by the way in which the illness model is so naturalised that students are defensive about diagnostic categories and psychiatric practices even when this jars with their newly found language of 'holism'. Students and, indeed, those charged with their education and training rarely engage with 'anti-psychiatry' ideas beyond their *cliché* status while, paradoxically, lauding the new language of 'user participation' and 'recovery' as if these virtuous terms render mental illness an uncontested concept. I have to admit that my own engagement with Szasz is a conflictual one because of the 'free-market' implications of his libertarianism. His thesis might also have more intellectual currency if it could be read sociologically as a deconstructivist theory about psychiatric ideas rather than a methodological argument about how scientific claims ought to be validated, even though the latter should have more weight, given the current emphasis on 'evidence-based medicine'. Ideological differences and theoretical fadism aside, I focus on the progressive import of Szasz's critique that, I argue, remains central to the challenge of shifting the dominant mentality in psychiatry in Ireland, as elsewhere.

We can describe a paradigm as a cognitive framework or worldview: those who are socialised within a particular worldview follow a standard repertoire in selecting, defining and responding to problems. In following Thomas Kuhn (1962), a 'paradigm shift' occurs when established knowledge claims undergo a crisis because problems can no longer be solved within the theoretical terms of the dominant paradigm. New ideas can better account for these problems and, in that process, create a new vision. Despite the new vision for mental health services and its repertoire of 'service innovation', 'user participation', 'experts by experience', 'recovery philosophy', 'therapeutic alliance' and 'partnership', there has been no radical shift in thinking, or what Kuhn would call a 'revolution'. Mental health services continue to be dominated by biomedical psychiatry and drug treatment, and psychiatry continues to wield considerable social and political power in shaping mental health policy – an influence that Szasz associates with the 'myth of mental illness' as a foundational belief system on which the power of diagnosis and psychiatry's extraordinary legal powers of detention and compulsory treatment rest. *The Myth of Mental Illness* has made a fundamental philosophical contribution to these issues, and any social movement or social critique of the mental health field should engage with it, if only to understand the cursory footnote on the history of ideas behind psychiatric dissent. This book is not an activist manual or toolkit, but a philosophical contribution to the politics of mental illness. While readers may not agree with all of Szasz's critique, in particular his individualist version of a free society, which pushes libertarian social thinking in the neo-liberal direction of privatised contractual relationships in capitalist free markets, he has been unwavering in his critique of psychiatric power.

Szasz's legacy

Szasz, a Hungarian-born American psychiatrist and professor of psychiatry at the State University of New York's Upstate Medical Centre (now, SUNY Health Science Centre), Syracuse (1956–90), is most associated with the so-called 'anti-psychiatry' intellectual movement of the 1960s. Reducing his life's work to an anecdote about his fame as an anti-psychiatrist is, as Szasz himself notes, enough to evoke an attitude of disengagement with the implications of his critique. He has always insisted that he is politically opposed not to psychiatry *per se* but to its coercive powers and practices. Szasz rejects the 'anti-psychiatry' label, which he sees as tainted by the counter-cultural liberal-left politics associated with the celebrity cult of R. D. Laing in Britain (Szasz, 2007). The fact that he objects to the label is not in itself sufficient grounds for rejecting the association of his work with an intellectual movement that brought dissent to psychiatry. Amongst contemporary critical and liberatory psychiatrists, Szasz is now more often reduced to a footnote and dismissed on the grounds of his 'conservative' and 'right-wing' libertarianism (Hopton, 2006). However, he remains a controversial figure and the most ardent critic of modern psychiatry, and his work continues to have international resonance with the psychiatric survivor and liberation networks that are the main voices of opposition to human rights abuses within psychiatric systems and whose campaigning efforts are issue-based rather than ideologically aligned.

The Myth of Mental Illness saw him both revered and despised as a critical voice within psychiatry. Szasz associates the impact of his book with the 're-medicalisation' of psychiatry (1997, Szasz in conversation with Alan Kerr; Szasz, 2002), which perhaps can be seen as a strategy for facing down dissension within the ranks. He did not set out to put forward a new theory of mental illness or a new type of therapeutic practice. Instead, he boldly announced that the emperor has no clothes and challenged the very basis of the clinical and political dominance of psychiatry within the mental health field. The stakes were high for Szasz in writing this book, and he was aware that his ideas would be received as 'an affront against the powerful institutions of medicine and psychiatry ... ' (1974 [revised edition]: 249). He insists that there are no biographical clues to unearth in explaining what led him to write *The Myth of Mental Illness*:

> I try to explain ... that I did not have any unusual 'experiences', that I did not do any 'research', that I did not 'discover' anything – in short, that I did not replace a belief in mental illness with a disbelief in it. (Szasz, 2004: 28)

Szasz's critique continues to be regarded as radical and controversial, not least because his libertarian humanist philosophy and political opposition to the social power that accrues to psychiatry through the medicalisation of what he famously termed 'problems of living' have remained consistent over five decades. A re-engagement with Szasz's original thesis would serve to reinvigorate debate about the ethics of psychiatry and challenge the degradations experienced within the mental health system.

Szasz in Ireland

In 2007, Professor Szasz was invited by the Department of Nursing at Dublin City University to address its conference on mental health (Health4Life), which involved the participation of a wide range of mental health professionals, academics and user and carer groups – all with very different philosophical orientations to mental illness. In his paper, 'Psychopathology: Mendacity and Metaphor', Szasz presented the essence of his classical work in the following terms: 'in *The Myth of Mental Illness* I took this semiotic bull by its horns and showed that it was bull indeed'.[1] My motivation for reintroducing his classical text in this volume stemmed from my experience of that event. While Szasz's fame as an 'anti-psychiatrist' drew the biggest crowd, the apparent confidence of the audience that a radical dissident was amongst us was not matched by a level of engagement that would suggest that the audience understood precisely what he was contesting and whether or not it was relevant to the kind of debates we ought to be having about the direction of mental health services in Ireland and the role of psychiatry in general. More curiously, I asked myself, where were Szasz's critics within the Irish psychiatric establishment, including those most publicly associated with maintaining the status quo, as well as those who see themselves as part of a changing agenda within mental health services? For the psychiatric establishment, Szasz's presence in Dublin may well have been viewed as an unwelcome distraction from the kind of issues it considers pertinent to the agenda of mental health reform: the need for more resources and services, the need to address 'undetected' mental health problems in the community in the name of prevention, and the need to address stigma as a social policy concern. In this agenda, as Pilgrim and Rogers (2005) point out, psychiatry is part of the solution not the problem, whereas for Szasz psychiatry is deeply implicated in his understanding of what the problem is. While Szasz would appear to offer much in clarifying what some mental health activists are against (non-consensual treatment), what his critique has to offer in clarifying what they are for appears more ambiguous. This is less a criticism of Szasz than the inevitable tension that arises for mental health activists in fighting for the right to services and, at the same time, critiquing the relevance of such a service or challenging the concept of 'illness' as a necessary precondition to making political demands.

Historical context

The Myth of Mental Illness was published against the background of the dawning of the era of antipsychotic and antidepressant drugs, which saw mental illness redefined in terms of neurochemical imbalances of the brain. At the same time, psychoanalysis had already gained a strong foothold in North American psychiatric training. The cleavage between psychoanalysis and the so-called 'organicists' (those who insisted that mental illness could only be understood in biological terms) reflected the social division between private and public systems of mental health. By Szasz's (2004) own account, North American psychoanalysis, contra the European psychoanalytic tradition, was deeply embedded in the medical model. Szasz's attack on psychiatric abuses is equally matched by his denunciation of American-styled

psychoanalysis, which he claims failed to question coercive psychiatric practices while masquerading as a liberal-left intellectual movement. He was
an early critic of the use of tranquillisers as 'chemical straightjackets' at a
time when the negative neurological effects of antipsychotic drugs were well
known but vehemently denied by psychiatrists (1997, Szasz in conversation with Alan Kerr). This new class of drugs had a ready-made market in
overcrowded psychiatric hospitals across the world and would soon become
part of the rationale for treating patients in the community when institutionalisation could no longer be sustained. Indeed, the weight of Szasz's critique against defining mental illness in the biological language of medicine
is best understood in relation to the strength of the emergent psychopharma-
cological agenda at the time rather than in the context of 'anti-psychiatry'
as a movement that found its mobilising strength in growing public and
professional unease with institutionalisation and the spirit of 1960s counter-
cultural movements.

The issues raised by Szasz about the validity of the concept of mental
illness, the challenges that he posed for orthodox psychiatry and, in equal
measure, his critique of Freudian psychoanalysis as the new orthodoxy in
North America would have had no significant intellectual impact in the Irish
context, not least because psychiatric training and education was seriously
underdeveloped. By the 1960s psychiatric training had quickly become
dominated by neurophysiology and psychopharmacology, while the professional practices of those recruited into the newly emerging community
services had already been formed within the custodial system of the psychiatric hospitals and dominated by pharmaceutical treatments (Browne,
2008). Reflecting on his experience of returning to Ireland from the USA in
the early 1960s, Ivor Browne wrote:

> I found myself in a foreign world with strange terminology and quite dif-
> ferent basic conceptions, virtually a separate psychiatric language [...] On
> this side of the Atlantic, where the influence of Freudian theory has been
> much less, psychiatry often seems to be arrested at the level of treating
> symptoms, without any real attempt to understand the patient as a human
> being. (Browne, 1964: 11, 15)

Given the political and intellectual conservatism of Irish psychiatry, the
absence of a psychosocial and psychoanalytical tradition and the dominance
of a custodial model of care, Szasz's invocation in the original preface to
The Myth of Mental Illness that psychiatry should be about 'understanding human beings' rather than 'understanding mental diseases' (1974: xiv)
would have had little ethical import. Indeed, in an Irish context, his critique
would have raised the ire of those institutions that propagated and defended
conservative social values. His anti-authoritarianism challenged two of the
key values that were prescriptive of the norms of social behaviour and public
morality in Irish society, namely family and religious values, just as today it
challenges our slavish adherence to the ideology of mental healthism – the

idea that positive mental health is itself an ethical choice about how we live our lives.

In what is now regarded as a classical text for psychiatrists, *Psychiatry in Dissent: Controversial Issues in Thought and Practice* (1976), by Ireland's most popularly acclaimed psychiatrist, the late Anthony Clare, Szasz's attack on the power and interests of psychiatry is dismissed as hyperbolic rhetoric. Clare's defence of psychiatry as an eclectic enterprise is argued from the standpoint of his experiences of working within the British mental health system where there was a more open intellectual tradition associated with the pioneering of therapeutic communities and social psychology. When Szasz was publishing his critiques of psychiatry in the late 1950s and early 1960s, medical directors reigned over mental hospitals in Ireland as if they were their personal fiefdoms (see Ivor Browne's (2008) memoir on his initial experiences of Grangegorman psychiatric hospital). Moreover, the large psychiatric hospitals that dotted the Irish landscape served an economic function within the communities that serviced them and there were few structures for psychiatric patients to represent their issues and concerns – a task that would have required those who were stigmatised to question the self-image of a society that defined them as 'other' and assumed that they could not speak for themselves. When Hanna Greally wrote about her detention in 1943 and the eighteen years that she spent in St Loman's Psychiatric Hospital in *Bird Nest Soup* (1971), a decade after the publication of *The Myth of Mental Illness*, the only acceptable narrative available for her to express her voice was a fictional one. Hanna's story is a reminder of the lack of authority that psychiatric patients had in providing testimony of their own experiences. While her story is one of survival, she did not have access to a politicised, collective identity as a survivor for there was no such movement, emergent or otherwise, in Ireland. Her resistance was entirely a personal journey, which did not have the authority of ideas such as 'self-advocacy', 'recovery' or 'expert by experience', which have become part of the shared language of mental health policy and the emergent user-movement in Ireland.

Let us now turn to the basic tenets of Szasz's argument in *The Myth of Mental Illness*, which have remained remarkably consistent in his large corpus of work spanning over half a century.[2] Indeed, we might well say that this man 'is not for turning'.

The Myth of Mental Illness: key mobilising ideas

In *The Myth of Mental Illness*, Szasz argues that 'talking' or communication is the fundamental therapeutic method of psychiatry, although few psychiatrists at the time would have accepted this and today it would appear difficult to defend given patients' experiences. For these very reasons, Szasz is correct in contending that modern psychiatry has been on the wrong side of science. He sees a more logical alliance between psychiatry and the human and social sciences. Instead, psychiatry has 'shackled' itself to a biomedical 'conceptual framework and terminology', which renders it 'fundamentally unfaithful to its own subject' (1974: 4–5). In critiquing the modern enterprise of psychiatry, Szasz asserts his philosophical frustration with deterministic cause–effect models of human behaviour. In this respect, he is best known for his critique of what we now call 'biological psychiatry' and its core hypothesis that the behaviours we observe and categorise as 'mental illness' are caused by underlying mental diseases. For Szasz, the complexity of human behaviour cannot be thought about in the same mechanistic terms that we might apply to physical and biological phenomena and, indeed, first-hand accounts and public testimonies of mental distress and experiences of psychiatric services (whatever model of explanation individuals ascribe to) remind us that emotional suffering and recovery are not reducible to biochemical imbalances and re-balancing. Moreover, he points out that the claims of psychiatry about the biological basis of mental illness cannot be proven by the methods of the scientific framework within which it seeks legitimacy for its claims. He argues that the search for the biological causes of mental illnesses was motivated by the prestige and power that accrued from claims grounded in the natural sciences at a time when a psychosocial viewpoint raised the spectre of 'charlatanry and quackery' (1974: 28). Szasz goes on to observe:

> this imitation of the natural scientist has been largely successful, at least in a social or opportunistic way: I refer to the widespread social acceptance of psychiatry and psychoanalysis as allegedly biological – and hence ultimately physiochemical – sciences, and to the prestige of their practitioners based, in part, on this connection between what they claim they do and what other scientists do. (Szasz, 1974: 77–8)

One of the more challenging aspects of Szasz's thesis are the ethical questions he raises about the historical project of psychiatric dominance in terms of how professional self-interests became incompatible with a humanistic sensibility. Szasz draws our attention to the 'dehumanised view' of the patient as a clinical, scientific case that entailed in the attitude of the great medical men concerned with the 'real' phenomena to which the science of neurology (and later neuropsychology) could speak. He also reminds us that this attitude has long been in danger of being naturalised as part of the ethos in which psychiatrists and therapists speak in terms of clinical cases rather than persons. Szasz invites us to address the history of modern psychiatry through an ethical lens: to what extent did medical knowledge of hysteria, which he discusses as the prototype of modern-day mental illnesses, reflect and reinforce the self-image of society at that particular point in time, and in what way did medical knowledge contribute to the well being of patients?

Szasz's critical observations were not just historical. Writing against the background of the emerging 'therapy culture' in North America, which now has such global reach, he saw the demand for psychotherapy as a product of affluent societies. He argues that in wealthy societies psychotherapy serves the social function of making people happy, and he points to a much-cited study at the time by Hollingshead and Redlich (1958) showing how social class influenced the type of treatment that psychiatric patients received. Not surprisingly, the wealthy were more likely to receive psychotherapy while the poor were treated by physical interventions (Szasz, 1974: 59). This has led Szasz to argue throughout his career as a heretic that some social groups are more vulnerable than others to being labelled mentally ill and subjected to psychiatric practices in which the psychiatrist acts as an agent of some other person or institution, but not the patients themselves.

A fundamental aspect of Szasz's argument is that the biological sciences have nothing to offer psychiatric practice, which he insists deals with a different order of problem from that normally addressed by 'medical methods' (1974: 9). He challenges the conventional understanding of psychiatry as a speciality of medicine 'concerned with the diagnosis and treatment of mental diseases' (1974: 1) and, instead, redefines behaviour associated with mental illness as 'problems of living'. While we might well argue that 'problems of living' is as nebulous a term as 'mental illness', it speaks more readily to a humanistic model of practice than a scientific model. In defining mental illness as problems of living, Szasz claims that his intention is to expand the 'conceptual framework and vocabulary of psychiatry' to take account of issues of 'freedom, choice, and responsibility' (1974: 6), which is the basis of his libertarian position. In describing behaviours defined as mental illness as manifestations of problems of living, Szasz does not subscribe to deterministic sociological arguments – the idea that there are law-like social structures (analogous to physical forces) working behind our backs and determining our behaviour. He is equally opposed to what we might call the psychologising and individualising of social and political problems, which he claims is an effect of defining certain behaviours arising from the complexity of the lives that people have to negotiate as forms of mental illness. For Szasz, the psychology of the individual is always about the social context and social relationships that the individual has to negotiate in terms of everyday living. In this respect, he observes:

> just as physical laws are relativistic with respect to mass, so psychological laws are relativistic with respect to social conditions. In short, the laws of psychology cannot be formulated independently of the laws of sociology. (Szasz, 1974: 8)

The fundamental error for Szasz is that psychiatry cannot understand the problems that it seeks to describe and explain, let alone cure, by reference to its knowledge claims, which are firmly rooted in a biological scientific paradigm. People should be able to seek help without the prerequisite of illness. Szasz sees numerous advantages in moving away from a medicalised context of care, not least of which is turning the paternalistic model of psychiatric care on its head – an idea that now appears less radical by virtue of the policy discourse about the patient as 'expert by experience'. He argues that value conflicts are never made explicit in the psychiatrist–patient relationship because this would undermine the 'prestige and power of the psychiatric profession' (1974: 215). While this situation may also pertain in the general medical case, values have a significant role in relation to the task of psychiatry, which is about understanding human behaviour. Arguably, values are qualitatively more pertinent in the context of psychiatry by virtue of the contradiction between its central premise that mental illness is akin to physical illness and, yet, psychiatric patients are not treated on the same basis as those with physical illnesses. This brings us to two of the more contentious claims arising from Szasz's thesis on the myth of mental illness. The first stems from what he defines as a categorical error in equating mental illness with physical illness. He states this provocatively in the distinction he draws between 'real' illnesses as bodily diseases and 'non-illness' or 'metaphorical illness', which has no known organic basis. The second claim raises the spectre of coercive practices and human rights abuses. Szasz contends that the fundamental difference between those who are physically ill and those who are labelled mentally ill is that the former enter the sick role voluntarily, whereas the latter may have the sick role imposed upon them.

Clare (1976: 33) and other critics (Glaser, 1965; Bentall and Pilgrim, 1993) argue that Szasz's conceptualisation of disease is based on a 'dualist philosophy' that jars with contemporary philosophies of 'holism' – what today we call the 'biopsychosocial' approach to health. In countering the mind–body split implied by Szasz, Clare (1976: 30) notes that psychological states are accompanied by physiological symptoms, and while accepting that this observation does not amount to proof that psychological states have a biological cause, he nonetheless insists that physical alterations 'serve as relatively objective identification markers of abnormality'. As an extension of this argument, Clare (1976: 34) points out that all diseases can be described in somatic and psychological terms and the idea that psychiatrists should choose between either a biological or a psychological language creates a false distinction within psychiatry between 'organic' and 'functional' disorders. Szasz (1974: 12–13) points out that the distinction between organic (bodily) and functional (mental) disease is the very basis of modern psychiatry, which served to secure its status as a medical discipline. Laying the charge of dualistic thinking at the feet of Szasz (when the history of psychiatry itself reflects modern Western thinking infected by Cartesian philosophy), and on this basis to suggest that the whole of his thesis is, at best, illogical or, at worst, deceptive, serves to undermine the political implications of the challenges he raises about the scientific authority that psychiatry claims as a branch of medicine. Moreover, much of Szasz's critique is based precisely on the baffling mix of biological and psychological terminology in the disciplines of psychiatry and psychoanalysis, which he claims has led to conceptual confusion evidenced by the wide variety of and disparities in theoretical explanations about the causes of mental illness.

Szasz insists that the analogy between mental and physical illnesses is a myth since there is no scientific basis for such a claim, only the promise that neuroscience and genetics will one day provide such unequivocal evidence. Hence, the kind of dualism that Szasz espouses is not between mind and body in an ontological sense, but one that calls for a clear epistemological split between psychiatry and medicine on the basis that the claims made by psychiatry cannot be verified by the same scientific criteria. Since mental illness cannot be objectively diagnosed against biological criteria but can only be judged against psychosocial and ethical norms, Szasz argues that psychiatric and medical practices are no more the same than the false claim that mental illnesses are akin to physical illnesses. He is adamant that there is a huge social cost to the 'illness' paradigm: presenting mental illness as the cause of problems in social living reinforces the notion that most people live harmonious lives, which obscures the inherently conflictual nature of human values, needs and desires and denies us an insight into the human condition. Those with a mental illness diagnosis carry the burden of this social cost: for Szasz this is at the expense of their liberty and dignity. This brings us to the fundamental difference between the ethical practices of medicine and psychiatry. It is only in the name of mental health that a citizen's human right to freedom and right to medical consent can be trumped.

Szasz's libertarianism, which advocates a minimum role for the state, has led his critics to argue that he is only concerned with advocating for negative rights. However, it is the state that legitimises psychiatric coercion and this legitimacy underscores the subtle forms of symbolic violence that operate when patients are denied a say in their treatment and when their resistance to institutional and treatment regimes is interpreted as proof of illness; or when blinded by its own authority rooted in claims about biology psychiatry denies, sometimes writ large, people's own stories of personal suffering. In medicalising problems of living, Szasz argues, psychiatry removes the ethical imperative to oppose coercive practices and to question the basis of its legitimacy. Psychiatry remains defensive about this kind of criticism, which strikes at the heart of the crisis of legitimacy within psychiatry. In this sense, Szaszian 'anti-psychiatry' challenges the very basis of the clinical dominance of psychiatry in terms of the claims that it makes to substantiate its medical status. The new dissenting voices within psychiatry – 'critical psychiatry', 'postpsychiatry' and 'liberatory psychiatry' – see themselves as moving beyond the legacy of anti-psychiatry, and from Szasz in particular. In presenting the postpsychiatry position, Bracken and Thomas (2005: 90) argue that Szasz's critique is 'limited' because 'it simply understands psychiatry as some sort of repressive force'. While their philosophical critique of psychiatric power does not engage directly with Szasz's central arguments here, elsewhere they claim that Szasz's dualistic distinction between how physical and mental illnesses are constituted amounts to an ontological dualism, which fails to recognise 'the reality of our embodied nature' (Thomas and Bracken, 2008: 47). Yet, while their critique works with different philosophical precepts and refuses to concede to Szasz's central argument that medicine and psychiatry are not the same, it shares many of the same political concerns about psychiatric abuses and scientific pretensions. Indeed, in echoing Szasz they challenge the notion that psychiatry can offer liberation (and this in a contribution to a book entitled *Liberatory Psychiatry*) and surely we find an endorsement of Szasz (however unacknowledged) in the statement that the task of critical psychiatry is 'to show how a great deal of psychiatric discourse is nothing more than mythology' (Thomas and Bracken, 2008: 37).

Contemporary context

So what has Szazs's thesis to offer today? Szasz is often misrepresented on his idea that mental illness is a myth, misrepresentations that imply or claim that he denies the ontological status of suffering, thus stripping those who suffer emotional distress of any kind of legitimacy in relation to those experiences. By defining mental illness as 'problems of living', Szasz insists that those experiences are better understood within the context of people's lives rather than in psychopathology or biological categories, which function to deny people insight into their own experiences of suffering and, to boot, deny them the dignity, respect and control over the medical situations in which they find themselves. More recently, we see this clearly articulated by the postpsychiatry perspective of Thomas and Bracken when they state:

> The single most harmful aspect of modern psychiatry is its failure to face up to and engage with personal suffering, stories of tragedy, loss, abuse, and oppression. The biological reductionism that now dominates has served to marginalize approaches that foreground these issues. (2008: 49)

Szasz did not set out to challenge the validity of the experiences of sufferers, as some of his critics would lead us to believe, but to challenge the self-perception and self-representation of psychiatry as liberatory. The cultural legacy of anti-psychiatry as a mobilising set of ideas centrally concerned the liberation of the patient. Of course the problem with this claim is that it is found in both Whig histories (where scientific advances in psychiatric knowledge are presented as motors of progressive reform) and in the claims of those who see themselves as part of a more radicalising agenda within psychiatry. For example, the editors of a recent book on liberatory psychiatry (of the same title) claim that 'the project of psychiatry has always been one of liberation' (Cohen and Timimi, 2008: 1). Szasz makes no radicalising claims for psychiatry, insisting that it can only be judged on its practices. He sees such claims as illusory and, therefore, politically dangerous or, at best, paternalistic. For Szasz, this is empty rhetoric and posturing unless psychiatry is willing to put the involuntary patient at the centre of its ethical project.

In 1960, when Szasz published an article titled 'The Myth of Mental Illness' in the *American Psychologist*, he wrote that the concept of mental illness had by then 'outlived whatever usefulness it might have had' and that its only function was to operate as a politically useful social fiction. On the social function of the fiction of mental illness, he wrote:

> Sustained adherence to the myth of mental illness allows people to avoid facing the problem [that 'life for most people is a continuous struggle'] believing that mental health, conceived as the absence of mental illness, automatically insures the making of right and safe choices in one's conduct of life.
>
> The myth of mental illness encourages us, moreover, to believe in its logical corollary: that social intercourse would be harmonious, satisfying, and the secure basis of a 'good life' were it not for the disrupting influences of mental illness or 'psychopathology'. (Szasz, 1960: 118)

Here Szasz expresses concern about the ever-expanding scope of the concept of mental illness, and not unlike Ivan Illich's (1976) insights into the medicalisation of society, he questions the implications of this for both individual and collective responsibility. Today the language of responsibility has conservative connotations and in the context of neo-liberal ideology it has come to operate as a value statement about who we are so that we can deride as 'other' those who fail to present themselves in such terms. Szasz uses the concept of responsibility in the classical liberal sense as a corollary of rights and as a prerequisite of autonomy and enfranchisement. He sees the cultural investment in psychiatry as a panacea for modern social ills all the more problematic because, while individuals invest in its modern myth of restitution or cure, psychiatry operates as an institution of social control in a manner in which the normal rights and duties of the 'sick role' do not always apply. The fact that psychiatric treatment allows for coercive treatment, which ethically distinguishes it from general medical services, is the core point for Szasz. This is consistently fudged in the analogy drawn between physical and mental illness, which, Szasz insists, draws its legitimacy from the epistemological claims of psychiatry rooted in the biological model of mental illness. The double fallacy here is that when illness is deployed in a mental health context, it can provide the excuse for coercion. Moreover, all the houses come tumbling down in the face of coercive practice in the sense that coercion has no 'hard' scientific basis (and it can only be politically legitimised) and claims to holism as a philosophy of practice pales when those who resist treatment are deemed to lack insight into their own condition.

In recent years in Ireland both those who seek validation for their suffering in the illness paradigm, which in a system that offers no alternatives is the only means of accessing support services, and those mental health activists who resist the illness label, have become politically active around the issue of social coercion. While user involvement is made more palpable in the health managerial speak of making services more efficient and consumer-orientated, the key challenge for policy-makers is addressing this issue. Szasz has always insisted that he is not opposed to psychiatry, hospitalisation or drugs but to those practices that undermine the liberty and autonomy of individuals. These include compulsory detention and treatment, as well as the threat of sanctions where the voluntary status of a patient operates as a reward contingent on medical compliance, which can be withdrawn if the patient is resistant to treatment. His critique rests on a fundamental libertarian principle – that the apparatus of the state should not be used to coerce people into any kind of treatment. Szasz strongly rejects the psychiatric counter-claim that individuals with symptoms of mental illness, usually the most severe forms of impairment, do not recognise that they are ill and are in need of treatment.

While psychiatrists insist that the approach of psychiatry is fundamentally a humanistic one and even stretch to the claim that it is more holistic than any other branch of medicine, Szasz begs to differ, as do many mental health activists and those with experience of seeking support from our mental health services. In the consultation documentation of the Expert Group on Mental Health Policy,[3] those dissatisfied with the services that they receive insist on the need for more 'talking therapies'. Mainstream psychiatrists shun the therapeutic value of counselling, especially for those with enduring mental health problems (Lynch, 2001), which suggests that a biological scientific model continues to define what it is that psychiatry does. Perhaps this should not be surprising given that the distinction between 'talking therapies' and 'psychiatry' is premised on a further division between the 'soft' and 'hard' sciences, which serves the authoritative claims underlying the professional strategy of the clinical dominance of psychiatry. Lest we are lulled into seeing 'talking therapies' as some kind of panacea or a radical alternative to the mainstream, Szasz stops us in our tracks. Those psychiatrists who practise as psychotherapists or psychoanalysts often give meaning to their practices by framing them in the biomedical language of diagnosis, treatment and cure, which Szasz insists serves to medicalise the problems that they seek to describe and understand. Furthermore, those working within the mental health system (including psychiatric nurses, occupational therapists and social workers) operate under the clinical direction of a psychiatrist, and while they may not subscribe to the disease model of mental illness, their practices operate within the clinical diagnostic categories of psychiatry and they are deeply socialised within professional organisational cultures that extol the authority of scientific expertise.

Discussion

Despite Szasz's disillusionment with the direction that psychiatry has taken since he first published what are essentially the most challenging epistemological and ethical questions for its practices, in an interview with Jacob Sullum in *Reason* he points to an even more important challenge:

> The encouraging development is essentially the uprising of the slaves, the increasing protestation by ex-mental patients, many of whom call themselves victims. Through all kinds of groups, they have a voice now which

they didn't have before. We should hear from the slaves. Psychiatry has always been described from the point of view of the psychiatrists; now the oppressed, the victim, the patient also has a voice. This, I think, is a very positive development. (Szasz, 2000: 34)

The Myth of Mental Illness is a potential resource for the 'uprising of the slaves' in articulating opposition to the coercive power of psychiatry, in developing alternative, autonomous spaces and peer-support outside the control of the state, and in mobilising strategies that attest to the personal stories of those who experience distress, which contest how psychiatry constructs mental illness. However, there is another aspect of mental health activism that centres on the state and that requires collective forms of action through alliances with progressive mental health professionals and carers to demand reform within the mental health system and welfare rights more generally. The current opportunities for the emergent mental health user movement in Ireland centre on reforming psychiatric services, and the policy rhetoric of change undoubtedly gives symbolic leverage to campaigning efforts

It should be pointed out that in the Irish context user-led organisations are far outnumbered by third-sector mental health voluntary organisations, and for this reason the language of 'user participation' can often appear tokenistic. The user-movement in Ireland is made up of different types of organisations with different philosophical understandings of mental illness. It includes the professionalised voluntary sector, which has traditionally seen itself as advocating on behalf of service users and works within a mental illness model, and for this reason it is less likely to demand radical change in terms of how we view and respond to psychological distress. Smaller, independent activist groups, which have developed since the late 1990s, are key to sowing the seeds of collective radical action because it is in these groups that personal disaffection is registered as part of a more collective experience. Groups such as the Irish Advocacy Network[1] and the Cork Advocacy Network, some of whose members went on to form MindFreedom Ireland in 2003 and Mad Pride (which hosted its first community event in Cork in 2008),[5] were founded on the social movement ethos of self-advocacy and are affiliated to a more radical international movement through, for example, the European Network of (ex)Users and Survivors of Psychiatry (ENUSP) and the World Network of Users and Survivors of Psychiatry (WNUSP). The various groups are involved in different types of alliances around a number of different campaigns in relation to mental health service reform, and much of this activity is now being coordinated through the National Service User Executive, which formalises user-participation within the mental health system. Amnesty International Ireland has also initiated an alliance amongst user groups in relation to service failure as a human rights issue. For now the agenda is set on service reform, not least because of the frustrations over the lack of change despite the rhetoric of a paradigm shift. However, our failure to raise, let alone address, institutional abuse within our psychiatric hospitals is testament to the powerful role that silence plays in the official story of Irish psychiatry, while the involuntary status of patients remains the most fundamental and difficult of issues to be addressed.

While user organisations in Ireland do not have a cultural legacy of psychiatric dissent or the oppositional politics of a pre-existing survivor movement to draw on, the globalisation of social movements and the reach of the internet and worldwide web provide links between peripheral and radical campaigning groups in Ireland and international organisations. For example, MindFreedom Ireland draws on the mobilising resources of MindFreedom International, which is clearly identified with anti-psychiatry ideas. The core ideas of Szasz's mobilising thesis are found in 'Coercion in Psychiatry' by Mary Maddock (2008), who is one of its founding members, on the MindFreedom Ireland website.[6] Maddock, in writing about her twenty years of experience as a psychiatric patient, describes mental illness as 'psycho-social problems', and objects to the diagnosis of such problems as 'medical disorders'. In constructs not dissimilar to Szasz's, she argues that 'coercive psychiatry' fails to recognise that patients have values, which serves to dehumanise them while, at the same time, psychiatry can ignore the implications of its actions by hiding behind its own aggrandisement and paternalism. In typical Szaszian style she quotes C. S. Lewis: 'of all tyrannies, a tyranny sincerely exercised for the good of its victims may be the most oppressive'.

MindFreedom is an activist rather than a user-led service or support group and campaigns on the issue of human rights abuses within the Irish psychiatric system. The issues on which it campaigns include drawing public attention to the continuing use of electroconvulsive therapy (ECT). Under the current Mental Health Act (2001), ECT can be forced on unwilling patients on the authorisation of the patient's psychiatrist and a second consultant psychiatrist nominated by the patient's own psychiatrist. This issue goes to the heart of what makes psychiatry different from the general medical case. Section 59 of the 2001 Mental Health Act not only allows ECT to be administered to an involuntary patient who is unable to give their consent despite the absence of a legal framework for defining legal capacity, it also allows the same to apply where capacity to consent is not at issue but the patient is 'unwilling' to agree to treatment. In 2008, the Green Party, lobbied by mental health activist John McCarthy, introduced a Private Members Bill in the Seanad calling for the prohibition of the involuntary administration of ECT and allowing for the provision of an advanced directive.[7] Any fundamental change in relation to psychiatric coercion is unlikely to be led from within the ranks of mainstream psychiatry in Ireland, and Szasz provides us with some answers as to why this is the case.

The inevitable contradictions that arise for movement actors in fighting for the right to services and at the same, time challenging the very models that these services are based on arose at an alliance-building forum organised by the Cork Advocacy Network (CAN) in conjunction with Lydia Sapouna of the Department of Applied Social Studies at University College Cork in 2005. Dr John Owens, then chair of the newly formed Mental Health Commission, shared many of the concerns of service users and mental health activists. Amongst the problems that he identified was the narrow clinical focus of psychiatric treatment, with its overly medicalised approach that emphasised diagnosis, the lack of emphasis on recovery, limited user involvement and the absence of an advocacy service (personal notes). While Dr Owens spoke about the need to reform the psychiatric system to foster greater understanding of and empathy with user experiences, David Oaks, Director of MindFreedom International, spoke about the need for a 'revolution' in the mental health services (personal notes). Those who seek more radical change resist the language of mental illness and continue to foreground human rights abuses, which they see as the main impetus of a social change movement. Not unlike Szasz, MindFreedom argues that much of the debate is misguided in terms of emphasising the dominance of the medical model when the important question is whether treatment is voluntary or not and whether or not someone is punished if they reject a diagnosis of their problems as a mental disorder. Oaks describes this as the 'domination model' (personal notes). The key tension at that conference arose from how 'users' were perceived from the perspective of a reforming agenda that sought to empower them *within* the system, and how users presented themselves as political actors drawing on the confidence and authority of an international social movement. While the silence of users emerged as a theme amongst the speakers, the reasons for this silence were contested. Dr Woods saw it as arising because patients were 'too sick', 'disempowered' and 'stigmatised' (personal notes), while the international and local CAN speakers rejected the 'sickness' explanation, attributing the silence to the oppression of those labelled with a mental illness.

The reality of the mental health system in Ireland is that while it now appears more receptive to more critical perspectives that stress the importance of self-advocacy and user involvement, its philosophical outlook is dominated by biological psychiatry and its practices are driven by psychopharmacology. While mainstream psychiatry is willing to engage in debates about deficiencies within the public mental health system in relation to its institutional architecture, public stigma and staffing resources, it is less willing to engage with concerns about coercive psychiatric interventions and the theoretical assumptions that underpin psychiatric practice. Reading *The Myth of Mental Illness* is a good starting point since Szasz invites psychiatry to abandon its project of scientisation and re-engage with the human and social sciences.

Notes

1 See the video of his presentation at the Health4Life Conference, Dublin City University: www.dcu.ie/health4life/conferences/2007/Thomas_Szasz.shtml.
2 Thomas Szasz's Cybercentre for Liberty and Responsibility has an archive of his published work that is accessible at www.szasz.com/publist.html.

3 In drafting the new policy framework *A Vision for Change* (Department of Health and Children, 2007), the Expert Group on Mental Health Policy (set up by the Department of Health and Children in 2003) carried out a consultation process, the results of which are summarised in two reports, 'Speaking Your Mind' (2004a) and 'What We Heard' (2004b).

4 See www.irishadvocacynetwork.com

5 The first Mad Pride event organised by the mental health activist John McCarthy was aired as part of the RTÉ 1 *Nationwide* programme, which can be seen at www.rte.ie/new/2008/0818/nationwide.html.

6 See www.mindfreedomireland.com.

7 The Mental Health (Involuntary Procedures) (Amendment) Bill (2008) received its second reading in the Seanad on 25 June 2008. The bill also calls for the deletion of Section 58 of the 2001 Mental Health Act, which is anachronistic in allowing for psychosurgery, although this is framed as a protective measure in that it does require consent and authorisation by the Mental Health Commission. See http://debates.oireachtas.ie.

7

Kwame Ture and Charles Hamilton's
Black Power: The Politics of Liberation
Robbie McVeigh

Introduction

Black Power: The Politics of Liberation in America was first published in 1967.[1] It was authored by two African American activist intellectuals – Stokely Carmichael – later Kwame Ture – and Charles Hamilton.[2] *Black Power* is a key text in the social scientific analysis of racism – it should be an essential text in any institute of learning that takes the analysis of racism seriously. This is as true in Ireland as it is elsewhere. But its politics also remain immediately relevant. *Black Power* remains a practical as well as an analytical tool. I first came to *Black Power* as a text as a young Irish person in London in the wake of the Hunger Strikes.[3] This was an exciting time when people like me were searching for a language to explain the war in Ireland and our broader colonial history alongside other anti-racist struggles. *Black Power* made clear the nature of racism in its structural institutional form – this was a revelation in itself. But it also negated the idea that people in struggle cannot speak and theorise for themselves.

Black Power is thus simultaneously scholarly sociopolitical analysis and radical treatise. Fundamentally, however, its conceptualisation of race and racism was intended to *change* rather than merely interpret the landscape of race in the USA. Its key terms made a significant contribution to the sociology of race, but their intended outcome was political action rather than academic reflection. This is precisely why the book still matters. It remains doubly-coded. It moved the analysis of racism definitively beyond 'race relations' – the implicitly sociobiological assumption of the specificity of some kind of social relations following from the juxtaposition of two or more 'races'. But the publication also involved much more than a theoretical advance. It introduced a praxis that was interested in theory and concepts only insofar as these helped generate, as the book's subtitle suggests, a *politics of liberation*.

Stokely Carmichael came to prominence in the 1960s as a SNCC (Student Nonviolent Coordinating Committee) activist and organiser of the Lowndes County Freedom Organization (LCFO).[4] The LCFO took a black panther as its symbol, later famously adopted by the Black Panther Party for Self-Defense.[5] In 1966 he was arrested in Greenwood Mississippi after he joined volunteers replacing James Meredith on his solitary 'Walk Against Fear' from Memphis to Jackson following Meredith's shooting. After his release from custody Carmichael made the definitive 'Black Power' speech:

> This is the twenty-seventh time I have been arrested – and I ain't going to jail no more ... We been saying 'Freedom' for six years and we ain't got nothing. What we gonna start saying now is 'Black Power'! (Carmichael and Thelwell, 2003: 507)

In 1967 Carmichael split with the SNCC and he became 'honorary prime minister' of the Black Panthers. Carmichael went back to Africa in 1968, a year after *Black Power* was published. He changed his name to Kwame Ture in honour of his two political heroes – Kwame Nkrumah and Sékou Touré. In July 1969, three months after he moved to Africa, he made public his resignation from the Black Panther Party because of what he called 'its dogmatic party line favoring alliances with white radicals' (Carmichael and Thelwell, 2003: 668). In Africa he organised the All-African People's Revolutionary Party and insisted that 'Black power can only be realized when there exists a unified socialist Africa' (Ture and Hamilton, 1992: 199). His marriage to Miriam Makeba the South African activist and singer symbolised his developing Pan-Africanism (Carmichael, 2007: 221–7). His journey also, of course, symbolised the union of Black radicalism internationally and no doubt presented the nemesis of White Power – a synthesis of Black liberation movements at home and abroad across Africa, the Caribbean and the USA. Kwame Ture worked in support of these principles until he died of prostate cancer in Guinea in 1998. His activism spanned a continuum of evolving Black Liberation politics throughout the 1960s like no other individual – ranging from reformism to US Black nationalism to Africanist and socialist internationalism. He was a leader in SNCC, the Black Panther Party and the All African People's Revolutionary Party. In later life he remained critical of the supposed economic and electoral progress made by African Americans since the 1960s. We can only speculate as to what his reaction to Obama's election might have been.

Kwame Ture's co-author Charles Hamilton was from an African American academic background. His experiences and struggles as a radical young academic in Booker T. Washington's segregated Tuskegee Institute are detailed in *Black Power*. After he wrote *Black Power*, Charles Hamilton became one of the first African Americans to hold a chair at an Ivy League Institution (Rich, 2004). He continued challenging on key issues of race and became an influential voice in liberal political circles.

Carmichael and Hamilton came from a generation which proved that the subaltern could speak – they represented an articulate people, literate in resistance and struggle. This is very clear in the dialectics of *Black Power* as a piece of writing. Carmichael was not simply the activist foil to Hamilton's academic intellectual. When Carmichael spoke and wrote he referenced Sartre, Camus and Fanon. The broader Black Power movement was associated with a whole outpouring of radical speech and writing

– Eldridge Cleaver, Angela Davis, Huey P. Newtown, Rap Brown – the subaltern speaking in engaged, articulate, passionate and theoretical ways. This
disproved once and for all the 'myth of coalition' so ably critiqued in *Black
Power*. These activists could speak and write – articulately, innovatively
and beautifully; they needed neither white academics nor white liberals to
represent them.

Black Power in the age of Obama

The epoch-defining election of a Black person as US president may make
this seem a particularly inappropriate time to try to 'open up' *Black Power*.
It might appear that the gloomier predictions of the book have been negated
while its reformist appeals have triumphed. Some of the hyperbole surrounding the election of America's first Black president might suggest a natural
closing of *Black Power* rather than any need for it to be opened up. Much
else has also changed over the past forty years. Short on the heels of Obama,
the British driver Lewis Hamilton became the first Black Formula One
racing champion and this was seen as nearly as symbolic a breakthrough in
some quarters. African American advancement – one key indicator of Black
Power in action – is evidenced elsewhere. One of Obama's key supporters
– Oprah Winfrey – has the highest-rated talk show in the history of television and has been characterised as, 'arguably the world's most powerful
woman' (*Time*, 2001).

It would be palpably untrue therefore to suggest that *nothing* has changed
over the years since *Black Power* was published. Amid the celebration of the
dawn of 'post-racism' America, a text which speaks directly to the subordination of people of colour might appear woefully out of date. For all
the hyperbole, however, the USA in 2008 remained a country profoundly
divided and hierarchised by race. Much of the progress on racism has been
contradictory and symbolic at best. The world-champion racing driver may
be black, but the *de facto* 'crime' of 'driving while black' remains a key
issue for many people of colour. And behind the reality of contemporary
everyday racism, a series of political defeats mark a retrenchment of White
Power rather than the triumph of equality. Ironically, the vision of Martin
Luther King – that children be judged not by the colour of their skin but
by the content of their character – has become a maxim of right-wing anti-
affirmative action. The 1960s discourse of racial equality has often been
appropriated by the racist right.

At the same time, there is no doubt that the 2008 presidential election
marked a monumental step on a dialectical journey towards freedom and
equality. A couple of years ago I was told by an expert in US community-
based murals that the only image that remained taboo in the USA was a
'Black man with a gun'. Now, ever-pioneering, the country has given us a
Black man with his finger on the nuclear button. This signals an apposite
time for opening up *Black Power* and its unfinished revolution. For all the

furore and condemnation that the publication of *Black Power* generated, the analysis was not self-consciously revolutionary. In fact it offered, 'the last reasonable opportunity for this society to work out its racial problems short of prolonged destructive guerrilla warfare' (Ture and Hamilton, 1992: xi). In terms of the Black Panther Party, which Carmichael was to join shortly after its publication, the *Black Power* analysis was on the Black nationalist rather than socialist revolutionary wing. In its own terms *Black Power* was a realistic prognosis for peace, not a call to arms. So we may take the out-working of reformism leading to the election of Obama as, at least in part, an indication of the success of radical reformism.

More importantly, however, we have to insist on the partial nature of this reformism. Any less cursory glance at contemporary America confirms that notions of the end of racism are overstated. For example, Obama himself was only the fifth Black senator *ever*. In a country in which there are 100 senators at a given moment this is a startling reminder of both the achievement of Obama and the continuing exclusion of other Black people – especially when we remember that fifteen per cent of the US population is African American and approaching half of all Americans are people of colour. In the trumpeting of Obama's election to president, it was lost that his election also meant that the US Senate had *become an exclusively white domain once again*. In other words, Black power in its political sense is far from triumphant. African Americans and other people of colour also remain profoundly unequal across a range of other indices. From this perspective, the Obama story is as much a reminder of how far the USA has to go on the road to racial equality as an indication of how far it has come.

Towards a 'politics of liberation'

So what were the key concepts developed in *Black Power*? First up, it named the USA as a 'colonial situation'. Alongside its theorisation of institutional racism, the book is packed with the conceptual tools for transformative praxis: there are groundbreaking definitions of 'racism', 'white power' and 'black power'; there are incisive critiques of the 'myths of coalition', 'integration' and 'the politics of deference' in Black academia and the 'black ghetto' and urban uprisings. The 1992 edition also carried two key afterwords in which the authors reflected on and critiqued the original publication. Ironically, perhaps, the theoretical and academic contribution of the book was by then far more tangible than its transformative contribution.

The preamble, dated August 1967, made clear the project:

> This book presents a political framework and ideology which represents the last reasonable opportunity for this society to work out its racial problems short of prolonged destructive guerrilla warfare. That such violent warfare may be unavoidable is not herein denied. But if there is the slightest chance to avoid it, the politics of Black Power as described in this book is seen as the only viable hope. (Ture and Hamilton, 1992: xi)

The book then proceeded to deliver a whole series of tools for this project. For example, it names racism immediately and more usefully than any literature that has emerged from the 'race relations' paradigm – either previously or subsequently:

> What is racism? The word has represented daily reality to millions of black people for centuries, yet it is rarely defined – perhaps because that reality has been such a commonplace. By 'racism' we mean the predication of decisions and policies on considerations of race for the purpose of *subordinating* a racial group and maintaining control over that group. (Ture and Hamilton, 1992: 3)

So racism is not nasty ideas about people but rather a system of subordination. It is by definition about inequality and its reproduction. It is not simply about prejudice which may be held by any group about any other group but rather about systemic inequality which, by its very nature, impacts differently on different 'races'.

The book also developed the concept of 'Black Power' itself. The phrase has been used with great rhetorical effect by Stokely Carmichael and others, but here it began to have conceptual substance. It was

> a call for black people in this country to unite, to recognise their heritage, to build a sense of community. It is a call for black people to begin to define their own goals, to lead their own organizations and to support those organizations. It is a call to reject the racist institutions and values of this society. The concept of Black Power rests on a fundamental premise: *Before a group can enter the open society, it must first close ranks.* (Ture and Hamilton, 1992: 44, original emphasis)

At one level this was the revolutionary watchword that so threatened the US establishment. At another, however, this was a very American notion of reformist political organisation:

> Studies in voting behaviour specifically, and political behaviour generally, have made it clear that politically the American pot has not melted. Italians vote for Rubino over O'Brien; Irish for Murphy over Goldberg, etc. This phenomenon may seem distasteful to some but it has been and remains today a central fact of the American political system ... Black Power recognizes – it must recognize – the ethnic basis of American politics as well as the power-oriented nature of American politics. Black Power therefore calls for black people to consolidate behind their own, so that they can bargain from a position of strength. (Ture and Hamilton, 1992: 45, 47)

In this sense the argument was closer to Tammany Hall than Mao. But the book also made a key distinction between Black Power and 'black visibility':

> It does not mean *merely* putting black faces into office. Black visibility is not Black Power. Most of the black politicians around the country today are not an example of Black Power. The power must be that of a community,

and emanate from there. The black politicians must start from there. (Ture and Hamilton, 1992: 46)

This distinction assumes a sharp new focus in the 'age of Obama'. Few would dispute the difference in *visibility* associated with the election of a Black president. An African American is now probably the most instantly recognised *person* in the world. But the question remains whether this indicates any meaningful advance in the exercise of Black Power.

The analysis in *Black Power* also forcefully rejected the common attempt to equate Black Power with white racism:

> There is no analogy – by any stretch of definition or imagination – between the advocates of Black Power and white racists. Racism is not merely exclusion on the basis of race, exclusion for the purposes of subjugating or maintaining subjugation. The goal of the racists is to keep black people on the bottom, arbitrarily and dictatorially, as they have done in this country for over three hundred years. The goal of black self-determination and black self-identity – Black Power – is full participation in the decision making processes affecting the lives of black people, and recognition of the virtues in themselves as black people. The black people of this country have not lynched whites, bombed their churches, murdered their children and manipulated laws and institutions to maintain oppression. White racists have. (Ture and Hamilton, 1992: 47)

The only concept developed in *Black Power* that has not survived the test of time is the notion of 'taking care of business' (Ture and Hamilton, 1992: 178–85). 'TCB' was a phrase that had some reference among African Americans at that time as shorthand for 'self-determination'. But for me it does little to further the project as presented in *Black Power*. The rhetoric employed to frame TCB made a clear reference to Malcolm X – 'by whatever means necessary'. But it is also a perhaps unexpected pre-echo of Obama – 'in this time and in this land' sounds surprisingly contemporary. For me, however, the phrase TCB does little to illuminate or mobilise. This is the one trope in *Black Power* that seems underdeveloped and shallow. It was with some irony therefore that I read the *Daily Mirror* banner headline on the morning after the Obama inauguration: 'It's the first day in his new job, he's at his desk by 8.35am, and already the new President is ... TAKING CARE OF BUSINESS' (*Daily Mirror*, 2009, original emphasis).

Institutional racism and institutional racism-lite

The most important theoretical formulation of all in *Black Power* was that of *institutional racism*. It provided the language that allowed us to move beyond liberal excoriation of racism – the 'one side is as bad as the other', 'ebony and ivory' constructions. In this context it remains both exciting and poignant to revisit Carmichael and Hamilton's original definition of institutional racism to examine how different it is from safer and more academic notions:

> Racism is both overt and covert. It takes two closely related forms: indi-
> vidual whites acting against individual Blacks, and acts by the total white
> community against the Black community. We call these individual racism
> and institutional racism ... When white terrorists bomb a Black church
> and kill Black children, that is an act of individual racism, widely deplored
> by most segments of society. But when in that same city – Birmingham,
> Alabama – five hundred Black babies die each year because of the lack
> of proper food, clothing, shelter and proper medical facilities, and thou-
> sands more are destroyed or maimed physically, emotionally, and intel-
> lectually because of conditions of poverty and discrimination of the Black
> community, that is a function of institutional racism. (Ture and Hamilton,
> 1992: 4)

This conceptualisation of *institutional racism* as understood in *Black Power*
still throws remarkable clarity on the nature of contemporary racism – both
in the USA and elsewhere in the world. If we ask how many babies continue to die because of a lack of proper food, clothing, shelter and proper
medical facilities around the world – and then ask how this is colour-coded
– we begin to understand the reality of contemporary institutional racism.
The inspired simplicity of this approach also profoundly critiques the now
hegemonic and state-sanctioned 'institutional racism-lite' which dominates
contemporary theory and practice.

In terms of the legacy of the intervention, 'institutional racism' has
become perhaps the key concept in the analysis of racism and anti-racist
praxis within Western democracies. Its adoption by the British government
signalled a radical shift in the analysis of racism and the state's acknowledgement of state racism.[6] But this shift was contradictory the 'institu
tional racism' of MacPherson was not the same as the institutional racism
of Carmichael and Hamilton. The shift in the MacPherson Report *disguised*
as much as it revealed:

> We have been concerned with the more subtle and much discussed concept
> of racism referred to as institutional racism which (in the words of Dr
> Robin Oakley) can influence police service delivery '*not solely through the
> deliberate actions of a small number of bigoted individuals, but through a
> more systematic tendency that could unconsciously influence police per-
> formance generally*'. (MacPherson, 1999: para. 6.5)

There is something particularly disturbing about this. First the source of
the theorisation in Carmichael and Hamilton and wider Black struggle
is not acknowledged; second, the concept is neutralised. These two misrepresentations are both cause and consequence of each other: the source is
not acknowledged because this would allow easy critique of the distorted
use of the term in the report; the distorted use of the term is only possible
because the concept is – wilfully or not – profoundly misunderstood.

Thus the acknowledgement of the state in MacPherson was itself an
indication of the radical nature of this intervention. But it also changed
Ture and Hamilton's theorisation profoundly. In naming the state it clearly

moved British state analysis forward in a radical manner; yet it proceeded to let the state off the hook. The institutional racism-lite identified here was pretty small stuff – *unwitting racism*. It reduced the notion of institutional racism to a very English construction of *racism as absentmindedness*. The MacPherson reconceptualisation of institutional racism had a wider impact in terms of discussions of race and racism around the world. Moreover the widespread interest in and reporting of the inquiry ensured that it would have implications in other jurisdictions, not least Ireland, north and south. Here too the MacPherson definition of institutional racism has been adopted, albeit in a slightly altered form (Ionann Management Consultants, 2004; An Garda Síochána, 2005: 5; Department of Justice and Equality, 2005: 59; McGill and Oliver, 2002).

Arguably the institutional racism-lite aspect of MacPherson was further diluted in the Irish context. Thus in the north, McGill and Oliver in their report for the Equality Commission for Northern Ireland on the implications of the MacPherson Report for institutional racism in the north said *almost nothing* about policing. It bears emphasis that this was in an explicit response to MacPherson – a report that was all about institutional racism in policing. Moreover, it was supposed to look at the implications of MacPherson for Northern Ireland – a context in which policing was even more contested and more militarised than in London where Stephen Lawrence was killed (McGill and Oliver, 2002). In the south, the Garda construction of institutional racism added further inanity. By 2005 a spokesperson felt able to announce with a straight face that 'We have put in place procedures to ensure there is no institutional racism in *An Garda Síochána*' (*Irish Examiner*, 2005). This kind of statement was possible because the notion of 'institutional racism' has ceased to have any reference to the Carmichael and Hamilton definition. While Irish usage draws on MacPherson, *Black Power* is nowhere to be seen. Thus the Garda human rights audit suggests that 'identifying and tackling institutional racism' becomes a key element within its 'priority area' of 'policing a diverse community'. But there is little evidence of any understanding of 'institutional racism' as conceptualised by Carmichael and Hamilton. The phrase is so diluted that it now refers to unpleasant ethnic stereotypes about Nigerians and Travellers held by some police officers (Ionnan Management Consultants, 2004: 128). As we have seen, this was *not* how Carmichael and Hamilton conceptualised and described institutional racism. Theirs was an altogether more fearsome and malign social phenomenon. The concept as understood in *Black Power* throws remarkable clarity on the nature of contemporary racism – both in the USA and around the world. But it is the radical conceptualisation of *Black Power* rather than the phrase 'institutional racism' that matters. In other words, people need to return to source if they are serious about dismantling institutional racism.

Critical reflections: the limitations of *Black Power*

There is no question that *Black Power* is an intellectual *tour de force*. This is all the more remarkable given that it emerged in the middle of so much other political activity. It also bears emphasis that the book emerged *because* rather than despite of revolutionary ferment. Of course, the text is not revealed truth – it had plenty of errors and omissions – it was imperfect at the time and history has exposed other flaws. Ture himself was fond of quoting Castro in his own critique of the limitations of the text: 'only history will absolve us'. Some of the most serious of these errors and shortcomings were addressed by the authors in two afterwords published in a new edition of the book in 1992. (Although no obvious schism marks their different contributions, it was, no doubt, telling that they did not provide a joint afterword at that time.) Some elements of the analysis have stood the test of time better than others. The book was undoubtedly 'US centric' (not simply in the sense that this was the subject of the analysis but also more critically in the sense that it downplayed the connection between racism in the USA and events and relationships outside the country). But the authors recognised this in the text and in subsequent reflection. The title changed subtly from *The Politics of Liberation in America* to the *Politics of Liberation* in the 1992 edition of the book, and both 1992 afterwords expressly address the centrality of internationalism to their understanding of Black Power.

It is also true of course that the social conditions the authors analysed have not stood still. The USA today looks very different from the USA of over forty years ago. It has been commonly observed that something has changed profoundly when the leading rapper in the world is white and the leading golfer is Black. There is a profound distance between the Black Power salute at the 1968 Olympics and the election of a Black president in 2008. All the reformism symbolised by these changes is – in part at least – a reflection of the restructuring of the US state in the face of the radical challenge posed by Black Power in the late 1960s. In his afterword, Kwame Ture recognised the successful historical role of the Black nationalism mobilised in the book: 'We can say today that the need for an ideology coming from our culture and in which nationalism played its necessary role was met' (Ture and Hamilton, 1992: 188). Rather than being mellowed by age, however, he repudiated the reformist impulse of *Black Power*: '[We] clearly stated ... that only these reforms could avoid Revolution. Here [we] were in error. The reforms advocated in the book will not *avoid* Revolution, rather, they will help *advance* the African Revolution and consequently the world socialist Revolution' (Ibid.). In contrast Hamilton's retrospective assessment emphasised the continued possibility of radical reform: 'The ultimate goal remains ... *an open society*. Such a process, properly pursued, could be more revolutionary in the long run than anything this country has seen in its two-hundred-year history' (Ture and Hamilton, 1992: 218). Hamilton also tellingly reminded us that:

there was nothing inevitable or self-evident about the *economic* policy preferences of a coherent Black Power movement ... Black Power advocates on the left saw the conservatives as equating Black Power with Black Capitalism ... What was needed, they assumed, and often as not articulated, was black empowerment that ultimately would challenge and change the basic dominant-subordinate relationship embedded in an institutionally racist and exploitatively capitalist system. Black Power advocates on the right were more inclined to view the need in less holistic and 'revolutionary' terms. Blacks needed to organise their own resources, to accumulate capital, to be enabled to function better – as individuals and collectively – in a market economy. [Our book] was not sufficiently attentive to this predictable dichotomy. (Ture and Hamilton, 1992: 209–11)

Hamilton also criticised the book's lack of historical context, arguing for a more grounded 'historic perspective, the progressive continuity of our struggle' (Ture and Hamilton, 1992: 211–12). Certainly for many African Americans the 'progressive continuity' in Black struggle in the USA reached its apogee in the election of Barack Obama as President (Obama, 2009).

Arguably, however, the real shortcoming of book was not its vision or its analysis or its predictions, but rather *in the issues it failed to address*. Crucially here it never addressed the nature of *power* with the same incision as it did race and racism. This is equally true of notions of both Black Power and White Power. In terms of *Black Power*, the irony is that the rise of the intellectual significance of the book – even if we regard this as plagiarism rather than intellectual debt – was mirrored by the implosion and collapse of the radical and revolutionary African American movement with which Stokely Carmichael was associated. There is no questioning the widening reference to 'institutional racism' as the key paradigm in the sociology of race; but less evidence of the relevance of the radical political programme this analysis implied. Insofar as Black Power was realised, it was much more conservative and much less empowering than either author had anticipated. For every Jesse Jackson and Barack Obama the subsequent years produced, there was a Clarence Thomas and a Colin Powell. The book fails to help us to anticipate or understand this process. It maintains its optimism of the will to the expense of a necessary pessimism of the intellect. In other words – and with appropriate recognition of the not insignificant advantage of hindsight – we need to critique the book because of its failure to understand the collapse of the Black Power movement.

At this point it becomes clear that the implosion of the movement was not an accident. The US state violently confronted the Black Panther Party and other broader manifestations of Black Power. This impacted directly on the biography of the authors. Stokely Carmichael went back to Africa specifically in the wake of 'dirty tricks' from the Federal Bureau of Investigation (FBI). Here we begin to identify some of the limitations of the publication in terms of its unpacking of 'White Power'. Arguably the core weakness of the book is that in naming and confronting overt White Power it ignored covert White Power. Of course, it is asking of a lot of any publication to anticipate the next stage in the dialectic. Moreover, given that Stokely Carmichael in particular was intimately involved in confronting the visceral racist violence of 1960s America – from the murder of Medgar Evans and Martin Luther King and the shooting of James Meredith – asking that he also hypothesise the nature of covert power of the state might seem unfair. Nevertheless it is striking that the element of White Power which subverted and undermined the Black Panther Party and Stokely Carmichael himself is hardly addressed in the book at all. And here is the rub – the *contretemps* around the phrase 'Black Power' and the title of the book was focused on the word 'Black': was it Black capitalism? Was it Black nationalism? Was it Black 'race hate'? In truth, however, the key issue it addressed was the nexus of race and *power*. It both demanded an analysis of the complexity of the whiteness of contemporary power as well as provoking the question of what the reality of Black Power might actually look like.

It was in speaking truth to power that the book is most revelatory; equally in understanding the increasingly covert nature of power it was at its weakest. Carmichael and Hamilton made a huge breakthrough in tracing the institutionalisation of racism. But their approach suggests that we need to go further and deeper in understanding racism in the contemporary world. We might argue on re-opening *Black Power* that it teaches us that racism is hardest to resist at the point at which it stops being overt and blunt and *easy to read*. Racist power stops blowing up children in churches, but it kills far more with 'Structural Adjustment Programs'. 'Fortress Europe' takes over from *apartheid*. The Dred Scott decision of the US Supreme Court is replaced by COINTELPRO and Homeland Security.

Counter-insurgency and racism – the new white power?

COINTELPRO (an acronym for Counter Intelligence Program) was a series of covert and illegal projects conducted by the FBI aimed at investigating and disrupting 'subversive' political organisations within the United States. This activity was investigated in the wake of Watergate by the Select Committee on Intelligence Activities and the Rights of Americans, 1975 – commonly referred to as the 'Church Committee' – although much of this activity continued to be classified (US Congress, 1976a,b,c). The Church Committee Report specifically investigated a series of operations against Black organisations and individuals – including Martin Luther King. These African American organisations and individuals were collectively identified as 'Black Nationalist Hate Groups'. The Church Committee summarised the FBI memorandum expanding the programme described its five 'long-range goals':

> 1. to prevent the 'coalition of militant black nationalist groups' which might be the first step towards a real 'Mau Mau' in America;

2. to prevent the rise of a 'messiah' who could 'unify and electrify' the movement, naming specifically Martin Luther King, Stokely Carmichael and Elijah Muhammad;

3. to prevent violence on the part of black nationalist groups by pinpointing 'potential troublemakers' and neutralizing them 'before they exercise their potential for violence';

4. to prevent militant groups and leaders from gaining 'respectability' by discrediting them to the 'responsible' Negro community, to the white community (both the responsible community and the 'liberals' – the distinction is the Bureau's), and to Negro radicals; and

5. to prevent the long-range growth of these organizations, especially among youth, by developing specific tactics to 'prevent these groups from recruiting young people'. (US Congress, 1976c: 20–2)

The Report confirmed that the 'targets of this nationwide program to disrupt 'militant black nationalist organizations' included groups such as the Southern Christian Leadership Conference (SCLC), the Student Non-violent Coordinating Committee (SNCC), the Revolutionary Action Movement (RAM), and the Nation of Islam (NOI). COINTELPRO was expressly directed against leaders such as Martin Luther King and Stokely Carmichael (US Congress, 1976c: 20). This bears some deconstruction. The range of 'Black Nationalist Hate Groups' targeted covered the entire continuum of African American political activity in the 1960s – from conservative and religious reformism to nationalist and separatist revolutionary politics. In other words, from this perspective almost any African Americans organising politically became a 'Black Nationalist Hate Group' *whatever their politics.* Never mind the aspiration to Black Power: *to address racism was to be a Black Nationalist Hate Group.*

Here we begin to speak truth to a different kind of power. In the 1960s the US state was prepared to prevent African American advance 'by any means necessary'. Black nationalism, revolutionary socialism *but also religious reformism* would and could be regarded as subversive and undermined in the most profound ways. Thus Martin Luther King was to be attacked and smeared – and perhaps ultimately assassinated – by a state supposedly governed by democracy and civil rights. With the brief window of the post-Watergate period, we can trace a continuum from COINTELPRO to Homeland Security, from Birmingham to Guantanamo Bay and Abu Ghraib. The real weakness in *Black Power* was that it only spoke directly to overt, crude and openly racist power – those who were, as it Dylan described it, 'only a pawn in their game'. From this perspective, the real White Power structure emerged from the 1960s almost unchanged.

Black Power survived as a text, and this is why it remains so important – the text couldn't be repressed or censored or destroyed. Nevertheless the organisational manifestation of Black Power *was* destroyed. By 1970 neither Stokely Carmichael nor King nor Malcolm X was part of the struggle in the

USA. The 'messiah' that the FBI had feared would not reappear for another generation. Moreover the covert state exposed in the COINTELPRO files was subsequently reinforced exponentially under the Bush administration. Thus when we anticipate the performance of Barack Obama, we must gauge this as much in terms of his vulnerability to the repressive state apparatus he notionally controls as Commander-in-Chief and President as in his ability to deal with economic crisis or war or injustice or inequality. Without succumbing to hyperbole, we might anticipate a continuing embedded 'White Power' that has two choices with Obama: it must either co-opt him – or remove him by whatever means necessary.

Lessons for Ireland

The politics of *Black Power* remain immediately relevant to two broad constituencies in Ireland. The first is the new people of colour population in Ireland – people who came as immigrants and refugees and migrant workers and now consolidate into a relatively large Black and minority ethnic Irish population. This population is increasingly confronted by Irishness as whiteness and has to negotiate its relationship with racism in Ireland. The second relevant constituency is the Irish left – the 'unfinished revolution' – those of us who continue to engage with the question of the continuing legacy of British colonialism in Ireland.

For both of these two – largely unconnected – groups, *Black Power* remains a key text. In Ireland in the 1960s, the Black Power model had been answered in a parallel fashion with rise in civil rights and anti-imperialist politics. Though it seems unbelievable now, until the 1960s the nationalist voice in the north had seemed bumbling and incompetent compared to the sophistication of unionism. This was all transformed by Bernadette Devlin as a young woman speaking in her own terms. Others followed of course: articulate, theorised, writers like Eamonn McCann and Bobby Sands, who located their politics in relation to African American struggle. Here was evidence – if it were needed – that the subaltern could speak. People in struggle can do 'theory', but they do it in a way that is engaged and relevant and about praxis.

Black Power is also a reminder of the complex intertwining of American and Irish politics. America continues to lead and influence liberation movements around the world. But the civil rights/USA/Ireland interface was much stronger than this. The Irish civil rights movement modelled itself on the USA's counterpart; the left of this movement in both countries was also keenly aware of the similarities. Bernadette Devlin famously donated the keys of New York to the Black Panthers and she spoke alongside Stokely Carmichael and other Black Power leaders. The key difference between the USA and the north of Ireland was that the two situations quickly diverged. In the words of *Black Power,* Ireland did 'fail to work out its racial problems' and quickly descended into 'prolonged destructive guerrilla warfare'.

But it is perhaps the ongoing and deepening elective affinity between Irishness and racism that needs the insights of *Black Power* most immediately. In a context in which Roma European citizens are being forced out of Ireland through racist violence and in which minority ethnic political representatives are being death-threatened and minority ethnic organisations bomb-threatened, contemporary Ireland presents a scenario that is all too familiar to the reality addressed in *Black Power*. One of the key challenges for Irish social sciences and Irish anti-racism is that Black Power placed Black people right in the centre of the analysis – it was their struggle and they would define the parameters of the struggle. Irish anti-racism has still failed to do this. It is white-focused and white-dominated. In particular, the role of the Black Irish intellectual and activist needs to be articulated. And *Black Power* still provides the template.

The key consequence of the intervention on racism in Ireland was to create jobs for white Irish people – white academics, white quangocrats, white integrationists on the ground. Not surprisingly this mirrored developments in terms of the Irish anti-racism articulated around Traveller support a generation before. Once the case for justice for Travellers became irresistible, it was transmogrified into an analysis of cultural difference with large numbers of settled experts who were able to not only identify but construct a subculture of poverty. In other words, they become a self-fulfilling prophecy that confirms that minority ethnic people are incapable of liberation 'on their own'.

Here we return again to the *Black Power* thesis – this is primarily about a *politics*, not a philosophy or a sociology or a government programme. The key question begged in re-reading the book is: where is the broader politics of liberation in Ireland? And once this is asked, the supplementaries are: first, how do people of colour in Ireland relate to this wider politics; and second, how does that politics relate to them?

This raises profound questions in terms of the place of people of colour and migrant workers within Ireland and Irishness. As we have seen, Ireland adopted its own notion of institutional racism and celebrates its own notion of integration. However, the current fetishing of diversity and integration is the very antithesis of the anti-racism conceptualised in *Black Power*. It allows the state to be 'doing something' on race as it continues to do nothing on racism. The state in Ireland, north and south, remains institutionally racist as this was conceptualised by Carmichael and Hamilton.

Finally, in Ireland in particular, the analytical gaps in the book alluded to early also speak to progressive politics in Ireland. We too need to understand and critique our own 'counter intelligence programme' – the 'dirty war'. Moreover we must do this not as a minor footnote to Irish history but as a central challenge to what has happened to the politics of liberation. As in the USA, this is the point at which subordination stops being overt and blunt and *easy to read* and becomes something else. The mechanisms of subordination continue, but they are no longer crudely racist and they are no longer uncomfortable with having a Black – or a Catholic – about the place.

We have observed this process in Ireland over recent years as evidence has emerged of the exact nature of the 'dirty war' conducted by the British state in Ireland. The British state has been directing terrorism in the north of Ireland for the duration of the conflict. In Ireland, from the Littlejohns to Denis Donaldson, we find the British state disrupting republican and anti-imperialist political activity – and apparently preventing any possibility of progressive political activity. This raises profound questions about revolutionary praxis. The use of counter-insurgency becomes the key mechanism of counter-revolution. Moreover, it has been remarkably effective. In a state of emergency, a permanent state of exception, the traditional protections from state power are increasingly weak. The state can torture you, hold you without trial indefinitely, make you disappear and murder you with impunity. It has colluded with and directed the terrorism of loyalist paramilitarism in a whole series of ways over this period (Rowan, 2006; Police Ombudsman for Northern Ireland, 2007).

And here we begin to see the affinity of those two constituencies that I suggested should be 'opening up' *Black Power* for its politics. Ironically, these two separated constituencies – the Black Irish and the Irish left – have begun to meet through necessity rather than choice in the context of racism and covert action by the state. In 2006 the Independent Monitoring Commission – the body was charged by the British and Irish States with overseeing normalisation – quietly announced:

> One important step [toward normalisation] would be for loyalist para-militaries, including the UVF and RHC, to stop targeting nationalists and ethnic minorities. We hope the PUP will give a clear and robust lead on this   Another important step would be for loyalist paramilitaries, including the UDA, to stop targeting nationalists and members of ethnic minorities. We hope that the UPRG will give a clear and robust lead on this. (Independent Monitoring Commission, 2006: 23, 24)

There has been no sign of 'significant progress' since. In June 2009 as the world was trumpeting the decommissioning of loyalism, the north's only minority-ethnic MLA was being death-threatened by loyalists and UDA's youth wing was sending signed bomb threats to minority ethnic organisations across Belfast. This is a profoundly disturbing scenario – a paramilitary force often directed by the state and riddled with informers is acknowledged to be engaged in targeting minority-ethnic people in racist violence. Whether people like it or not, the vexed, sordid world of the dirty war now threatens a lethal combination of racism and sectariansm, loyalist paramilitarism and state collusion. *Black Power* begins with its analysis of the bombing of African American churches; in Ireland we now face the prospect of the bombing of mosques. The point is that the continuing 'dirty war' in Ireland is more than a simple irritant to progressive politics in Ireland. We have to profoundly reframe progressive political activity – and particularly anti-racism – in the context of this aspect of power. What this means will, of course, be worked out dialectically on a much bigger stage than Ireland. But we might begin by opening – or re-opening – *Black Power*.

Conclusions

I hope I have done *Black Power* justice. It is a *great* book and it is an *historic* book. It is history, sociology, social psychology, political analysis and political rhetoric all rolled into one. It is also simply a very fine read. When I re-opened the chapter on the Lowndes County Freedom Party and the 'Black Belt election' of 1966, it had the hallmarks of a gripping political thriller. You are reminded that the reality of racism in the 'deep south' provided just as powerful and dreadful a story as the idealised and whitened fantasy that appeared in the film *Mississippi Burning*. (Remember the COINTELPRO files have amply demonstrated what the FBI was *really* up to in terms of its relationship with Black struggle in the 1960s.)

An African American may become US president, an African American may be head of the US armed forces, an African American may be the most influential woman in the world, an African American may be crowned 'King of Pop' and a Black person can be world motor racing champion and US Masters golf champion. None of these things would have been possible in 1967 when *Black Power* appeared; none of these changes is trivial. Each represents Black Power in action. None of these changes was conceded willingly by the White Power elite – each emerged from Black struggle. But this journey is far from complete. Moreover, if it is unfinished in the USA, it has hardly started in places like Ireland. The start is – as with *Black Power* – for people in struggle to define their terms, to construct a politics of liberation.

In this regard, the publication of *Black Power* was not simply an interesting moment in the history of ideas. It remains a living tool for transformation; it retains its status as a 'dangerous book'. Ironically from this perspective the preamble cited earlier becomes strangely apposite – even though at first glance it appears the most dated aspect of the book. Of course if 'this society' is the mainland USA, it can be argued that it has significantly 'worked out' its 'racial problems' without either conceding 'Black Power' or 'prolonged destructive guerrilla warfare' – it has avoided the doomsday scenario. Moreover, its reformism is more than tokenism – it may have taken over forty years but it has elected its first Black president. If, however, 'this society' is the globalised world, then Carmichael and Hamilton look a lot closer to the mark. The USA – alongside its white allies – is now fighting a prolonged war around the world. Strangely, therefore, when we return to the preamble to *Black Power* – which appears the most millenarian section when we first re-open the book – we find the prophetic voice true. A 'destructive guerrilla war' is being fought not in the streets of the USA but elsewhere within the writ of the US Empire – in Afghanistan, in Iraq, in Iran, in Palestine. And this war remains inescapably and undeniably colour-coded.

Meanwhile around the world ideas of race and racism – and anti-racism – remain refracted through the USA. This is, of course, not entirely positive: in one sense it reflects the level of organisation and vanguardism of organised peoples of colour in the USA, in another it merely reflects the hegemony of all things American. We now do anti-racism like the Americans because we do business and sport and culture and everything else like them as well. Once again the contradiction of Obama looms large and poses fascinating new questions. Of course he speaks as a Black person. And for the first time there is an American President who looks like he belongs to the Majority World. But the degree to which he can speak *for* the world remains much more problematic and contentious. From this perspective, what and who Obama represents – *Black Power or Black visibility* – remains the key semiotic and political question of our time. And anyone interested in answering this question would do well to begin by opening and reading *Black Power: The Politics of Liberation*.

Acknowledgement

The author would like to like to thank Gwen Patton – 'movement warrior', LCFO activist and friend of Stokely Carmichael – and Catherine Flowers – Lowndes County native and activist – for their inspiration and insights as well as their comments and support. He also wishes to thank the editors for their helpful comments and support.

Notes

1 I use the 1992 Vintage Edition as definitive (Ture and Hamilton, 1992).

2 Stokely Carmichael was born in Trinidad where he lived for the first ten years of his life. This aspect of his biography placed him in a specific relationship with mainstream 'African America' at that time. His self-identification was as 'African' and towards the end of his life he used the term 'Africans in America' rather than African Americans.

3 The other key concept which emerged from the Black Panther Party was Huey P. Newton's (2009) notion of 'revolutionary suicide'. This has specific reference in the Irish context. While not theorised thus at the time, the struggle of the hunger strikers is paradigmatic of this particular notion of revolutionary sacrifice.

4 The Lowndes County Freedom Organization (LCFO), also known as the Black Panther Party, was started in 1965 under the direction of Stokely Carmichael and became an example of Black Power in action. In Lowndes at that time a tiny white oligarchy owned ninety per cent of the land in the county and controlled local government in a county that was around eighty per cent African American. Despite the 1965 Voting Rights Act, very few black residents were registered to vote. The LCFO organised African Americans to register to vote and stand

for election to county office. Racists in Lowndes County reacted brutally to the LCFO.

5 Kwame Ture also locates the formation of the Black Panther Party in this southern context (Ture and Hamilton, 1992: 192).

6 This analysis emerged from the MacPherson Report – the British government-established inquiry into the murder of black teenager Stephen Lawrence and the subsequent shamefully botched police response to his death (MacPherson, 1999).

8

Paulo Freire's *Pedagogy of the Oppressed*
Mark Garavan

Introduction

When the contemporary reader first approaches Paulo Freire's *Pedagogy of the Oppressed* there may be some initial barriers to be confronted. First, precisely what kind of book is it? Is it an education textbook providing instructions for achieving adult literacy? Is it a manifesto for a 'new person', a quasi-religious exhortation to social and political justice? Is it a call for revolution outlining a radical new method for achieving 'bottom-up' social transformation? Second, in the light of so much history and horror since 1970, the book may strike the reader now as a naïve attempt to combine elements of Marxism and Christianity to create a 'new man' devoid of evil and self-interest. The positive references in the text to figures such as Mao Tse Tung may sound now as deluded or even sinister. Finally, the book may also seem dated and surprisingly limited in its set of concerns. For example, there are no explicit references to gender or to the environment, no recognition of these issues as warranting specific attention within a liberation process. Instead, there appears to be a gender blindness throughout and a simple faith in the old modernist project of fashioning the natural world to enhance human progress.

Of course, the book is a product of its time and circumstances. Freire's work is rooted in the concrete social, economic and cultural reality of 1960s Latin America. This was a reality marked by, above all else, poverty and oppression. As much as eighty per cent of the population of Latin America was living in conditions of dire poverty. This was the overwhelming reality that any book purporting to describe and contribute to social understanding had to confront.

Freire himself was no detached theorist. The book was written while he was in exile in Chile following the Brazilian military coup of 1964. Published in 1970, it was based on many years of direct experience of working with the poor of Brazil and Chile. Freire was born in 1921 in Recife, Brazil. While initially he taught Portuguese in secondary schools, from 1946 he began developing adult literacy programmes. That work was brought to an end with the military coup. Following a brief imprisonment he went into exile in Chile. After the Portuguese-language publication of the *Pedagogy of the Oppressed* he was invited in 1969 to Harvard as a visiting professor. He later moved to Europe as a special education advisor to the World Council of Churches. Returning to Brazil in 1980, Freire took up again his work in adult pedagogy. In 1988, he was appointed Secretary of Education in São Paulo by the Brazilian Workers Party. Freire died in 1997.

We still live in a world marred by widespread and systematic poverty. Added to the threats posed by war and nuclear proliferation is the realisation that the planet's ecology is in crisis as a consequence of human action. In this context, Freire's book offers the modern reader enduring and significant ideas regarding the importance of developing a critical consciousness; the necessity of affirming the project of humanisation; and the centrality and necessity of dialogue as the key tool for social progress. It seems to me that these are three values of the utmost importance, values which can act as essential tools to assess the competing political ideologies confronting us today. Freire opposed all received and dogmatic versions of social reality, from both left and right – 'They both suffer from an absence of doubt' (Freire, 1972: 18).[1]

In fact, the book is a ringing invocation of the necessity (both empirical and normative) for human freedom. Throughout the text, Freire contrasts oppression and liberation. These are the two polarities of the human existential condition. On the one hand, the poor are oppressed by virtue of their poverty and are unable to be themselves as free, human subjects. Yet they may accept this situation as fated or unalterable. They may even fear freedom because it carries risk and the potential for conflict. In addition, in situations of objective oppression and mass poverty, the rich are not free either. They too live in fear and destroy their own humanity by their violent suppression of their fellow human beings. Freire's book can be understood as providing a method to enable the poor to understand the structural reasons for their poverty so that they can begin to liberate themselves and become free, autonomous human beings. By so doing they liberate the oppressors too.

The key tool identified by Freire for achieving this liberation is education. Freire argues for a new type of education – an education or pedagogy *of* the oppressed, i.e. one constructed by themselves, out of their lived experience. Conventional education is critiqued by Freire as embedded within oppressive structures. Such education is designed to pacify, to render the student a compliant object to be controlled. To overcome this reality, Freire develops a number of key concepts – problematisation, de-mythologisation, conscientisation, and the culture of silence. It is here above all else I think that we might find the book's contemporary relevance and enduring inspiration. Our education system remains co-opted into an economic imperative centred on growth and inequality. Certain voices and certain words are today reduced to silence in the public sphere. How to speak straightforwardly out of one's direct experience remains problematic. Oppressed groups are obliged to translate their concerns into another language, especially the language of economics and business. Even the term 'the oppressed' is politically potent and almost never used to designate an empirically identifiable group of people. Thus, officially, we don't have 'oppressed' people in Ireland.

A key moment in the path of liberation is when the poor ask what the nature of the social world is. Is it really like the 'natural' world, governed by laws and irrevocable processes? Or is it malleable – subject to human agency – and capable of being constructed and re-constructed? The realisation that social reality is constructed and that we can understand how it is constructed and how it may be changed is the key moment when one moves from a naïve, mythical view of the world to an analytical understanding. Freire's normative or ethical claim is that the social world should not have 'oppression', i.e. any curtailment of freedom. The goal of a proper social system should be maximum humanisation.

I first encountered Freire's work as an undergraduate student in University College Galway in the early 1980s. Its vision of humanisation, both as the end of political activity and as the criterion for determining the means by which political action is conducted, seemed to me particularly exciting. Here was an approach which combined political, philosophical and cultural processes to achieve radical social change but refused to subordinate means to ends. In my subsequent work with homeless people in the Dublin Simon Community I glimpsed the value of Freire's emphasis on reading reality 'from below': from the perspective of the poor and oppressed, rather than imposing theoretical frameworks of liberation on them. Many times I was rightly rebuked by homeless people, Travellers and prisoners for my earnest claims that I could understand their reality. The need for political and intellectual elites to recognise the intrinsic value of the voices of the poor and oppressed has, I believe, enormous modern potency and value. Indeed, Freire's work continues to challenge many of the orthodoxies of contemporary social theory. I will make some remarks on this below and explore whether his core ideas continue to have resonance and application by examining aspects of the well-known and ongoing conflict between Shell, the multinational group of energy and petrochemical companies, and a small, rural community in North Mayo. But first, it may be of value to briefly outline the key ideas in Freire's text.

Pedagogy of the Oppressed

Pedagogy of the Oppressed is a short book. Freire states:

> This book will present some aspects of what the writer has termed the 'pedagogy of the oppressed', a pedagogy which must be forged *with*, not *for*, the oppressed (be they individuals or whole peoples) in the incessant struggle to regain their humanity. This pedagogy makes oppression and its causes objects of reflection by the oppressed, and from that reflection will come their necessary engagement in the struggle for their liberation. And in the struggle this pedagogy will be made and remade. (Freire, 1972: 25)

Freedom

The core problematic addressed in the opening pages is what it is to be human. Key to this for Freire is freedom, 'the indispensable condition for the quest for human completeness' (Freire, 1972: 24). The struggle to be human begins in the struggle to be free. One can detect in Freire's work here a very strong influence from French existentialism, especially ideas developed by Sartre regarding how the human subject is made through one's actions and choices. However, in the Latin American situation, this question is posed in the context of empirical dehumanisation through poverty. In every situation and conflict, the issue of humanisation is always at stake. In claiming their humanity, the oppressed should not themselves become oppressors (Freire, 1972: 21). This is a risk because initially, in liberation, the oppressed are tempted to become like their oppressors because this is their model for what it is to be human and free.

Crucial to beginning the process of liberation is the awareness of oppression, which is defined as 'Any situation in which A objectively exploits B or hinders his pursuit of self-affirmation as a responsible person' (Freire, 1972: 31). Oppression interferes with wo/man's ontological and historical vocation to be more fully human. It is kept in place by fatalism – the belief that one's social condition is the result of destiny, fate, fortune, God's will, magic or myth. Self-depreciation and feelings of worthlessness accentuate this passivity. What is required to overcome this is a new liberating praxis – 'reflection and action upon the world in order to transform it' (Freire, 1972: 28). This can happen when people realise that it is we who produce our social reality. Thus we can change it.

The key to awakening awareness and liberation among the oppressed is critical and liberating dialogue. This is a point of the utmost importance for Freire. 'One must trust the oppressed and in their ability to reason' (Freire, 1972: 41). Action must be based on pedagogy not propaganda. Simplistic programmes, slogans, political templates are not of value. In fact, they can form part of the oppressive disempowerment of the people.

Pedagogy

Freire then turns his attention specifically to the education system and models of pedagogy. He asserts that contemporary education has a narrative character – it suffers from 'narration sickness'.

> Narration (with the teacher as narrator) leads the students to memorize mechanically the narrated content. Worse still, it turns them into 'containers', into receptacles to be filled by the teacher. The more completely he fills the receptacles, the better a teacher he is. The more meekly the receptacles permit themselves to be filled, the better students they are. (Freire, 1972: 45)

In this style of 'banking' education there is a focus on memory, repetition and rote learning. The objective is to turn people into automatons. 'The educated man is the adapted man, because he is "more fit" for the world'

(Freire, 1972: 50). For this reason, banking methods cannot be used for the purposes of liberation because its objective is to change the consciousness of the oppressed so they adapt to the situation of oppression (Freire, 1972: 47–50).

The alternative to this is 'problem posing' education engaged in through dialogical relations. Dialogue is the critical method involving an engagement between student-teacher and teacher-student. The goal of liberatory education is the end of the teacher–student contradiction. The objective is to achieve critical cognition, where the students are 'critical co-investigators in dialogue with the teacher' (Freire, 1972: 54). The consequence of 'problem-posing education' is that

> men develop their power to perceive critically *the way they exist* in the world *with which* and *in which* they find themselves; they come to see the world not as a static reality, but as a reality in process, in transformation. (Freire, 1972: 56)

Banking education mythicises reality, whereas problem-posing education de-mythologises it. People come to realise that they can control social reality. In this context, the subversive power of the question 'why' is revealed – 'No oppressive order could permit the oppressed to begin to question: Why?' (Freire, 1972: 59).

Dialogue
A key further concern of Freire's text is dialogue.

> Dialogue is the encounter between men, mediated by the world, in order to name the world ... If it is in speaking their word that men transform the world by naming it, dialogue imposes itself as the way in which men achieve significance as men. Dialogue is thus an existential necessity. (Freire, 1972: 61)

For Freire, '[t]o speak a true word is to transform the world', and '[t]o exist, humanly, is to name the world, to change it' (Freire, 1972: 60–1). For dialogue to be genuine and possible there must be love, faith, hope, humanity and trust. 'To glorify democracy and to silence the people is a farce; to discourse on humanism and to negate man is a lie' (Freire, 1972: 64). Likewise he states: 'If I do not love the world – if I do not love life – if I do not love men – I cannot enter into dialogue' (Freire, 1972: 62).

The objective of the pedagogy of liberation is now revealed as 'the dialogical man'. No libertarian programme can be imposed – that would simply be a return to banking. Instead, freedom is to be uncovered through the process of dialogue and engagement with the people. Any failure to respect the view of the world held by the people is 'cultural invasion'. The purpose of this process is to allow one to see critically. 'Conscientisation is the deepening of the attitude of awareness characteristic of all emergence' (Freire, 1972: 81). This method puts the student at the centre of the process.

Social change

Finally Freire outlines how radical social change can occur in situations of deep oppression. His concern however is to outline a process not a programme. Revolution, he asserts throughout, can only emerge from dialogue with the people. 'Dialogue is a fundamental precondition for their true humanisation' (Freire, 1972: 107). The characteristics of anti-dialogical action carried out either by the oppressors or by would-be saviours of the people include: *conquest*, a key method of which is by inculcating myths; *divide and rule*, which includes not just dividing the people but also dividing up social problems and social perspectives by not seeing the connections between issues; *manipulation*, one component of which is the false image of the people inculcated in them from the oppressors; and *cultural invasion*, by which the invaders 'impose their own view of the world upon those they invade and inhibit the creativity of the invaded by curbing their expression' (Freire, 1972: 121).

By contrast, dialogical action – the object of which is to get the oppressed to transform unjust reality – is characterised by: *co-operation*, whereby 'subjects meet in cooperation in order to transform the world' (Freire, 1972: 135); *unity for liberation*, which is achieved not by slogans or empty manifestoes but through dialogue and critical engagement; *organisation*, involving leaders being with the people not over them; and, finally, *cultural synthesis*, through which the people come to understand the integrated and systemic nature of the problems confronting them and the resultant need for both political-economic and cultural revolution.

Critique

It is important, in the spirit of Freire's work, to subject this account to an initial critique. On the positive side, Freire confronts two dominant myths still prevalent in contemporary Western society. First, is the myth of the individual as a kind of free-floating asocial being and second, that of the social world as static and 'natural', in the sense that its present form is inevitable and obvious. These myths taken together amount to a powerful ideological justification for a view of the world that posits personal effort and endeavour as the key criteria for achieving material and social success within a fixed and naturally constrained social world. The implication of this is that the poor are poor because of personal failure on their part and the rich are so because of personal virtues and talents. This view of the world, if internalised by the poor, can become a key component of the passivity, fatalism and low self-value which Freire identifies as inimical to their capacity to understand and change the world.

However, there may also be a number of reasonable objections to the universal reach of Freire's arguments that warrant acknowledgement. The first might be to enquire whether, in the context particularly of European social democracy, the categories of oppressed and oppressor are so clear.

Might there be a dichotomisation here not readily applicable outside of the poor Southern nations of the world? In this context the only options may not be between oppression and revolution. A middle-way may be possible. In addition, what happens if the people want reform, not revolution? Will this be dismissed as evidence of false consciousness on their part? Is there a latent arrogance in the Freirean view that the people need to be brought to a similar stage of enlightenment as the critical pedagogue? This danger may be more acute if the pedagogue is seeking to 'humanise' or 'modernise' indigenous cultures who may wish to retain cultural structures that may appear objectively 'oppressive' against the Western standard of freedom implicit in Freire's anthropological assumptions.

A second issue that may be raised is whether the 'new man' heralded and lauded by Freire is possible outside of a religious ethical framework? The invocation to faith, hope and love made by Freire clearly ring of Christian moral virtues rather than proletarian class consciousness. Once again, the foundation of these ideas within a specifically Christian Latin America may hinder their easy translation or application to societies whose religious and cultural ethos is non-Christian or even non-religious. In addition, Freire may be accused of being utopian in this regard. Will human beings really behave in this virtuous manner once material deprivation has been overcome?

Finally, one may also question whether Freire's pedagogical ideas themselves can have universal application. Is his depiction of 'banking' education a fair characterisation of contemporary pedagogical practice? Some might reasonably argue that new educational theories now animate and inform practice in the Western world. In addition, a teaching methodology of teacher–student dialogue may not always be appropriate for every academic discipline and setting. One thinks of mathematics for example, or many of the natural sciences. In these instances the teacher is required to be didactic in order to equip the student to understand and operationalise core concepts and tools. It may not be fair to characterise such pedagogy as necessarily oppressive.

These points serve merely to temper a facile universal application of Freire's ideas. However, Freire was clear that his analysis and concepts grew out of a specifically Latin American context where overt and extreme social deprivation was the norm. Within this context, and within any context of oppression, it seems proper to ask what type of education should be applied, what its purpose should be, and what is the model of the human being implied by our pedagogical practice.

Contemporary Irish relevance

How inspirational or relevant has this text been within the Irish context? The general principle might be that these ideas are most receptive to those who are objectively in a state of oppression. One of the most notable applications of Freire's methods in an Irish setting occurred in the 1980s when returned Columban missionary John O'Connell established an educational programme with twenty four Traveller activists in Dublin. O'Connell had worked in the Philippines and was anxious to apply Freire's pedagogical ideas in Ireland. With others he established the Dublin Traveller Education and Training Group in 1985[2] and set out to create Freirean-based consciousness awareness groups. These were hugely successful and had a major impact on Traveller understanding of their social position and oppression in Irish society. It is clear that this early Freirean programme was a decisive moment in creating the modern Traveller rights movement. Until this time, Travellers were characterised by attitudes of fatalism regarding their position, invoking 'God's will' as an explanatory framework for their disadvantage. The immediate effect of the programme was to change this language. From then, Traveller activists spoke of oppression and characterised their campaigning as a struggle for liberation. As Martin Collins said when addressing the opening session of the National Seminar of Traveller Parents and Learners in 2004, 'Education needs to be about liberating Travellers, not about domesticating them. True Education will give Travellers the tools to challenge their oppression rather than teaching them how to become acceptable in a settled world'.[3] Collins has asserted to me in a conversation in 2008 that Freirean concepts and language are now embedded into Traveller activists' psyche and mode of understanding the world. On the face of it this is quite a startling claim which suggests either a striking fit between Traveller experiences and Freirean pedagogy or the possibility that a Freirean framework can be imposed by Freirean-inspired pedagogues which constructs a discourse for articulating and organising experiences of oppression.

Nonetheless, the impact of O'Connell's work alerts us to the important role played by Irish missionary and development workers as a conduit for Freire's ideas into Ireland. Even as a minor member of the Irish El Salvador Support Group in the late 1980s I well remember the energising impact of people returning and visiting from Latin America. Many of them were imbued with the concepts and value of cultural and pedagogical action for freedom largely derived from Paulo Freire. Crucially, they brought with them not merely theoretical frameworks and templates but lived experiences and empirical verifications of this pedagogical approach.

Some of this energy was manifested in the founding of the Partners Training for Transformation, a series of development education programmes which began in 1981. This initiative, instigated both by people working in Ireland and returned development workers, set out to develop programmes for community education and empowerment focused on drawing from people's own experiences. It grounded its approach specifically on the work of Freire. Apart from their direct involvement in communities, the training manuals developed by the Partners further transmitted Freirean ideas in Ireland.

Reading reality 'from below'

As a working sociologist in contemporary Ireland, teaching in a small rural campus in the West of Ireland, Freire's work continues to present me with a significant challenge. Much current sociology and social theory, especially in its 'post-modernist' and 'globalisation' approaches, gives the appearance of theorising from on high. As a consequence, it may seem that the lives and experiences of people may be elided and constructed to fit into macro-deductive theoretical frameworks. In this sense, social theory may resemble the utterances and perspectives of those from the world of the wealthy and powerful (Sobrino, 2008). Michael McCaughan, a correspondent of many years on Latin America for *The Irish Times*, reminded me recently of the distinction drawn there between the 'real world' of the people and the 'shadow world' of the wealthy and 'glamorous'. This latter world – the realm of celebrity and media – can give the appearance of substantiality in a culture where form dominates over substance such as is often the case in our own.

However, if we wish to correctly grasp the true reality of our interlinking social worlds then we need to do sociology 'from below', i.e. a sociology from the position of the poor. This involves a shift of perspective, moving from a new epistemological and methodological platform. Thus, our new generating questions become: what does this society or world look like from the reality of the poor; and how do we judge this society from their perspective? The social condition of the poor can then become a measure of the actual efficacy of 'progress' and 'development' and can serve as the empirical judge of whether we have truly achieved humanisation, freedom and justice for all. Their very reality (they are, after all, the global majority) can puncture the illusory bubble within which is contained our perceptions and errors about what is really going on in our world.

Freire and the Corrib gas conflict

Let me attempt to put this argument to the test by examining the conflict between a small rural community in North Mayo on the one side and the Irish State and Shell Oil on the other. Read 'from above', this is about a small group of recalcitrant malcontents holding up progress and development for irrational and increasingly perverse reasons. But seen 'from below', it is about a small community's efforts to be the agent of its own development, to be protected in the continuation of its indigenous forms of life and not to be subjected to 'cultural invasion'. While the community here has not drawn explicitly on Freire's work, it is clear that for me, in attempting to understand the dynamics of what is going on, Freire's approach offers a crucial method by which we might achieve understanding. Above all, examining this conflict through dialogue with the community gives rise to the critical data from which to construct a sociology 'from below'.

In addition, an examination of the conflict permits us to enquire whether Freire's pedagogical claims regarding the process of learning and liberation can be empirically verified in a contemporary Irish campaign. Do 'oppressed' actors undergo the type of developmental process suggested by Freire? If so, then Freire's approach can still serve as a potent resource for Irish social movement actors.

The conflict in North Mayo has arisen because of the proposal by a consortium of oil and gas corporations, led by Shell, to situate a gas-processing refinery and associated high-pressure pipeline nine kilometres inland within a culturally and environmentally sensitive part of North Mayo. Initially, the proposal was imbued with all of the most potent contemporary mythologies of progress, development and wealth. Yet despite this, the local community soon mobilised to resist the development. In understanding this process of resistance, I believe we can utilise Freire's key concepts of problematisation, conscientisation and dialogue to analytically unravel what has occurred. In the spirit of Freire, and to avoid a deductive theoretical analysis, I propose to largely rely on the direct words of local inhabitants rather than my own commentary or analysis. This excavation and presentation of people's actual and articulated views breaches the culture of silence, restores people's voices to them and provides us with the empirical resources to construct a sociology 'from below'. This serves to me as an important working methodology.

Problematisation of the project

Initially, as a consequence of the twin perceptions that the area was economically 'undeveloped' but culturally and socially distinct, the community was uncertain and ambivalent in its interpretation of the gas refinery development. On the one hand, there was an immediate receptivity to the promise of development:

> We need this here for our children and grandchildren. I want them to grow up around me.

> We have nothing here. This is what we need. It will bring roads, jobs. (Fieldnotes, Pollathomas, Rossport, Ceathrú Taidgh, January to March, 2001)

On the other hand, there was anxiety that the impact of the project might change something fundamental and important about the area's way of life – social, economic and cultural. These opposed sets of concerns highlight an ambivalence that 'marginal' societies may possess regarding 'development'. 'This results in the duality of the dependent society, its ambiguity, its being and not being itself, and the ambivalence characteristic of its long experience of dependency, both attracted by and rejecting the metropolitan society' (Freire, 1972: 59). However, the key to local mobilisation against the project was the perception that their locality was under threat from the company's proposal.

> Why I'm opposed? One – the people. Two – the scenery. I mean health,

especially the children. (Interview, local resident, Ceathrú Taidgh, March 2001)

It's the health issue really that has got people together. There are over 700 signatures in the area gathered. People don't realise how big this is. (Interview, local resident, Ceathrú Taidgh, March 2001)

We saw things [in the Environmental Impact Statement] like mercury and nitrogen oxide and things like this until the sweat broke through. (Resident on Mid-West Radio, June 2001)

If the proposal to dump wastewater into the sea goes ahead it could sound the death knell for inshore fishing. (Interview, Rossport, April 2001)

I cannot understand why anyone would want to spoil an area as beautiful as this. (Fieldnotes, Glengad, June 2002)

In order to further trace the process of problematisation, the following citations are drawn from the text *The Rossport Five: Our Story*. These are recorded interviews that I conducted with five local men and their wives. The five men were imprisoned for 94 days in 2005 for breaching a court order which had forbidden them to prevent Shell from laying the high-pressure pipeline.

> At first we were naïve. You wouldn't take a lot of notice of those things. We heard that there was gas found and it was coming in to Erris or Mayo somewhere. (W. Corduff, in Garavan, 2006: 19)

> The parish priest in particular was the first to be talking about it. He announced it from the altar. He gave the impression to the people that your poverty is over ... They were used big time and they were told that whatever was going to be needed in the area this was going to be the answer to it. I'd say that's what really happened. The people heard the parish priest announcing this from the altar, that poverty was over. You just take it that if you were in poverty for thirty or forty years, struggling to live, with hard work, and you have nothing, and to hear the parish priest coming to the altar saying this is it, it's over. The benefits that were going to be from it were going to be unreal. (W. Corduff, Ibid.: 20)

> What worried me all the time was that there was nobody asking questions. There were no questions. 'We were going to be rich. The schools will be full of kids'. But there were no questions being asked about the project or the dangers or the chimneys. That worried me. (C. Ó Seighin, Ibid.: 65)

> I don't know what got into us, to give us the confidence to stand up. It's hard to pinpoint it. I saw harm in it from the word go. I don't know was it the fear of gas. I don't know if it was something like that that made us fear it. I think it was the One Voice for Erris[4] that sparked us off. We felt that these people were trying to downgrade us. They felt that we know nothing. You looked at yourself and you'd say well I have to look at my end of the story. We figured where are the benefits as such. We were being told that there was going to be good. But when you asked the questions

you wouldn't be answered. You kind of know when there are people beginning to pull the wool over your eyes. That's one thing I cannot stand for.
You have to be straight and clean with somebody. You could see what was
going on there. Also, it probably was the love of the land and the love of
the place. We loved the place so much and we were both from the area.
(W. Corduff, Ibid.: 26–7)

Conscientisation

This extraordinary problematisation of the project was rapidly followed
by a deepening conscientisation of many within the local community. This
occurred as a direct result of their own ongoing experiences of interact-
ing with Shell and various organs of the state, and their engagement and
exchanges with many outside actors involved in similar disputes worldwide.
A particularly close identification was made with the Ogoni experience in
the Niger Delta.

For Freire, the process of problematisation arises when human subjects
no longer perceive events or projects to be inevitable, certain or inherently
'good' (as part of a 'mythologisation of reality') but rather begin to reframe
them as issues warranting critique and examination. Problematisation
involves a form of phenomenological enquiry.

> That which had existed objectively but had not been perceived in its
> deeper implications (if indeed it was perceived at all) begins to 'stand out',
> assuming the character of a problem and therefore as challenge. Thus, men
> begin to single out elements from their 'background awarenesses' and to
> reflect upon them. These elements are now objects of men's consideration,
> and, as such, objects of their action and cognition. (Freire, 1972: 56)

It is possible to discern in this campaign a cognitive progression among
the protest actors from an initial *reaction* to the gas proposal, towards an
affirmation of a particular set of values, such as sustainability and solidarity,
suggested to be exemplified in the local community. The project came to be
seen, to employ Freire's phrase once more, as a 'cultural invasion' and was
resisted accordingly.

> It was hard to accept that our government was willing to let this happen.
> You'd feel that the government should be there to protect the citizens
> and they weren't doing it. They were helping out a multi-national oil and
> gas company above ordinary Irish citizens. It's hard to accept that kind
> of thing. You'd feel like you shouldn't really have to put up a fight. We
> weren't only fighting the gas company we were fighting the government
> and even lower levels of the State such as the county council. (M. Corduff,
> in Garavan, 2006: 31–2)

> It has made us aware of the wealth that's out there off our coast. All that's
> going to be done for us is that we're going to be used for access and then
> it will be sent off to benefit other countries. Even Norway is getting a
> percentage of this. We can't gain one cent from it. You just wonder what

kind of mind-frame would be on someone to give that kind of gift away. I know the Irish were always classed as a generous people and friendly and easy going but there's a limit to friendship! You can't give everything away for nothing. (M. Corduff, Ibid.: 58)

I could say honestly that I regretted having wasted my time contributing all my life to this awful system, to this denial, to this con democracy, this cod democracy, that was being administered by cod civil servants, cod public servants. Because that is all I could call them. I mean contributing both as a teacher and even in just living here. In a way I had wasted forty years functioning in an environment that I found out didn't exist. (M. Ó Seighin, Ibid.: 75)

Our attachment to place comes into it too. According as we were going on bit by bit and learning more it was obvious that it was the end of the place as somewhere to which the next generation could return whether visiting or otherwise. This was the end of it. It wasn't just a matter of new industry coming in – that alone is no problem – but that it would be the end of millennia of culture. For us, the cultural aspect was very simple. When people talk about culture it's a page in The Times that no one reads or the Sunday newspaper. But for us it's a different thing, it's all of living, everyday survival. (M. Ó Seighin, Ibid.: 78)

I think the conclusion is that it is a banana republic at the end of the day. You saw that especially when the men were sent into prison. You don't know the sinking feeling I've had for the last six years about this country that had been fought and died for. It would leave you now lifeless almost. I loved history when I was going to school and I was nearly out there fighting the battles. And then to see what has happened! We were told for as long as I remember that there's nothing in Erris, there's nothing in Mayo. But now there's billions of euros worth of oil and gas just a couple of miles there off our shores here. And we're not going to benefit one bit except for a couple of jobs. They would take it and walk on us and take it through Erris and through Mayo without gain for the country or Erris or Mayo except that they will destroy this area. And whoever would live to see the day in thirty or forty years time there will be nobody living along Sruhwaddoccon and that area. If this happens and the big pipe goes in and the terminal in Ballinaboy, people will not be there. Number one, they won't get planning permission anyway for their house and two, they wouldn't want to live there. As a parent I wouldn't want to see my children building a house along Sruhwaddoccon or Glengad. This is not the country I thought it was. It's an awful shock and shattering experience. Life is gone from us. (C. Ó Seighin, Ibid.: 79)

What type of Ireland do we want? This is why people of so many different political ideologies are very comfortable in this campaign. Because what it's dealing with is the context – the context is the big thing, the important thing, what should be the important thing, for everyone. And the context is what kind of Ireland do we want? What kind of Ireland do we want for the people after us, what kind of Ireland do we want to leave? Do we want to leave it to a new landlord grouping that the next generation or the generation after that are going to have to get rid of? Do we want to leave a legacy after us that can only be solved by violence? To me this is all about context. The people realise that the politicians will have to come back and function within a context that's real. And the context is what kind of Ireland do we want and not what kind of Ireland is most convenient for making money at a particular time. It's not awfully relevant whether it's for multinationals or for Irish companies. (M. Ó Seighin, Ibid.: 95)

One result of our experience is that I look differently on people elsewhere who are fighting for causes. Before I wouldn't have taken any notice really. All we can do now though is offer our support. (P. McGrath Ibid.: 131–2)

But in our case neither the Government nor the oil companies could buy our dignity nor could they buy our freedom. (V. McGrath, Ibid.: 208)

We don't trust any of the authorities to monitor them [Shell] on our behalf. The bottom line is we trust ourselves to protect our environment and to protect ourselves. We are the people who live here. It makes sense that we are the ones who have the interest of our environment at heart. This is where we live and where we want to live and live safely. There is no chance now of Shell coming in here at all. This whole experience has reinforced my belief that the Irish people have a sense of justice and that they will stand up for what is right and that they will not be pushed against their will. People aren't going to go to jail lightly. People don't just go to jail without good reason. They do so only when they feel strongly and when the law and the authorities have failed them. It's up to the government and the State and the authorities to listen to those people and to take their concerns into account. I think people will assert their dignity and their rights more and more and I think the governments will have no choice but to listen. I think that's the big lesson. The rural community here has been radicalised, particularly those people who always voted Fianna Fáil or Fine Gael and who are now saying that they will not vote for them again. Another thing is that the women have been politicised. Women may be slow to get involved in social and political campaigns but when they do they won't let their bone go with any dog. And maybe they're slower to compromise as well. (V. McGrath, Ibid.: 206–7)

Dialogue and anti-dialogue

One of the most overwhelming characteristics of the Corrib gas conflict has been the consistent refusal by Shell or the state to enter into meaningful dialogue with the local community (Garavan, 2008). Local concerns were stereotyped, misrepresented or ignored. The refusal to engage in dialogue, and the capacity to proceed in the absence of dialogue, indicates the existence, and exercise, of power (Haugaard, 1997). The gas project was to be determined through a series of 'objective' tests managed by various administrative bodies and could proceed accordingly if judged appropriate by these tests, irrespective of community consent. In this way, through the application of a series of procedural mechanisms, popular dissent and resistance to the project were controlled and rendered, in appearance at least, unreasonable.

The capacity to establish the conventions under which communication between citizens and decision-making bodies can occur is a key contemporary form of power. It is conventions (often legislatively set) that determine the test of relevancy adopted by decision-making or policy-making bodies. In the gas refinery conflict, questions of health, for example, were strictly speaking irrelevant for all the administrative bodies involved and could not become relevant for any of them even though it was of central concern to the local community. Therefore, by determining that certain topics and concerns are irrelevant (i.e. outside the scope of consideration), the actors raising them are rendered silent. In this way, the empirical plurality of views on development projects, and dissenting views particularly, can, through the application of a predetermined *method*, be excluded from consideration (Peace, 1993; Taylor, 2001).

In addition, the gas developer consciously chose not to engage in open, public dialogue.

> On the whole, we felt that the public meeting forum was not working as not everyone had the opportunity to give their view in such a large forum. Therefore, we began a process of meeting with smaller groups who shared similar concerns. In this way, it is possible to talk to everyone and everyone has the chance to give their view. We feel this has worked much better and we are still in discussion with locals in the area in this way. (Email to the author, 29 June 2001)

These claims of widespread consultation were judged as far-fetched and highly implausible by local residents. However, this reply presents a rationale for limiting the structure of consultation to small-scale, private encounters rather than open, public meetings. Many local activists perceived this strategy to be one of 'divide and conquer'. Furthermore, by not engaging in *public* discussion, the true state of collective public concern could not be brought to bear on the corporation.

> When you see someone starting to bully you to get something that really gets to you. If somebody wanted something off me and they go to bully me I'd just stick my heels in. You don't act that way. There's something wrong then at that stage when you ask questions and no answers but you get 'we're going to do it anyway.' When we did start keeping them off the land, the Shell man told me 'look it, we'll get it there anyway, regardless of what you're going to do'. That really gave you strength. (W. Corduff, in Garavan, 2006: 31)

> They never wanted to meet those who weren't in favour. (C. Ó Seighin, Ibid.: 72)

> Because the pipeline wasn't going through our land Enterprise Energy Ireland (they sold to Shell in 2002)[5] didn't require our consent. They had been speaking to other landowners but they hadn't come near us. It angered me though because we learned later how dangerous the gas was and here we were the closest to the pipeline route and yet we were being completely

ignored. As far as they were concerned we didn't matter. That still seems
to be their position today. In their public pronouncements they talk about
engaging with the local community and consulting with stakeholders but
if they don't have to deal with you they just ignore you. A *stakeholder* is
somebody affected by a project but the Company's definition appears to
be somebody who helps them to get the project through. At least that's
how they have acted. But here we were, the local residents, closest to the
pipeline, the people who would be in most danger if an accident happened
and yet they ignored us. The only information we ever got directly was in
February 2005 when they were about to start laying the pipeline in front of
our house. They informed us then by letter about the noise levels we would
experience. That was it. *Fait accompli.* If you don't wish, they said, there
will be no work on Sunday. Alleluia! … That was the whole approach – a
fait accompli. It's coming in anyway. Everything they did came from this
idea they had planted in the public mind. Even Frank Fahey, the Minister
for Marine and Natural Resources and the man who gave the go-ahead to
the Plan of Development, said in the Dáil that the people of Erris were entitled to object but they couldn't hold up the project. That was the message
that was going out, the psychological message. We'll take on board your
concerns but the project is going ahead as planned. You cannot do anything about it. It's too important. The interests pushing it are too powerful.
You're only a little guy. That's it. (V. McGrath, Ibid.: 164–5)

We were never consulted about the route. There was not a word. It was
as if we didn't exist. On one occasion their local rep visited the house but
I realised later that it was probably to see how near we were to the route.
I remember during the 2002 election Fianna Fáil canvassers called and
remarked on how we had a lovely view. I said to them what about that
Terminal. They said, 'oh, we won't talk about that'. They said that it would
be coming in anyway. (M. McGrath, Ibid.: 164–5)

Conclusion

While community activists in North Mayo did not consciously deploy Freire's
ideas in their campaign, nonetheless I think it evident that the Freirean framework does help us to understand the process of consciousness-raising that
can unfold within oppressed communities, thereby showing how Freire's
text remains a viable and relevant resource for social movement activists
and theorists. Their nine years of meetings and internal dialogue amounted
to, in the Irish context, an extraordinary exercise in problematisation and
conscientisation. It is clear to me from close observation of this process that
the transformation and radicalisation of the community activists involved
provide clear evidence of the fundamental insight and validity offered by
Freire's pedagogical framework. Whether it be Travellers or vulnerable
communities, it is in the awareness of oppression that a pedagogy of the
oppressed can be formed and practised. In this specific sense at least, Freire's
book retains a significance and vitality for progressive social movements.

His work serves both as a method to change awareness, as has been the case with Irish Travellers, and as a tool to analyse and illustrate the process of awareness itself.

Notes

1 The pages numbers cited are from Freire (1972).
2 In 1995, this later became Pavee Point.
3 See www.paveepoint.ie.
4 One Voice for Erris was a pro-project support group initially established by the local parish priest. It disbanded in due course due to a loss of local support.
5 The leading company in the original consortium developing the Corrib gas field, Enterprise Oil, was bought by Shell in 2002.

9

Ivan Illich's *Tools for Conviviality*
Orla O'Donovan

Introduction – Ivan Illich comes to Corofin

I wish I had been in Corofin, County Clare, on the evening in May 1989 when Ivan Illich spoke to a large crowd in the village hall and caused pandemonium and consternation. At that time, I had only vaguely heard of Illich, and it would be a few years later before I began to read and be both invigorated and vexed by his work that questions the innocence of what passes for 'development'. Illich was in Ireland as a guest of campaigners for alternatives in education, many of whom drew inspiration from his 1971 book *Deschooling Society*. An experiment in co-operative living, known as The Shed, was sited in Corofin. Part of this was a school, an autonomous educational zone of sorts that sought to provide a collective formative experience to young people to continue learning where they lived. The school functioned for over a decade without financial support from the state, enduring reprobation from the local Catholic hierarchy which was – and continues to be – accustomed to a privileged position within the Irish public schooling system. The local Catholic hierarchy's disapproval of the co-operative because its school did not incorporate Catholic religious instruction into its curriculum was extended to its guest, and parishioners were (unsuccessfully) discouraged from attending the gathering in the hall. The Shed was one of a number of workers' co-operatives established in Ireland in the 1980s. While many of these co-operatives received official endorsement as vehicles of job creation at a time when unemployment and emigration were rife in Ireland, others had more utopian visions and saw them as a means of achieving economic and participatory democracy and justice, and as a continuation of the Irish co-operative movement dating back to an experiment at Ralahine, also in County Clare, in the 1830s (Mac Eoin, 1982; Tucker, 1983). Although the workers' co-operatives of the 1980s were a distinct movement, they were regarded as part of the co-operative tradition that also included the Irish agricultural co-operative movement, which similarly originated in the nineteenth century. Reflecting the different neo-liberal mood of our times, many of the workers' co-operatives of the 1980s have since been disbanded, including the co-operative school in Corofin, while some of the surviving agricultural co-operatives have mutated into global corporations.

Renowned for his disruptive ideas and ways, Illich that evening did not adhere to the conventions of a good guest, beginning with a refusal to use a microphone to facilitate the recording of the evening's deliberations for broadcast by RTÉ Radio 1. On his arrival in Ireland two days previously, he had already refused to participate in the making of a television programme, one of the activities scheduled by the organiser of his short visit.[1] As recounted to me by Michael Neylon,[2] a founder of the Corofin co-operative, the two days Illich spent with members of the co-operative had entailed a series of informal and intimate gatherings, which contrasted sharply with the 'set up' in the local hall aimed at facilitating a didactic exchange and the production of a radio programme. Thankfully for those of us who were not present but would like to have been, Illich conceded to the recording of the radio programme so long as the programme-makers assumed a 'fly on the wall' stance.[3] Complete with the sounds of crying babies, chesty coughing, chair shuffling and murmured asides, the unavoidably poorly recorded 'Ivan Illich comes to Corofin', forms part of the significant volume of books, essays and recorded conversations involving this highly prolific and influential theorist. Celebrated by many as a twentieth-century 'intellectual superstar' (Kahn and Kellner, 2007: 438), Illich (1973: 50) himself acknowledged that his ideas exposed him to the 'painful criticism of being not only anti-people and against economic progress, but equally against liberal education and scientific and technological advance'. As he mentioned in Corofin, Illich was also accustomed to dismissals for being mad and having little understanding of the human condition.

Explaining his abhorrence of microphones, Illich made it clear that he had no desire to 'speak at' people for the evening in Corofin, preferring instead to engage in conversation. What followed was far from the conventions of polite conversation, with Illich's ideas and intimidating conversation style living up to the reputation of being more barb than balm. In addition to being a troublesome guest logistically (as well as refusing to use a microphone he asked that the seating arrangement in the hall be changed), the recording of the 'conversation' reveals that while some participants responded with delight, many were left aghast and others insulted. Others still could not hear or follow what was being said. So what did he say that caused such a stir?

Consistent with his writings and self-identification as a medieval historian,[4] Illich began by telling two short stories. One was set in Florence in 1317 and the other in France in 1777, and he told them to illustrate how contemporary understandings of wage labour are both 'crazy' and relatively 'new fangled'. Based on empirical evidence, the stories indicated that in medieval Florence wage labourers were regarded as being amongst the 'miserable' in society, but a few centuries later the previously disparaged wage labour began to be actively promoted by the French state as means of doing away with begging. This, Illich argued, was the beginning of the establishment in Europe of a totally different set of certainties about work, including that work is a prerequisite of human fulfilment – where to be human is to be *homo labora*, that dignified work is wage labour, and that work is only productive when it is performed as paid employment. He went on to argue that contemporary common-sense ideas about developed and underdeveloped countries, in which dependency on wage labour is a key distinguishing feature, are even more novel. In line with the ideas of his friend the Mexican post-development theorist Gustavo Esteva (1992), Illich pointed to the invention of the contemporary concept of 'development' in a 1949 speech by the US president Harry Truman. Launching the project of development, Truman had urged Western governments to embark 'on a bold new program for making the benefits of our scientific advances and industrial progress available for the improvement and growth of underdeveloped areas' (cited in Esteva, 1992: 6). Reformulating history in Western terms, as pointed out by Esteva (1992: 9), on the day of Truman's speech, two-thirds of the world's population became 'underdeveloped' and the 'industrial mode of production, which was no more than one, among many, forms of social life, became the definition of the terminal stage of a unilinear way of social evolution'.

In the wide-ranging and heated conversation provoked by Illich's stories and opening comments, topics discussed included domestic appliances, education and professionalism. Unlike lectures in more rarefied settings in which no one dared to challenge Illich (Bowles, 1983), in Corofin a few took him on. One man suggested that in light of new technologies developed through human ingenuity, such as the washing machine and dishwasher, labour is increasingly becoming a thing of the past. Responding to what he described as this 'magnificent macho statement', Illich questioned the labour-saving consequences of these domestic appliances and furthermore, the assumption that they have liberated women from housework. As elsewhere (Cayley, 1992), Illich referred to Ruth Schwartz Cowan's (1976; 1983) historical research on the effects of the twentieth-century industrial revolution in the home for North American women who could afford newly available household technologies. Initially Schwartz Cowan was ambivalent about the washing machine, arguing that it did reduce the drudgery of washday, but at the same time was associated with changing standards that led to an almost fetishistic preoccupation with cleanliness and consequent increases in the amount and frequency of laundering. In a similar vein, Illich urged people to question intuitive ideas about modern appliances, the effects of which may be more dubious than they first appear. However, in encouraging such important questioning, he underplayed the drudgery and romanticised public washing at rivers and wells where women allegedly had 'the possibility of having fun while doing so … chatting and telling stories'. While stressing that tools such as domestic appliances are not just passive instruments but have 'a life of their own' and can organise our work in unanticipated ways, Schwartz Cowan (1983: 216) later emphasised that it is possible to revise the unwritten rules that govern their use and, in the case of the washing machine, neutralise the gendered and 'senseless tyranny of spotless shirts'. Indeed, what Illich did not mention was that despite her initial technological pessimism, Schwartz Cowan found little evidence of resistance from domestic artisans and that the vast majority of women were perfectly delighted with many modern household technologies.

Another aspect of modern life widely regarded as indicative of progress discussed that evening in Corofin was schooling. Citing historical evidence of autobiographies written by people in the seventeenth century who had received a maximum of eight months' formal schooling, Illich asserted that there is something crazy about a society in which it takes more than eight months to teach a child how to read and, more broadly, where people come to believe that, in order to learn, children have to be incarcerated in schools. Contrary to common belief and to the high esteem in which educational credentials tend to be held in Ireland, Illich argued that schooling undermines people's capacity to learn, stifles their intellectual curiosity and leads to 'stupidification'. This provoked a teacher in the audience to accuse Illich of suggesting that teachers are stupid. He replied, 'they are not stupid; they are professionals', inducing laughter and applause from many present. The key problem with modern professionals, he explained, is their claim to a monopoly on what they do. Just as professional teachers claim a monopoly on education and thus belittle all learning outside of the context of the school, modern medical professionals claim a monopoly on healing and deride all other forms. Medical professionals, he argued, one of the many professional groups that proliferate in modern societies, are members of a state-sanctioned association that claims a monopoly not only on defining what constitutes a disease but also on judging whether or not someone suffers from it and how it should be treated. In tending to his own health, Illich resisted the radical monopoly of Western medicine; he drew on a number of forms of treatment for the large cancerous growth on his jaw that was clearly evident during his visit to Corofin and that caused him considerable suffering.

Some of the participants who spoke indicated their accord with Illich's arguments. One woman, for example, spoke with exasperation about her son's schooling in which not only was his reading prescribed but so too was his interpretation of the compulsory readings. Others confronted him, including one who pointed to the inconsistencies between his close associations with academia (including three doctorates) and his critique of schooling, and enquired if Illich ever considered de-schooling himself. Illich irked many present by referring to the Irish dancing that was performed by local children in advance of the 'conversation' as an upsetting example of curricular management of a traditional art. Emphasising that he was grateful for the gift of the performance, he nonetheless likened it to the efforts of professional teachers in Mexico who, in attempting to preserve some of the many indigenous languages, were teaching and thus transforming them, and destroying their survival capacity. As mentioned at the end of the recording by John Quinn, the maker of the radio programme, the music of two local fiddle players who also performed that night in Corofin was needed by many to calm down after hearing Illich.

Reading Illich

Although in both media we miss the embodied Illich – 'tall, aquiline, smiling affably, gesticulating with long, gangling arms, conversing in five languages at once' (du Plessix Gray, 1970: 273) – reading Illich strongly resembles listening to him in the recording of 'Ivan Illich comes to Corofin'. One similarity is that many of his books and essays are presented as the results of conversations. Several of his best-known books, including *Tools for Conviviality*, which is the focus of this chapter, are offered as thoughts on conversations that took place in the Centre for Intercultural Documentation (CIDOC) in Cuernavaca, Mexico. Illich, who was born in Austria in 1926 (into a privileged family that included in its circle of friends prominent intellectuals such as Rudolf Steiner) and died in Germany in 2002, lived a largely nomadic life with no fixed abode (du Plessix Gray, 1970; Tijmes, 2002). However, for the ten years of its existence he spent much of his time in CIDOC. Having worked as a Catholic priest in New York and Puerto Rico, Illich settled in Cuernavaca in 1961 partly because the bishop there, a self-declared Zapatista, was like-minded and supported his plans to establish the Centre. Illich described CIDOC as a 'thinkery' and 'a meeting place for those who, long before it had become fashionable, questioned the innocence of "development"' (Illich, 2002: 235). Amongst the people who frequented this meeting place were the Brazilian educationalist Paulo Freire and the Austrian political ecologist André Gorz.

The Cold War was a crucial aspect of the context in which Illich established CIDOC. Extending Truman's 'bold new program', in 1961 US president John F. Kennedy launched the Alliance for Progress, an ostensible development programme for Latin America aimed at countering the communist threat perceived to be emanating from Cuba. This coincided with the 'Papal Plan', a call from the pope for the North American Catholic church to send ten per cent of its personnel to Latin America to offset the continent's shortage of clergy. Illich saw this coincidence as ominous, with both plans motivated by US latter-day imperialism. CIDOC, in his view, was a centre of 'de-Yankeefication' where would-be missionaries and development workers would get cultural lobotomies and shed their saviour do-gooder complexes. The Centre, 'part language school, part conference center, part free university, part publishing house – was not so much designed to train missionaries, as to keep all but the most progressive of them away' (du Plessix Gray, 1970: 253). After all, for Illich missionaries were 'ecclesiastical conquistadores' (du Plessix Gray, 1970: 244). Following the Vatican's attempts to subject Illich to a medieval-style inquisition because of his – amongst other charges – 'dangerous doctrinal opinions', and the banning in 1969 of Catholic clergy from attending courses at CIDOC, Illich resigned his clerical status. By that time, however, he had gained an international reputation as an intellectual and went on to hold a series of prestigious academic positions in Germany and the USA, while retaining an ascetic lifestyle.

Tools for Conviviality is offered as a progress report on conversations that were taking place in CIDOC in the early 1970s. Reflecting the fluidity of these conversations and also Illich's willingness to change his mind and engage with his critics in dialogical theorising, the text was repeatedly revised as it was published in different languages, with new prefaces added. The last republication with a new preface was a German version published in 1998 (Mitcham, 2002).[5] As pointed out by Erich Fromm of the Frankfurt School of critical theory, who wrote the introduction to a collection of essays by Illich published in 1971, Illich's views on some of the issues addressed in the essays had changed by the time they were published. However, what remained unchanged was his radical attitude. Fromm explains that this attitude is primarily characterised not by a set of ideas but by radical questioning, a process captured by the motto '*de omnibus dubitandum*; everything must be doubted, particularly the ideological concepts which are virtually shared by everybody and have consequently assumed the role of indubitable common sense axioms' (Fromm 2001: 7–8). Just as Illich's writings elude classification by academic discipline, they are not easily classified according to their political orientation. Frequently his work is associated with anarchism; Richard Kahn (2009) argues that his Christian anarchism closely resembled that of the anarcho-pacifist Catholic Worker Movement, a movement that became high profile in Ireland in 2003 due to its members' opposition to the US army's use of Shannon Airport as a stopover in the war in Iraq. But Fromm (2001: 9) identifies Illich's political orientation as humanist radicalism defined by a questioning of 'every idea and every institution from the standpoint of whether it helps or hinders man's [*sic*] capacity for greater aliveness and joy'.

I should note that the irritating patriarchal habit of using 'man' to refer to women and men that features in Fromm's writings is also evident in Illich's work. Significantly, in the 1970s this was one ideological concept virtually shared by everyone – except feminists – that neither of these influential thinkers questioned. Despite this and Illich's disinclination to recognise patriarchal oppression, glimpsed in the conversation in Corofin about the washing machine, Illich's provocative ideas about overdeveloped societies and self-interested professionals have nonetheless been welcomed by many feminists. Although his 1982 book *Gender* is an exception to this and has been read as part of the backlash against feminism and upholding the gender-caste system (Hochschild, 1983). Radical feminist Mary Daly (1979) recommended his writings on modern medicine as a 'springboard' for feminist analysis. But then, Daly's is an open attitude that does not rely exclusively on feminist works for insight – 'I'll take it wherever I can get it. If there's an insight, I'll take it' (Daly in Madsen, 2000: 340). Reading *Tools for*

Conviviality, and many of Illich's other works, therefore can be approached as momentarily eavesdropping on an ongoing conversation (albeit mainly between men with patriarchal habits), but also as reading a manifestation of a radically questioning attitude that, to use Daly's language, can springboard our thinking over the walls of mindbinding established wisdom.

In an era such as ours when feminist and socialist movements in Ireland and many places elsewhere are widely believed to be moribund or at best in abeyance, springboards such as those offered by Illich and his co-conversationalists are badly needed. Experiences of institutionalised socialism have become more a source of disillusionment than inspiration, and many of the victories of feminism have failed to live up to our expectations, making the imagination of alternatives to the world as we know it all the more pressing. As pointed out by Nancy Fraser (Alldred, 1999: 128), the collapse of communism in 1989 – the year Illich was in Corofin – did not just entail the delegitimisation of the Soviet Union; it was also associated with a crisis in confidence and, even more crucially, of vision on the left. While recognised as flawed, institutionalised socialism had at least served as evidence that capitalism was not inevitable. A decade after the collapse of Soviet communism, Fraser continued to describe herself as a socialist-feminist but asserted that neither she nor anyone else any longer knew what was meant by that label. The 'postsocialist condition' is the term she employed to refer to the absence of a broad vision of an alternative to the present order. Fraser's ongoing theoretical work (Olson, 2008) that strives to conceptualise injustice in a way that incorporates the *injuries* inflicted by capitalism and the *insults* of cultural domination, together with the harms of political subordination, points to the ongoing project for the left of re-examining what count as genuine injustices, not to mention how to overcome them.

The stalling of capitalist globalisation in recent years due to a crisis of overaccumulation (Bello, 2006) has undermined celebrations and declarations of the inevitability of neo-liberalism, prompting a more widespread acknowledgement of the need for an alternative order. In the context of debates and national referenda about the future of the European Union, endeavours to move the left beyond the condition of visionlessness have led to emergent formulations such as 'alterglobalisation' and the casting of an 'alter-European vote' for a different, humane, democratic and social Europe (George, 2008). This revisioning of the 'big picture' can at times be overwhelming and many people engaged in egalitarian redistributive politics concentrate their efforts on specific local campaigns, several concerned with trying to prevent the reversal of previous victories. For example, in Ireland, some on the left have been mobilised around campaigns opposing state-sponsorship of the privatisation of hospital care, such as the Campaign for a Real Public Health Service launched in Dublin in 2008. For the remainder of this chapter, I hope to show how Illich's *Tools for Conviviality* can be a resource for big picture revisioning and rethinking injustice, but also, and perhaps this is where it is of more immediate relevance, for local struggles concerned with defending and transforming different aspects of the welfare state. For political activity aimed at figuring out what is it that we want, I will outline how Illich offers us the broad ideal of a 'convivial society' and also a methodology for distinguishing between 'convivial' and 'anti-convivial' tools.

Illich's attitude and ideas are particularly useful for those of us involved in defending principles such as universal entitlement who have found ourselves in the existential quandary of campaigning for equal access to things about which we have reservations and have been confronted with the question: to what do we want everyone to have universal entitlement? Do we want all women to have equal access to dubious biomedical procedures, such as mammography screening and the associated slash, burn and poison treatments for breast cancer? Is equal access for all young girls to the latest pharmaceutical formula that promises to reduce their risk of dying from cervical cancer something that we want? Do we want all women to have free access to the latest contraceptive medical technologies? Do we want universal entitlement for our children to psychiatric assessments for recently invented, stigmatised and medicalised disabilities? Should we be mobilised around campaigns for universal entitlement to free nursing home 'care' in which older people are literally bored to death? Is it worth fighting for universal entitlement to free university education when it is increasingly shaped by the priorities of private corporations and run like a credentials production line? In *Tools for Conviviality,* Illich (1973: 12) challenges us to consider that campaigns such as these may debase justice 'to mean the equal distribution of [professionally prescribed] institutional wares' and demean the definition of 'the maximum satisfaction of the maximum number as the largest consumption of industrial goods'. Anticipating the intensification of consumerism, Illich cautioned against a circumscribed and deformed political imagination in which securing equal access to 'ordering from an all-encompassing store catalogue' is the objective. In addition to helping us radically question past campaigns, it offers ideas about how people on the left might work out how to position themselves in respect of more recent and troubling 'tools', such as genetic screening and stem cell research. In light of complex arguments about the relief of human suffering, reproductive choice, eugenics, disability rights, the commodification of human biological material and bioprospecting, to say the least, what constitutes a left opinion on these technologies is far from self-evident. In my experience, the kind of doubt and questioning suggested by Illich is sometimes strategically avoided for fear of arming opponents of the left with arguments that undermine ours; such avoidance can result in a pursuit of pyrrhic victories and also a facile positioning on issues determined by a logic of – if our usual opponents are for it, we're against it. As noted by Fromm (2001: 10), the importance of Illich's writings lies 'in the fact that they have a liberating effect on the mind by showing entirely new possibilities ... they open the door that leads out of the prison of routinized, sterile, preconceived notions', including about what is and is not worthwhile fighting for.

Tools for Conviviality

Like many of Illich's other publications, *Tools for Conviviality* is a short book running to just 110 pages. As already mentioned, it can be approached as 'ideas in progress' with many of the arguments considered in it further developed in subsequent texts. For example, a line of thought in the arguments about health and medicine can be followed between it and the book *Medical Nemesis: The Expropriation of Health*, first published in 1976, and his 1990 essay 'Health as One's Own Responsibility – No, Thank You!'

It was through *Medical Nemesis* that in the early 1990s I first encountered Illich's unsettling ideas. I have no doubt that my alienating experience shortly beforehand of giving birth to my first child in a hospital *qua* industrial reproduction line was partly responsible for the initial personal resonance of his ideas about doctor-inflicted injuries. Subsequently, his ideas about the shaping of needs by professional design helped me to understand aspects of what we were up against in my involvement in various reproductive rights campaigns. A feature of these struggles, particularly in respect of abortion, was and continues to be the Irish state's consistent privileging of the 'masters' of maternity hospitals and members of the almost entirely male obstetric profession in defining women's reproductive health needs. Later still, my and many co-activists' involvement in pharma-politics have drawn on his ideas about consumerism, medicalisation and the pharmaceutical invasion.

In elucidating what I regard as the key ideas elaborated in *Tools for Conviviality*, a short but not-to-be-speed-read text, let me start by clarifying the concepts used in its title. As can be discerned from the account above of the evening in Corofin, Ivan Illich had strong views about commonly used appliances such as washing machines and microphones, and encouraged us to reflect on the potential consequences of their use at practical, social relational and ideological levels. However, his use of the term 'tools' was not confined to tangible artefacts but also included what he referred to as productive institutions and systems. He provided a clear explanation of this broad conceptualisation of tools as follows:

> I use the term 'tool' broadly enough to include not only simple hardware such as drills, pots, syringes, brooms, building elements, or motors, and not just large machines like cars or power stations; I also include among tools productive institutions such as factories that produce tangible commodities like corn flakes or electric current, and productive systems for intangible commodities such as those which produce 'education', 'health', 'knowledge', or 'decisions'. I use this term because it allows me to subsume into one category all rationally designed devices, be they artifacts or rules, codes or operators, and to distinguish all these planned and engineered instrumentalities from other things such as basic food or implements, which in a given culture are not deemed to be subject to rationalization. School curricula or marriage laws are no less purposely shaped social devices than road networks. (Illich, 1973: 20–1)

The book thus offers reflections on tools or technologies such as cars and telephones, but also social technologies such as healthcare and educational systems. Not restricted to tangible machines, tools include any planned and engineered means to an end.

While frequently misrepresented as a technophobe who regarded all modern technologies as socially pernicious, Illich (1973: 20) argued against such an attitude; just as he rejected the automatic assumption that all modern tools are 'progressive', he warned that 'we must guard against falling into the equally damaging rejection of all machines as if they were works of the devil'. What is crucial, he argued, is the distinction between convivial and anti-convivial tools, and this brings us to the second key concept in the book's title, conviviality. Unlike common parlance, he used convivial as a technical term to refer to tools and societies, not people, and explained that conviviality or a convivial society designates the opposite of modern indus-trial society. As in Charlie Chaplin's classic film *Modern Times*, in which the leitmotif of modernity is the factory assembly line, but also anticipating the intensification of consumer capitalism and the 'MacDonaldization' of society (Ritzer, 1993) in late modernity, Illich characterised modern society as industrial society in which the role of people is increasingly reduced to that of mere consumers enforced to consume standardised products. He likened the frustration and alienation of individuals in industrial society to that felt by Sisyphus in Greek mythology, who was forced to engage in an unending, repetitive and pointless task. Industrial society is one that places an exaggerated value on standard products, uniformity, and professionally certified quality. A core ideological belief in industrial society is that more is better, thus leading to growth mania, but where 'no amount of indus-trial productivity can effectively satisfy the needs it creates among society's members' (Illich, 1973: 11). When using conviviality in the broad sense to refer to a society, Illich explained that he employed it 'to mean autonomous and creative intercourse among persons, and the intercourse of persons with their environment; and this [is] in contrast with the conditioned response of persons to the demands made upon them by others, and by a man-made environment. I consider conviviality to be individual freedom realized in personal interdependence and, as such, an intrinsic ethical value' (Ibid.). Resembling the spirit of recent alterglobalisationists' envisioning of 'another world', *Tools for Conviviality* represents a 1970s effort to imagine a post-industrial and convivial world. It also suggested how trends in industrial society can be reversed, how industrial tools can be substituted by convivial ones, a change without which, Illich asserted, the transition to socialism cannot be effected.

Guidelines for recognising convivial tools

Before considering Illich's guidelines for recognising convivial tools, let me get one possible misconception out of the way. When considering tangible artefacts, conviviality is not determined by the low-tech nature of a tool. Illich (1973: 22) emphasised that in principle 'the distinction between convivial and manipulatory tools is independent of the level of technology of the tool'. Illich's idea of conviviality, therefore, is not based on a romantic hankering for a pre-industrial world. This is illustrated for example in his assessment of the telephone as it was widely used in the 1970s as a tool for conviviality. The publication of *Tools for Conviviality* predates many information and communication technologies that are now widely used. However, Kahn and Kellner (2007: 439) claim that in later years Illich was 'aware of how tools like computers and other media technologies could themselves either enhance or distort life's balance'; he recognised the positive potentialities of these technologies, and *Tools for Conviviality* in particular anticipated the democratising social networking opportunities afforded by the Internet through blogs, wikis, chat rooms and listservs. This needles the tendency towards fetishism of the past in left and green activism, and equally towards doom predictions of emergent technologies.

At the heart of *Tools for Conviviality* is an attempt to provide a methodology to recognise the difference between convivial and anti-convivial tools, guidelines for recognising when means have been turned into ends. The purpose of the text is to 'lay down criteria by which the manipulation of people for the sake of their tools can be immediately recognized, and thus to exclude those artifacts and institutions which inevitably extinguish a convivial life style' (Illich, 1973: 14). The criteria that he offered are not meant as a set of prescriptions to be mechanically applied. Illich was emphatic that the text was not intended as 'an engineering manual', or as a 'sales campaign' for a particular convivial lifestyle. Instead, he asked that the criteria for conviviality be considered as guidelines for an ongoing process by which a society's members can envision and enact its unique convivial social arrangements.

Illich argued that the envisioning of new and diverse social possibilities requires recognition that tools can be used in at least two opposite ways. The first of these 'leads to specialization of functions, institutionalization of values and centralization of power and turns people into the accessories of bureaucracies or machines. The second enlarges the range of each person's competence, control and initiative, limited only by other individuals' claims to an equal range of power and freedom' (Illich, 1973: xxiv). Generally, tools are not inherently convivial or anti-convivial – this depends on how they are used and whether or not the range of their use crosses over certain critical limits. Later in the text he offered another formulation of the difference between convivial and anti-convivial use of tools as follows:

> There are two ranges in the growth of tools: the range within which machines are used to extend human capability and the range in which they are used to contract, eliminate, or replace human functions. In the first, man as an individual can exercise authority on his own behalf and therefore assume responsibility. In the second, the machine takes over – first

reducing the range of choice and motivation in both the operator and the client, and second imposing its own logic and demand on both. (Illich, 1973: 84–5)

Examples of anti-convivial tools that Illich discussed are compulsory schools systems and multilane road networks aimed at producing education and transport respectively. Emphasising that public ownership of the means of production does not ensure the conviviality of tools he argued these are destructive tools no matter who owns them. Regardless of their ownership by 'the Mafia, stockholders, a foreign company, the state, or even a workers' commune', they are productive systems that 'must inevitably increase regimentation, dependence, exploitation, or impotence, and rob not only the rich but also the poor of conviviality' (Illich, 1973: 26). The primary question to be addressed in the alternative politics mapped out by Illich, therefore is 'what tools can be controlled in the public interest. Only secondarily does the question arise whether private control of a potentially useful tool is in the public interest' (Ibid.). He pushed this issue of ownership further, arguing that the search for conviviality involves identifying the characteristics of some tools that render ownership of them impossible, a point that I will return to shortly in respect of healthcare.

Not all schools and high-speed roads are incompatible with conviviality; this is only the case when these tools rule out other forms of learning and transport. A tool that dominates alternatives and exercises exclusive control over the satisfaction of a pressing need establishes what Illich referred to as a 'radical monopoly', one of the hazards of industrial societies. A transport system geared towards cars and that rules out travel on foot or by bicycle is a radical monopoly, as is a schooling system that deems all those who have learnt elsewhere uneducated. So too is a medical system that belittles forms of healthcare not prescribed by doctors. A crucial feature of radical monopolies is their imposition of compulsory consumption of a standard product that only large institutions can provide. One has only to think of the widening array of vaccinations that parents are encouraged to 'voluntarily' agree to for their children to appreciate Illich's point that, in the case of medicine, underconsumers risk being blamed for social sabotage, and resistance to its consumption becomes an act of public immorality. In convivial societies, political control of tools protects people against such compulsory consumption.

The idea that there are critical limits within which tools should be used is central to Illich's thesis, and he encourages us to interrogate every step along the way all processes regarding whether or when they cross the line. Returning to the example of genetic screening, we might ask: does pre-implantation genetic diagnosis take this tool too far? With his usual dramatic flourish, he asserted that a 'tool can grow out of man's control, first to become his master and finally to become his executioner' (Illich, 1973: 84). In contrast to this scenario, a convivial society is characterised by responsibly limited tools. The new politics of conviviality that he proposed aims to exclude the design of tools that are obstacles to the exercise of personal freedom. Such politics aims 'to evaluate the structure built into tools and institutions so they can exclude those which by their structure are destructive, and control those which are useful' (Ibid.). In the field of social science known as science and technology studies (STS), the authoritative knowledge and technological artefacts that are the products of science have been shown to embody beliefs 'not only about how the world is, but also how it ought to be' (Jasanoff, 2005: 19). The assumption that tools have an in-built structure or inherent tendencies has been regarded as a feature of an 'intentionalist perspective', and *Tools for Conviviality* is recognised as an early articulation of this approach. This perspective is 'based on the idea that technological innovation entails the materialization of values by means of technological choices' (Nahuis and van Lente, 2008: 560). It also highlights how power relations can be materialised in artefacts. For example, nuclear and solar energy technologies have been contrasted for the different politics they imply, where the requirements of the former are more compatible with bureaucratic organisation, and the latter potentially lends itself to more democratic organisation. In the language of STS, it is suggested that a 'script' reflecting a specific vision of the world, cultural values and ideas about their future use and users is 'inscribed' in technologies by those involved in their design. Anita Hardon (2006), for example, has considered the gender and doctor–patient relations inscribed in certain contraceptive technologies. However, rather than being fixed or inevitable, many STS studies trace how these scripts can be contested and altered, highlighting that artefacts are 'flexibly interpretable' and the possibility of resistant readings. For example, earlier we saw how the rules that govern the use of the washing machine can be revised. At the risk of stretching this metaphor, for Illich the politics of conviviality aims in the first instance to identify and exclude tools with an indelible script of environmental and social destruction; secondly, it aims to identify useful tools whose script – especially in respect of its range of use and relationship with alternatives – can be politically controlled.

Fundamental values

Illich suggested that fundamental values for the political control (as distinct from the technocratic management) of tools are survival, justice and self-defined work. These he explained as follows:

> Each of these three values imposes its own limits on tools. The *conditions for survival* are necessary but not sufficient to ensure justice; people can survive in prison. The *conditions for the just distribution* of industrial outputs are necessary, but not sufficient to promote convivial production. People can be equally enslaved by their tools. The *conditions for convivial work* are structural arrangements that make possible the just distribution of unprecedented power. A postindustrial society must and can be so constructed that no one person's ability to express him- or herself in work will

require as a condition the enforced labor or the enforced learning or the enforced consumption of another. (Illich, 1973: 13)

Heeding the warnings of the 1970s environmental movement, Illich argued that in industrial society the relationship between people and their tools is 'suicidally distorted'; nearly everyone is a destructive consumer and the prevailing fundamental structure of industrial tools 'menaces the survival of mankind' (Illich, 1973: 45). Convivial or what might now be referred to as sustainable survival of all people requires sacrifices and renunciation of many of the taken-for-granted aspects of industrial life. Environmental crisis can only be averted, he argued, by limiting consumption, waste and (controversially) procreation. But equally, it requires change at another dimension; we must alter 'our expectations that machines will do our work for us or that therapists can make us learned or healthy' (Illich, 1973: 49–50). Environmental degradation, Illich argued, is only one of a number of hazards created by industrial development or 'over growth'. In addition to radical monopolies discussed above, another hazard is economic polarisation whereby the poor grow numerically and the rich grow in affluence.

Illich was not just concerned with the survival of the human race, but with survival in justice and freedom. The political limitation of tools, he argued, cannot be effected prior to the operationalisation of a new just economic order. However, he emphasised that the proposed methodology for distinguishing convivial from anti-convivial tools requires recognition of the value of both distributory and participatory justice, where the latter ensures individuals' capacity to define their own work, but also their needs and interests. Justice is undermined, he argued, by imperialism on three levels: 'the pernicious spread of one nation beyond its boundaries, the omnipresent influence of multinational corporations; and the mushrooming of professional monopolies over production' (Illich, 1973: 43). The new politics of convivial reconstruction must especially face professional imperialism, he argued, and it is this threat to participatory justice that he discussed at length in *Tools for Conviviality* and many of his subsequent texts.

For Illich, a prerequisite of participatory justice is de-professionalisation, whereby the quasi-religious authority of the certified doctor and other professionals is removed, along with their professional monopoly of tools and their ability to enforce compulsory consumption. The time has come, Illich asserted, 'to take the syringe out of the hand of the doctor, as the pen was taken out of the hand of the scribe during the Reformation of Europe' (Illich, 1973: 34). Convivial tools are not professionally controlled but are accessible. They do not require certification of the user, and can be used as often or as seldom and for the purpose chosen by the user. Furthermore, and perhaps especially relevant in respect of scientific innovations, their existence does not impose an obligation to use them. The de-professionalisation of healing, for example, which requires recognition of how complex medical rituals mask the simplicity of its basic procedures, would re-establish people's capacity for self-care and healing. In turn, it would make 'healing so plentiful that it would be difficult to turn this competence into a monopoly or to sell it as a commodity' (Illich, 1973: 35–6). Thus, de-professionalisation similarly can be crucial to rendering the ownership of tools impossible.

Convivial reconstruction

Not surprisingly given his aversion to coercion and professional paternalism, Illich did not envision the transformation of industrial into convivial society being accomplished through the use of force, nor by means of professionally managed change. Instead, he envisioned this change, which can be neither imposed nor engineered, happening organically. In line with Marxist ideas about the contradictory dynamics of capitalism and its inevitable structural crises, Illich predicted a catastrophic crisis of overgrowth in industrial society akin to the Great Depression triggered by the Wall Street Crash of 1929. The current crisis in global capitalism, which in Ireland has profoundly undermined the logic of stockbroker economists that prevailed in the short-lived Celtic Tiger era, has been likened to the Great Depression. It remains to be seen, however, if this crisis will result in the widespread and fundamental questioning of the industrial way of life anticipated by Illich. The crisis that he predicted will result in a sudden and profound crisis of legitimacy for the major institutions of industrial society (as has occurred in respect of the Irish banking system) but also, crucially, to people being confronted with a choice between 'convivial tools and being crushed by machines' (Illich, 1973: 107). The crash he predicted will

> render publicly obvious the structural contradictions between stated purposes and effective results in our major institutions. People will suddenly find obvious what is now evident to only a few: that the organization of the entire economy toward the 'better' life has become the major enemy of the *good* life. Like other widely shared insights, this one will have the potential of turning public imagination inside out. Large institutions can quite suddenly lose their respectability, their legitimacy, and their reputation for serving the public good. It happened to the Roman Church in the Reformation, to Royalty in the Revolution. The unthinkable became obvious overnight: that people could and would behead their rulers. (Illich, 1973: 103)

A key task for the new politics of conviviality, he argued, is the preparation of groups of 'clear-thinking and feeling' people who can communicate a coherent analysis of the crisis in industrial society. He was not advocating a new kind of expert, nor a political party, but a political process. While awaiting the profound crisis in industrial society, Illich argued that the project of conviviality could be advanced in three ways, the first of which is the de-mythologising of science, which in the current Irish context crucially needs to include the imperfect science of economics. What he proposed bore little resemblance to efforts to promote 'public understanding of science' that assume if people are 'properly informed about scientific facts, there should be no cross-cultural variation in their perceptions of science' (Jasanoff, 2005: 250). Rather, it is delusions about the objectivity of scientific knowledge and the view of it as a commodity that can be constantly improved, accumulated and fed into decision-making processes that need to be dispelled. This de-mythologising of science was regarded by him as concurrently entailing a revaluing of currently belittled forms of everyday evidence. Secondly, Illich advocated a 'recovery of language', an alteration of our habits of speech that reflect industrial habits of thought. In particular, he argued, we need to rid ourselves of the language of ownership and reverse the shift from verb to noun where, for example, work, education, fun and even sex are things that we *have* rather than *do*. The commodification of education, he argued, is evident in the transformation of the phrase 'I want to learn' into 'I want to get an education', a shift whereby credentials and 'having been' at college become more important than the experience of being there. This proprietary language, according to Illich, has contributed to blinkering the public of the destructiveness of industrial society and crippling our political fantasy. Finally, Illich called for a 'recovery of legal procedure' whereby the law can become a revolutionary tool if it is de-mystified, de-centralised and de-bureaucratised. He recognised that the body of laws in industrial society reflects and reproduces its ideology and class structure, but argued that this can be subverted, that the current corruption of legal procedures does not rule out the possibility of their use for a different purpose. His thesis is that 'any revolution which neglects the use of formal legal and political pro-cedures will fail' (Illich, 1973: 99). Akin to many proposals for deliberative democracy, Illich endorsed formal adversary procedure as the paradigmatic tool for people to engage in direct opposition to the limitations of their liberty by industrial tools and institutions.

Conclusion

Unquestionably, the politics of conviviality proposed by Ivan Illich – and only briefly sketched out above – are complex and enormously ambitious. For example, his calls for the de-mythologising of science and the revaluing of everyday evidence raises difficult questions about how technoscientific decision-making can be democratised, or how the tensions between exper-tise and democracy can be resolved. The 'problem of extension' has been the focus of much rumination as those who recognise multiple forms of expertise beyond the credentialised version seek to 'identify how far these different forms of expertise legitimately extend' (Sismondo, 2008: 23). Like-wise, the democratisation of legal procedures faces many obstacles inclu-ding the obvious one of variations in peoples' communicative competencies, where members of privileged groups are more likely to feel better equipped to engage in adversarial deliberations about their interests. Indeed, there is no shortage of critics of Ivan Illich's ideas, nor of his own habits of thought and speech. I myself am uncomfortable with what he had to say about a number of matters, not least gender issues. Also, even though many of those who knew Illich personally write about him with tremendous affection (Hoinacki and Mitcham, 2002), you have probably noticed that aristocratic insinuations can be discerned in his work and social interactions, where he appeared to set himself not only apart from but also above others, a problem that besets many involved in alternative politics (Duncombe, 2007a). This is evident for example in the quotation above in which he noted that the profound contradictions of industrial society are evident to only a select few, himself included. Apparently, it was these elitist insinuations that irked some of the participants in the 'conversation' in the hall in Corofin. However, we should not assume that in Corofin the inspiration was one-directional. It would seem that Illich was inspired by the members of the co-operative who attempted to engage in the search for conviviality, against considerable odds and opposition, and without the academic accolades and membership of an internationally renowned intellectual set that he enjoyed. And of course it is not necessary to idolise Illich in order to value his work. I agree with Mary Daly that we should take inspiration wherever we can get it.

Notes

1 For an account of Ivan Illich's visit to Ireland in 1989, see the obituary written by Dara Molloy, who invited him and organised his itinerary, at www.daramolloy. com/DaraMolloy/Writings/IllichObituary.html. Accessed 9 November 2009.

2 My sincere thanks to Michael Neylon for sharing with me his recollections and wonderful photographs of Ivan Illich's visit to Corofin.

3 I am hugely indebted to John Quinn, the maker of this radio programme, for supplying me with a copy of the recording.

4 In the paper 'Health as One's Own Responsibility – No, Thank You!' Illich describes himself as a medieval historian. However, his work eludes classification according to conventional academic disciplines, as it is all at once philosophical, theological, sociological, historical and educational, to say the least.

5 The version of *Tools for Conviviality* to which I refer in this discussion was published in 1973 by the New York-based publishers Harper & Row.

10

Adrienne Rich's
On Compulsory Heterosexuality and Lesbian Existence
Tina O'Toole

Introduction

The 1980s are unlikely to be remembered positively by Irish feminists[1] as it was a decade characterised primarily by a series of defeats such as the 1983 Pro-Life Constitutional Amendment and ensuing court cases taken by the anti-abortion movement against groups providing abortion information (Connolly, 2002: 155–84); by the death of Ann Lovett and the Joanne Hayes case;[2] and by high unemployment and the concomitant re-emergence of mass emigration. Yet, despite this challenging context, by the end of that decade Ireland had seen the emergence and consolidation of lesbian activist groups, academic discourses and communities, in tandem with a contemporary investment in identity politics internationally. These new formations were doubtless due at least in part to the increase in emigration, as those social radicals who left the country during the period tended to stay in touch with friends back home, sending back what Peggy Levitt (2001) calls 'social remittances'. In other words, this interaction between individuals and groups here and in Britain and North America predominantly, meant that such social remittances, that is ideas, policies, actions and texts developed by theorists and activists abroad, became common currency within lesbian and feminist activist groups on the island of Ireland during the 1980s.

One such broadside was Adrienne Rich's important essay 'On Compulsory Heterosexuality and Lesbian Existence'. While Rich is a poet and literary critic whose essay related specifically to lesbian feminist politics, this text had a reach which extended right across the spectrum of feminist thought and activism. Written in 1978, first published in the feminist journal *Signs* in 1980 and reproduced in a pamphlet series and a number of different collections throughout the 1980s, the essay sustained interest into the following decade and since. It remains in the top five most-cited articles from *Signs*, and several of the key terms introduced by Rich have since become part of mainstream critical discourse. In an Irish context, while it was doubtless read on an individual basis when first published, it would take several years before the essay, or indeed sexual identities more generally, could be publicly addressed by Irish feminists. By the late 1980s, the central arguments propounded by Rich's essay had entered mainstream feminist discourse here, by which stage the essay had become a central text within lesbian discussion and activist groups, as well as in the feminist classroom and other contexts, principally as a means to mobilise discussion of sexualities and lesbian politics. Texts such as this gave a theoretical perspective to the work going on in feminist groups in Ireland, as I will elaborate on below, in particular its core definition of heterosexuality as a constructed, rather than a 'natural', sexual identity, and the notion that lesbian feminists could use the terms of their oppression to redefine the social world.

My interest in Adrienne Rich's work derives in part from my own long-standing commitment to feminist and LGBTQ[3] scholarship and activism, and in part from a study I carried out with Linda Connolly on the second-wave Irish Women's Movement.[4] That project (and subsequent publication, *Documenting Irish Feminisms* (2005)) relies principally on primary archival material and interviews with 1980s movement activists. I first read 'On Compulsory Heterosexuality and Lesbian Existence' as an undergraduate student at University College Dublin (UCD) in the early 1990s, when it was passed on to me by a feminist friend, thus replicating the process by which the transmission of ideas generally takes place within activist movements. Yvonne Ivory recalls, 'At the time I had never read anything like it, and was completely seduced by its language and ideas. I remember recommending it to so many friends around that time' (personal communication, 1 February 2009). Joan McCarthy, likewise, remembers teaching the text in the early 1990s in Cork, situating it as part of the feminist history of ideas: 'I remember using Rich's essay on a Lesbian Studies Course I offered and taught in the Other Place in 1992. Then, it was critically considered alongside the likes of Wittig and de Beauvoir and thought of very positively' (personal communication, 19 January 2009). It cropped up again for me as a set text on the MA in Women's Studies at UCD, and over the intervening years I have seen it on countless reading lists for feminist education programmes at all levels. That this essay, first published almost thirty years ago, continues to find a place within the canon of feminist texts is testament to the groundbreaking nature of Rich's ideas but also to its ongoing resonance within feminist discourse.

Much-cited by Irish poet Eavan Boland as an important influence on her own work, a generation of Irish feminist writers and activists were familiar with the poetry from the fifteen collections Adrienne Rich had published between 1951 and 1990. This work was read on an individual basis, as well as in feminist reading groups, at conferences and in creative writing workshops in Ireland during the 1980s. Rich's prose collections, particularly *Of Woman Born* (1977), were also very well known and well read at the time. Rich opens her 1986 prose collection *Blood, Bread and Poetry*, in which the essay under discussion appears, with the following curriculum vitae:

> These essays were not written in an ivory tower. But neither were they written on the edges of a political organizer's daily life, or a nine-to-five manual or clerical job, or in prison. My fifteen or so years in the women's

liberation movement have been spent as a writer, a teacher, an editor-publisher, a pamphleteer, a lecturer and a sometimes activist. Before and throughout, I have been a poet. (Rich, 1986: vii)

Rich having gained a reputation first as a poet and later as a feminist activist, before coming out as a lesbian, those reading this article in the 1980s would almost certainly have been aware of her as a literary writer first and would have been familiar with, or would themselves have shared, her radical feminist politics. This suggests that they read it in something of a different context from those later readers who encounter this lesbian feminist essay for the first time in a classroom setting, perhaps as part of a list of required readings from different (and often unfamiliar) feminist authors from an earlier generation. Needless to say, the reception of the text and the meanings constructed by its readers are impacted by these different contexts, but a detailed analysis of this reception is beyond the scope of this chapter.

Irish feminist reading contexts in the 1980s

When we reflect on the venues within which previous generations of activists were educated about the history and development of counter-cultural resistance, at least in the feminist case, we often tend to place the academic Women's Studies model at centre-stage. However, Irish feminists had developed their own learning programmes in less formal ways during the 1970s and 1980s, which anticipated the development of academic Women's Studies programmes in the 1990s. In the early 1980s, feminist ideas were transmitted and debated in reading and discussion groups such as the Women's Place discussion group in Cork and the UCD Women's Forum, as well as in women's libraries such as the Women's Centre shop at 27 Temple Lane, Dublin, and the Women's Place library in Cork. Spaces such as these carried catalogues from emerging feminist publishing houses and made available a wide range of feminist reading material, as Róisín Conroy makes clear in the notes to a bibliography she published in 1980: 'While working on this bibliography I decided to compile a more comprehensive list of essential reading for feminist studies. This list will be available shortly from the Women's Centre Library Group' (Conroy, 1980). The Women's Place in Cork also published a newsletter which reviewed new books and articles relevant to their feminist readers. Thus, making a wide range of materials available either on loan or at second-hand prices meant that feminist theories were accessible to a wider number of people. The need for such libraries is reflected in a leaflet advertising one such resource:

> We now have the following range of books, pamphlets and magazines available, and will be selling them from a stall in the Dandelion Market at the weekends, as well as at meetings and conferences, and in the Resources Centre [at Rathgar Road] itself [...] If there is material which you find difficult to get through straight bookshops, let us know, and we'll do our best to get it for you.

The list carried by the Resource Centre includes periodicals such as the feminist newspapers *Banshee* and *Spare Rib*, also pamphlets and books on a wide range of political and social issues, including material relating to abortion, which was and remains illegal in the Republic of Ireland. Many of these 'pamphlets' were little more than stapled-together photocopies, sometimes with handwritten titles on the front, as anyone who consults the Irish Women's Movement Archive (IWMA) at University College Cork can see for themselves.[5] The hand-turned Gestetner machines which produced many of the original pamphlets did not always make for entirely legible script, or durability. The demand for such resources is reflected in one file of remaining letters held in the IWMA: dated 1978–79, these letters are from individuals and women's groups throughout the country, writing to ask for information or reading lists. This dissemination of feminist ideas demonstrates the ways in which Irish activists developed counter-arguments to those proposed by the dominant culture in Ireland in the late-1970s, particularly in relation to core issues such as employment and equal pay, fertility and reproduction, and sexual identities. Social scientists construct this kind of knowledge transfer within social movements as the 'negotiation of shared meaning' (Benford and Snow, 2000). We can see this negotiation taking place in the process by which counter-cultural movements, such as Irish feminism, construct a common ideological space, share ideas and experiences, and experiment with new ways of being in the world. This counter-cultural space not only supported the individuals within it, enabling them to construct shared understandings of their social and political identities, but also became the basis for emerging political activism which challenged their oppression within the dominant culture.

On compulsory heterosexuality and lesbian existence

The opening of Rich's essay in the 1980 special issue of *Signs* on the theme of 'Sexuality' fired an opening salvo in which she takes issue with 'the virtual or total neglect of lesbian existence in a wide range of writings, including feminist scholarship' (Rich, 1986: 27).[6] Citing a number of well-known publications from the 1970s by feminist scholars including Bridenthal and Koonz (1977), Chodorow (1978), Dinnerstein (1976), Ehrenrich and English (1978) and Miller (1976), and even the first edition of the hugely influential *Our Bodies Ourselves* (1976),[7] to name just a few, Rich states:

> In none of them is the question ever raised as to whether, in a different context or other things being equal, women would *choose* heterosexual coupling and marriage [...] In none of these books, which concern themselves with mothering, sex roles, relationships, and societal prescriptions for women, is compulsory heterosexuality ever examined as an institution powerfully affecting all these, or the idea of 'preference' or 'innate orientation' even indirectly questioned. (Rich, 1986: 28–9)

In much of what follows in the first section of her essay, Rich works through some of these texts in more depth, deconstructing individual approaches, teasing out the heteronormative construction of this feminist work, and offering alternative histories or counter-readings at key points. Her critique of this work is based on the central premise that heterosexuality, far from being a 'natural' state or a normative sexual identity, is in fact constructed and rigidly upheld by social laws and mores. As I discuss in more detail below, Rich's essay discusses heterosexuality as a powerful hegemony, the dominant means for the social regulation of relationships, and she goes on to outline a range of means by which this powerful institution has been maintained over time. The silencing of same-sex possibility is one such means. Rich discusses in some detail Dinnerstein's 1976 call for an end to current sex-roles and division of labour which, Dinnerstein suggests, are supported by women's collaboration with patriarchal power. Here, Rich points out that Dinnerstein has wilfully sidelined 'the history of women who – as witches, *femmes seules*, marriage resisters, spinsters, autonomous widows, or lesbians – have managed on varying levels not to collaborate' (Rich, 1986: 31).

From the perspective of those Irish lesbian feminists reading this, it seems to me that Rich's focus on the erasure of lesbian experience at the heart of feminist discourse would almost certainly have chimed with their experience of mainstream activist feminism at the time. While lesbians had been actively involved in second-wave feminist activism since the founding of the Irish Women's Liberation Movement (IWLM) in 1970, lesbian issues were not on the agenda. With solidarity a core principle of women's liberation, those joining the IWLM tacitly agreed to focus on what they had in common rather than on potentially divisive matters (sexuality and nationalist politics appear to have headed that list in the period). Mary Dorcey, recalling her experience of joining the women's movement on her return to Ireland, writes: 'to my surprise [there was] no one declaring themselves lesbian or speaking about it' (Dorcey, 1995: 35). Lesbian issues were not named within the 'seven minimum demands' of the IWLM manifesto, or in the charter of Irishwomen United, the organisation which followed on from IWLM, although Irishwomen United did call for the 'right of all women to [their] own self-defined sexuality'. This may have been prompted by a number of lesbian feminist activists who were involved in Irishwomen United, or by the fact that lesbian sexuality was addressed, among other issues, at consciousness-raising sessions run by that organisation. Nonetheless, lesbian politics *per se* were not specifically part of the mandate of either group, both of which were foundational to second-wave feminism in Ireland.

Ultimately, this began to cause dissent between lesbian feminists and their heterosexual sisters. Irish lesbian activists who had been engaged in a wide range of political campaigns throughout the 1970s and early 1980s began to realise the dearth of support that existed in the wider activist sphere when it came to organising on issues directly related to lesbian lives and experiences.

The first Irish lesbian conference was held in Dublin in May 1978, and the flyer announcing the conference touches on some of these issues.

> Lesbianism has not been explored by public debate or within the women's movement here. Lesbians have been in the vanguard of the fight for radical change – the struggle for an autonomous lifestyle for women will not be complete while lesbians are oppressed, therefore we should not be disclaimed publicly or in the context of women's liberation. We feel this conference will break down the barriers of silence and ignorance surrounding lesbian sexuality. We invite all women to participate in a sharing of lesbian experience and sensibilities, rather than in defence of your own sexuality – whatever it is! (IWMA, 1116)[8]

Lesbian activist Joni Crone saw this conference as a watershed, as she recalls: 'The 1978 conference [...] had a lasting effect on the community. Lesbian feminists now recognised the contribution we had already made to the Women's Movement since 1970' (Crone, 1995: 65). This had an impact on the wider feminist movement, as Irish lesbian activists began to suggest that their issues and experiences were being sidelined by the wider movement. At the time, Crone put this point forcefully in a 1980 article in the Trinity College Dublin Women's Group magazine, *Elektra*:

> Why has it taken ten years before the word 'lesbian' could be uttered at an Irish feminist meeting? Why, even in the most radical group yet – Irish-women United – was the existence of lesbians ignored? [...] Veiled references and tokenism after years of activism is just not good enough. For ten years we have struggled alongside our sisters for contraception, divorce, justice for deserted and battered wives, equal pay, and every legal and social issue that has arisen. We've given a large degree of energy and ideas, time and commitment. Most of the time these issues have not been central to the lives of lesbians.

This statement finds common cause with Rich's assertion that lesbian experience was an 'absent presence' (Lather, 1994) at the heart of feminist scholarship. Rich's clear statement, 'I believe that much feminist theory and criticism is stranded on this shoal' (Rich, 1986: 27), backed-up by her delineation of this using a range of contemporary feminist sources, could readily be applied by Irish lesbian activists to the manifestoes and public statements of the women's liberation groups they were involved in at that time.

While it took some time for ideas such as these to gain momentum, by the late 1980s, many lesbian activists had turned away from the mainstream women's liberation movement in Ireland to set up groups or work on projects within their own communities, establishing social and political networks for lesbians around the country.

Heterosexuality as political institution

The construction of heterosexuality as a political institution is fundamental to Rich's project in general in this essay: 'I am suggesting that heterosexuality, like motherhood, needs to be recognized and studied as a *political institution*' (Rich, 1986: 35). Her opening question as to why 'species survival, the means of impregnation, and emotional/erotic relationships should ever have become so rigidly identified with each other' (Ibid.) is answered by positing heteronormativity as a powerful hegemony. Drawing on Kathleen Gough's 'The Origin of the Family' in the second section of the essay, Rich identifies a range of 'violent strictures' by which the dominant culture enforces the heterosexual institution (Rich, 1986: 36–7) and underpins women's subjection to male power. For instance, she discusses clitoridectomy which, she points out, not only is a form of 'woman torture' but also, using Kathleen Barry's work, 'intends that women in the intimate proximity of polygynous marriage will not form sexual relationships with each other [so] that [...] female erotic connections, even in a sex-segregated situation, will be literally excised' (Rich, 1986: 39). Rich connects clitoridectomy, the chastity belt, child marriage, rape and sexual slavery with issues of pornography and sadomasochism (hotly-contested topics in feminist circles during the 1970s and 1980s), constructing all such 'forms of compulsion' as the strong-arm tactics of the heterosexual institution. Turning to an economic and labour model, Rich cites Catherine A. MacKinnon's research on sexual harassment and discrimination in the workplace, in which she states: 'Two forces of American society converge: men's control over women's sexuality and capital's control over employees' work lives' (Rich, 1986: 41). This underpins Rich's assertion that the institutional model of compulsory heterosexuality is key to an understanding of gender inequality in the workplace and in society in general (Rich, 1986: 40–1). Summing up this section of her argument, Rich concludes: 'it becomes an inescapable question whether the issue feminists have to address is not simple "gender inequality", nor the domination of culture by males, nor mere "taboos against homosexuality", but the enforcement of heterosexuality for women as a means of assuring male right of physical, economic and emotional access' (Rich, 1986: 49–50). It might be tempting for us, as it has been for other feminist theorists at the time and since, as I discuss below, to dismiss the lack of specificity of Rich's ideas here and in general. In this section in particular, her argument ranges from polygynous communities to urban work settings in the space of a few pages, without contextualising specific social or cultural settings. Nonetheless, her aim to provoke discussion and provide a series of rallying points for feminists was certainly achieved by this section of the essay. Of course Adrienne Rich was not the only feminist scholar in the period to suggest such a construction of heterosexuality-as-institution, which, as she acknowledges in the Foreword, had been posited by 'The Furies' a radical feminist collective (particularly in the articles by Charlotte Bunch in their publication, also called *The Furies*) in the early 1970s. Furthermore, in her 1978 presentation to the Modern Languages Association 'The Straight Mind' and her 1980 essay 'On ne nâit pas femme', Monique Wittig asserts that a lesbian is not a woman: 'for what makes a woman is a specific social relation to a man [...] a relation which lesbians escape by refusing to become or stay hetero-sexual' (Wittig, 1992: 20). Offering a radical analysis of Rousseau's social contract, which Wittig reads as a 'heterosexual contract', she argues that Lévi-Strauss's theory of the exchange of women 'exposes heterosexuality as a political régime', a social contract from which women are explicitly excluded from benefiting (Wittig, 1992: 40). However, while Rich was not alone in positing these ideas, her work appears to have been better known here in Ireland than that of the more activist Bunch, or the more scholarly Wittig. Perhaps her work was simply more widely available internationally at the time, or perhaps Irish familiarity with her poetry made her work seem more accessible than that of Wittig or Bunch, but for whatever reason, it seems to have been more widely discussed and had more resonance for Irish feminist activists at that time.

There was something of a time-lag between the publication of these radical feminist ideas in North America and their diffusion, even within a lesbian feminist context, here in Ireland. This was partly due to the resounding silence on the subject of lesbian (and other) sexualities, identities and issues in 1980. Anne O'Connor, then a member of the UCD Women's Forum, observes: 'For me personally, this article was transformational – it was inspiring and revolutionary. But I do not remember feminists talking about it openly until later in the 1980s' (personal communication, 14 January 2009). At local level throughout the 1980s in Ireland, texts such as this were shared, borrowed from women's libraries, and widely debated within feminist discussion groups. One experience of such a group (which came together c.1983 in Cork) is described here by Deirdre Walsh:

> I began reading the various authors discussed, Adrienne Rich being one of them. There was a classic feminist book on rape by Susan Brownmiller [*Against Our Will: Men, Women and Rape* (1975)], among many others, examining from a feminist perspective gender politics and the oppression of women by men [...] There were all these American and English feminist books around at the time being passed hand to hand. I can't remember them all now but [the] SCUM [Manifesto][9] is one that stands out which I was not altogether comfortable with. (personal communication, 15 January 2009)

That much of this feminist material was imported from abroad gives us an insight into the identity-formation of early Irish feminism and the kinds of influences which shaped the development of indigenous feminist politics. Róisín Conroy noted in the preface to the bibliography mentioned above (1980):

> Although I was asked to compile a bibliography dealing with the subject of

women in Ireland, I found that there is such a dearth of Irish material, both factual and theoretical, on topics such as Health and Sexuality that the 'Irish only' criteria has little or no relevance. Much of the theory, certainly, that has influenced Irishwomen has been written and published abroad.

Needless to say, the development of Irish feminist discourses in tandem with the establishment of Women's Studies programmes and centres in the academy over the intervening twenty years would change this, as Irish feminists themselves began to publish and read more specifically Irish material. Nonetheless, Conroy's assessment of the lack of available Irish publications contextualises the impact of ideas such as those of Adrienne Rich, along with a range of other international feminist writers and activists, on the thinking and praxis of Irish feminists during the period. The influence of international feminist frameworks at local level is apparent in the language and politics of early Irish lesbian activists. One example of this is the response of Mary Dorcey (one of the first Irish lesbian activists to come out publicly) when asked to define her own lesbian identity: 'the early 1970s phrase "women-identified-woman" probably expresses it' (Dorcey, 1995: 33). This phrase derives from the New York Radicalesbians' manifesto 'The Woman-Identified Woman' (1970) which had obviously been deployed by Irish lesbian activists in a local context. Likewise, Rich's writings, and specifically the term 'compulsory heterosexuality', was one which would be widely used and debated amongst feminists in Ireland.

However, this is not to suggest that such radicalism was simply imported wholesale from abroad and was inappropriate to the local context. Indeed, the level of contemporary debate and discussion taking place at local level relating to texts such as 'On Compulsory Heterosexuality and Lesbian Existence' indicates a vibrant context within which Irish feminists were taking these ideas and making their own of them. Deirdre Walsh describes this scene in mid-1980s Cork:

> There came to be an identifiable group of lesbian feminists as well as heterosexual feminists and socialist feminists and apolitical lesbians. There was always lively and heated debate [...] I remember many discussions informally amongst this group about compulsory heterosexuality and lesbian separatism and political lesbianism, all in the context of feminism and re-examining the world in that light. (personal communication, 15 January 2009)

Similarly within Irish academic feminism during the same period, international feminist ideas and theories were also being debated, although in this more public sphere there seem to have been more constraints on the kinds of discussion possible. Anne O'Connor comments:

> We had meetings, we held seminars on specific topics such as rape and violence against women; reproductive rights and reproductive technologies; divorce; abortion; etc [...] Literature and poetry and performance

were very important [...] We had international feminist academics visit and speak. Adrienne Rich's work was very important for us, especially *Of Woman Born* [1977] and the *On Lies, Secrets and Silence* [1979] collection as well as her poetry. But during 1983 I never heard lesbianism ever discussed out loud – of course some of us spoke to each other – but in general at that time it was a taboo. That was my experience. I suppose people were terrified of being labelled in that way at that time. (personal communication, 14 January 2009)

As is evident, it was through these groups at local level that Irish feminists encountered, sometimes at first-hand, the work of international feminist academics such as Rich, but more importantly, it was also within these groups that Irish feminists adapted these discourses for their own purposes.

Lesbian existence and lesbian continuum

The third section of Rich's essay is probably the best-known and is frequently reprinted as an extract in anthologies. This suggests that many readers today, perhaps in a classroom situation, read this part of Rich's argument in isolation from the broader context of feminist thinking within which Rich had very carefully situated it. In this section, Rich introduces two of the key terms for which her article is famous. The term 'lesbian existence' she uses very specifically, instead of 'lesbianism', to denote lesbian identity and experience, to construct 'both the [...] historical presence of lesbians and our continuing creation of the meaning of that existence' (Rich, 1986: 51). I will come back to discuss this term in more detail below, but suffice it to say for now that Rich's designation, far from being an essentialist one, is clearly marked out as one which is socially constructed, as is suggested by the phrase 'our continuing creation of its meaning'. Joan McCarthy points out: 'I think, for me at least and for others, the article also provided a positive self-affirming and feminist lesbian identity that seemed to be fuller and closer to my own experience than the more essentialist alternative' (personal communication, 19 January 2009).

The second term, 'lesbian continuum' is perhaps the most important term in this essay, and has been at the centre of robust debates within feminist and other circles ever since, as I discuss below. Rich's lesbian continuum opened up a way for women in general to strategically identify as lesbians, thus making the term 'lesbian' a political rather than a sexual category. Constructing an expansive category within which a range of 'woman-identified experience' was included within the sphere of this 'lesbian continuum', Rich created a space whereby 'female friendship and comradeship' constituted part of the continuum: 'If we expand it to embrace many more forms of primary intensity between and among women [...] we begin to grasp breadths of female history and psychology which have lain out of our reach as a consequence of limited, mostly clinical, definitions of *lesbianism*' (Rich, 1986: 51). In her Foreword to the 1986 edition of the essay, Rich indicates that her motivation here was primarily to 'sketch, at least, some bridge over the gap between *lesbian* and *feminist*' (Rich, 1986: 24) and as Imelda Whelehan suggests: 'Rich offers a point of contact between lesbian and heterosexual feminists upon the issue where the gulf between them was at its most treacherous' (Whelehan, 1995: 95). That gap in understanding between these groups of feminists centred on the way in which sexual identity had been constructed within feminist thought. As we can see from the first section of Rich's essay and the experience of Irish lesbian activists in the 1970s and 1980s, other feminists at the time had not yet begun to interrogate the hegemonic implications of heteronormativity. Thus, the sexual 'preference' of a minority of their number may not have seemed to them to have anything to do with the wider feminist project and, if anything, was a divisive and troublesome matter. This is evident in the public statements of US feminists such as Betty Friedan who in 1969 had attacked what she called the 'lavender menace', a view doubtless echoed, at least privately, in Irish feminist circles. As Yvonne Ivory points out: 'It was an important contribution to feminist theory at a time when lesbian was a dirty word – a slur to be feared – for most feminists' (personal communication, 1 February 2009). Rich's controversial contention suggested a new way forward by changing the terms of engagement altogether: by moving the discourse into a different frame, she suggested that heterosexual (and in particular, heterosexist) feminists needed to reconsider their own allegiances and reconstruct their own identities. Shane Phelan describes this understanding of the power of language by lesbian feminists in the period as 'a matter not only of ontology, but also of strategy'. She points out that such redeployment of language, the redefinition of the category of lesbian in this case, is consciously done: 'Arguments and definitions are proposed less with an eye to eternal truth than with a view toward their concrete implications for community membership and political strategy' (Phelan, 1989: 136). We can thus situate Rich's construction of the 'lesbian continuum' as an open invitation to all women to define themselves as lesbians, just as it was read (both positively and negatively) by many at the time.

The transformational nature of Rich's work, as described above, was central to the context of activist reading, discussion and political campaigning as discussed earlier, and her delineation of the 'lesbian continuum' provided a 'call to arms' for Irish feminist activists. As Anne O'Connor outlines:

> Within the feminist movement, the title 'woman-identified-woman' abounded, this meant someone who prioritised women or women's experience. Adrienne Rich wrote her famous 'Compulsory Heterosexuality and Lesbian Existence' article in the feminist journal *Signs* in 1980 which postulated a 'lesbian continuum' and was very powerful about the potential for women to come together to overcome their oppression. (personal communication, 14 January 2009)

While my focus here has chiefly been on lesbian community-building and political activism, it is *also* important to remember the role played by essays such as this in sustaining individuals who began to question their own sexual identities, who may have joined support groups and some of whom, perhaps later, became involved themselves in political activism. Furthermore, in comparing the location of Rich's article with the Irish social context in the 1980s, we must remember the relative size and character of Ireland and the USA. In other words, while Rich was writing in and for a defined and public lesbian community (both academic and activist) in North America, however marginalised, the prevailing social climate in which a woman might come out as a lesbian or become politically active as a feminist in Ireland in the 1980s was considerably more challenging. Anne O'Connor continues: 'Until 1983 I had never actually met any women who called themselves "lesbian" or "gay". In Ireland, [male] homosexuality was outlawed. Lesbianism was largely invisible. There were rumours about people being gay but it was not discussed openly' (personal communication, 14 January 2009). To be in the vanguard of feminist politics on a small island like Ireland then was not only to strike against the social order but to have to do so in the full glare of one's family and local community. Thus, the resonance of Rich's comment – 'we romanticize at our peril what it means to love and act against the grain' (Rich, 1986: 52) – must have rung true for many Irish lesbians at that time. Lesbian mothers with children had even more reason to be circumspect, as up until 1992, where custody battles came before the courts, they automatically lost the right to custody of their children by reason of their sexuality.[10] Thus, we might speculate that the possibility suggested by Rich's lesbian continuum – that of identifying *politically* as a lesbian – might have offered some Irish feminists involved in the movement a way to explore their own sexual identities and life choices. I have discussed elsewhere the strategic use of the term 'women' rather than 'lesbian' during the period as a means to disguise events aimed at a lesbian audience and thus enable all women to participate (Connolly and O'Toole, 2005: 173). As Joni Crone explains, in relation to a lesbian conference she organised in 1978:

> It was only quite late in the proceedings that we realized that if we called the event a 'lesbian conference' most of the organizing collective would be unable to attend because 'walking through the door would be a public statement' [...] it was sobering to discover that most of the lesbian women we knew were leading double lives. At home, at work, and even within the Women's Movement, they were open about their feminism, but they disguised their sexual identity. Our compromise solution was to call the weekend a 'Women's Conference on Lesbianism'. This meant that women of every sexual persuasion were free to attend. (Crone, 1995: 64)

In other words, defining a space or event as a 'women's space' – such as the 'Women's Place' in Cork, the Galway Women's Camp, and the Cork Women's Fun Weekend – were open to the participation of all women, irrespective of their sexual orientation.[11] Presumably the mobilisation of the lesbian continuum effected the same possibility for those who were unsure about their sexual identities to experiment in a supportive space, as Joan McCarthy suggests here: 'Certainly, the idea of the continuum was pretty well understood and, in my view, it gave a theoretical underpinning and kind of support that enabled straight women to own and express the "lesbian" in them, so to speak. That, in turn, enabled some straight women to eventually come out entirely' (personal communication, 19 January 2009). Endorsing this view, Deirdre Walsh recalls: 'There was a sense of women opening up to seeing each other as sexual beings and a challenging of the boundaries of sexuality from conventional (presumed) heterosexuality. It was a very exciting time' (personal communication, 15 January 2009).

Unreflective essentialism?

'On Compulsory Heterosexuality and Lesbian Existence' has been subject to much scrutiny and opposition since it first appeared. In fact, such was the barrage of criticism which greeted it in the first few years of its public life that the 1986 edition of the text (from *Blood, Bread and Poetry*), the version we are probably most familiar with today, is protectively book-ended by both Foreword and Afterword written by Rich to explain and defend her position. The essay was almost immediately constructed by opponents as having been high-handed and written from a position of privilege, and indeed Linda Garber's (2001: 127) categorisation of Rich as 'a (*the?*) white, middle-class lesbian feminist' is not unwarranted. This is perhaps why Rich was quick to state, in the Introduction to *Blood, Bread and Poetry*, that: 'these essays were not written in an ivory tower'; and to put forward her experience of fifteen years of activism in the women's liberation movement, in order to establish her right to speak and be heard on these issues. In response to the associated charge of having issued a lesbian imperative, in the Afterword to the 1986 text she goes on to say: 'My essay should be read as one contribution to a long exploration in progress, not as my own 'last word' on sexual politics' (Rich, 1986: 68). Apart from these skirmishes about legitimacy to speak, which are part and parcel of most activist movements (or certainly any that I have ever been involved with) critics have posited a number of key questions about the article which are relevant to its contemporary reception and possibilities as a future resource.

While embraced by many as a positive resource for change within both American and Irish feminist activism, as discussed above, the concept of the 'lesbian continuum' provoked a storm of criticism in the 1980s, with opposition coming from both heterosexual and lesbian feminists alike. For instance, Janice Raymond critiqued the imprecise nature of the concept, suggesting that it was 'morally short-changing to women who are lesbians and patronising to women who are not lesbians' (1989). Others felt that Rich's essay, in its efforts to build bridges with heterosexual feminists, elided the specificity of lesbian desire and rendered invisible those women whose social and sexual practices were not acceptable to mainstream society (such as sex workers, s/m lesbians and those involved in the butch/femme bar scene) (cf. Nestle, 2003: 52). Much criticism of the essay suggested that in striving to open up the category of lesbian to anyone who wanted to identify in this way, the specificity of lesbian experience was subject to further erasure: 'By so reducing the meaning of lesbian, we have in effect eliminated lesbianism as a meaningful category' (Zimmerman 1997: 205–6). However, it seems to me that while some of this criticism is valid, the suggestion that Rich eliminates the category of lesbianism is to negate or wilfully ignore Rich's category of 'lesbian existence', those whom Rich described as 'women who have made their primary erotic and emotional choices for women' (Rich, 1986: 74) and whose material existence she describes in the following way:

> Lesbian existence comprises both the breaking of a taboo and the rejection of a compulsory way of life. [...] lesbian existence has been lived [...] without access to any knowledge of a tradition, a continuity, a social underpinning. The destruction of records and memorabilia and letters documenting the realities of lesbian existence must be taken very seriously as a means of keeping heterosexuality compulsory for women, since what has been kept from our knowledge is joy, sensuality, courage and community, as well as guilt, self-betrayal and pain. (Rich, 1986: 52)

The specificity of Rich's fix on lesbian existence, it seems to me, answers some of the charges above. Furthermore, as I mentioned earlier, she clearly perceives lesbian existence as a non-essentialist category, an identity whose meaning is and can be constructed (and therefore presumably *deconstructed*). Furthermore, from a contemporary Irish point of view, the resonance of her description in the paragraph above of the erasure of lesbian traditions and history is particularly apt. There have been several Irish public figures (the author Kate O'Brien, to name one well-known such case) whose private papers were destroyed (often at their own request) following their deaths. This serves to remind us of the countless number of other women whose full stories can never be told.

More recently, the kind of radical feminist work we find in this essay has tended to be stereotyped by queer theorists as separatist and deriving from old-fashioned, unreflective essentialism. Linda Garber (2001: 128) points out that in some queer theory (citing Haraway) Rich is caricatured and 'reduce[d] to a sort of synecdoche for radical feminism'; while elsewhere (she cites Butler) key concepts such as compulsory heterosexuality are co-opted while their radical and lesbian-feminist roots are silenced or dismissed. While a full analysis of this phenomenon (which in any case Garber and others have more than adequately dealt with) is beyond the scope of this chapter, it is useful to focus on some of the key charges made by queer theorists here. Rich is very clear about her position on separatism. While she is committed to working within 'autonomous women's groups', she states: 'At no time have I ever defined myself as, or considered myself, a lesbian separatist. I have worked with self-defined separatists and have recognised the importance of separatism as grounding and strategy. I have opposed it as a pressure to conformity and where it seems to derive from biological determinism' (Rich, 1986: viii). An investment in identity politics was central to the community-building projects of the period and, as is clear from the discussion above, the deployment of categories such as 'women' and 'lesbians' during this period were a call-to-arms to those who self-identified as feminist and as lesbian. As postcolonial critics including Spivak have underlined, this strategic use of essentialism occurs frequently as a tool of marginalised groups as a way to raise consciousness and gather political momentum (Spivak, 1988). Thus, coming out, self-identifying as lesbian, or declaring an affinity with the lesbian continuum were all ways of redefining the terms of engagement with the social world in the 1980s in Ireland. Queer theory's subsequent questioning of the meaningfulness of terms such as 'lesbian', 'gay' or 'coming out', it seems to me, sometimes runs the risk of losing sight of the political and material usefulness of these terms, as well as rejecting the consciousness with which they were deployed. By inviting all women to become lesbians, or to participate in the lesbian continuum, Rich highlighted the social construction of identity, at a time when gay men's organisations, among others, continued to strategically employ the biological model as a basis for equal rights. This suggests that although essentialism may have been employed by lesbian feminists as a tool of identity politics, the charge of *unreflective* essentialism is without foundation. Furthermore, for lesbian feminist activists, one of the key disjunctures between queer theory and lesbian feminism is that the former frequently tends to remain in the realm of discourse, rather than being capable of translation in strategic ways to enable political or activist communities or campaigns. It seems to me that in order to resource twenty-first century theory and praxis in this field, the radical interaction of feminist, lesbian feminist and queer discourses are necessary, both to problematise heteronormative hegemonies and suggest ways out of binary thinking. By actively engaging with the fissures and disjunctures between these schools of thought we may construct a theory and a politics that *is* sufficient to fight oppression.

Conclusion

As I have demonstrated, writing and research about lesbian existence, how this changes over time and place, and the political struggles LGBTQ communities have faced in a variety of international contexts have been available in Ireland in a range of published documents *at least* since the late 1960s. One example of this in the collection at the IWMA is an undated photocopy of the Radicalesbian manifesto 'The Woman-Identified Woman', mentioned above, which demonstrates the availability of North American lesbian theory and politics to Irish lesbian and feminist groups in the period. However, to date, full-length publications on lesbian (and indeed, on bisexual and transgender) existence in Ireland north and south are few, although some research has emerged from Women's Studies centres on the island, from the annual Lesbian Lives Conference and the Queeries seminar series at UCD, and from a number of community-based projects such as L.InC in Cork and LASI in Belfast.[12] Such research, both practical and theoretical, provides a series of supports to ongoing activism in LGBTQ communities in various parts of Ireland and internationally. However, the O'Carroll and Collins edition of *Lesbian and Gay Visions of Ireland* (1995) remains one of the few texts relating specifically to the social and cultural history of Irish LGBTQ communities and while there have been more recent essays and chapters on lesbian social history in Ireland (McAuley and Tiernan, 2008; Connolly and O'Toole, 2005), there is still an obvious lacuna in the available history of sexuality and social movements in Ireland. Meantime, a transition has taken place from earlier work emerging from within lesbian feminist activism, which prioritised writing from the standpoint of experience, to feminist scholarship which analyses and problematises the representation of LGBTQ experience and identities in archival, (both oral and documentary) and cultural texts. While the latter is necessary and useful work, it is limited by being predicated, at least in an Irish context, upon a very limited body of primary archival material and a small number of published first-hand accounts of experience and activism, such as Nell McCafferty's autobiography (2004), the interviews carried out by Anne Stopper in *Mondays at Gaj's* (2006) and Anne Maguire's book on her experience of the US-based Irish Lesbian and Gay Organisation, *Rock the Sham!* (2005). With such a dearth of available sources, contemporary critics are more likely to focus on non-Irish sources and texts which, at the risk of seeming parochial, seems to be something of a pity in an area so starved of research and publications on Irish topics and themes. In this context, the availability of material at the Irish Women's Movement Archive and in the Irish Queer Archive (recently donated by the National Lesbian and Gay Federation to the National Library) is to be welcomed.[13]

 In the introduction to her history of the Lesbian Organisation of Toronto and its influence on Canadian social activism, Becki Ross (1995: 4) describes a scenario familiar to lesbian feminists and other activists in Ireland:

> Among those of us privileged to be out and to have access to [community] resources, there is little collective knowledge of how they came to exist, who was responsible for their genesis, and how fragile they continue to be. When I came out, even the immediate lesbian past seemed remote; I joined a collective state of unknowing that is both personally disabling and politically dangerous.

Ross goes on to emphasise the importance of a sense of collective and individual memory as a basis for future activism and political change. It seems to me that the kind of re-evaluation of key texts such as 'On Compulsory

Heterosexuality and Lesbian Existence', in tandem with the preservation *and use* of movement documents are vital for contemporary activists to recognise past achievements as well as failures, and by critically evaluating earlier strategies, to re-imagine and resource contemporary and future counter-cultural movements and campaigns.

Acknowledgements

My thanks to everyone who contributed to this essay, particularly to those whose first-hand accounts of engagement with feminist politics in Ireland breathed life into the material.

Notes

1 As is perhaps self-evident, the use of this term or references to an 'Irish feminist context' in the singular is a contested one, begging the question: which Ireland, or which feminists are under discussion? Definitions of Irishness are problematised not only by the division of Ireland into two states, north and south, and the various ways in which the label 'Irish' is used both within the country and abroad, but also by factors of class, location and, until recently, the frequent occlusion of Irish emigrants. In this discussion, I refer primarily to feminist activism in the south of Ireland and more specifically, to feminists involved in Dublin and Cork-based activist groups.

2 Anne Lovett and Joanne Hayes came to personify the bleakness of Irish social mores in the 1980s and to act as a mobilising impetus for change, as I have detailed elsewhere (Connolly and O'Toole, 2005: 65; 112–4). In 1984, Lovett, a teenage schoolgirl, bled to death beside her dead baby while attempting to give birth alone in a grotto in the town. She had carried the child to full term in a small village where no one would admit to having known she was pregnant. Joanne Hayes was the woman at the centre of the infamous 'Kerry Babies' case the same year, charged with the murder of a baby found with stab wounds on a beach in Cahirciveen. While finally cleared of all charges, she and her family were subject to public trial and scrutiny in a case in which the dire consequences of contravening Irish social law, particularly for women, was demonstrated to the full.

3 LGBTQ is a commonly-used acronym for lesbian, gay, bisexual, transgender and queer communities, in activism and scholarship.

4 This research was undertaken at UCC as part of the Irish government-funded HEA Women in Irish Society Project 1999–2002 (funded under PRTLI 1) which carried out a survey of the Irish Women's Movement Archive at the Boole Library, UCC. Our findings were published in Connolly and O'Toole (2005). During this project, I undertook related research at the Canadian Women's Movement Archive in Ottawa, as well as a number of feminist and LGBTQ archives in Montreál, Dublin, Belfast and London.

5 See http://booleweb.ucc.ie/index.php?pageID=260 for further information.

6 Page references derive from the *Blood, Bread and Poetry* edition.

7 Although Rich notes in the 1986 edition of her essay that the 1984 edition of *Our Bodies Ourselves* amended this, including a chapter on 'Loving Women: Lesbian Life and Relationships'.

8 Document held in the Irish Women's Movement Archive. For further information, see ee http://booleweb.ucc.ie/index.php?pageID=260.
9 The SCUM [Society for Cutting up Men] Manifesto, was published in 1968 by Valerie Solanas (who famously shot Andy Warhol) and called for the obliteration of men.
10 In May 1992, for the first time, the Irish courts awarded full custody of her children to a Cork lesbian mother.
11 The Cork 'Women's Weekend' in particular is remembered fondly by Irish feminists as a space which welcomed heterosexual, bisexual and lesbian feminists down through the years. Now in its twenty-sixth year, the event maintains the same name but is now primarily aimed at a lesbian audience.
12 Such as the *L.Inc* magazine which appeared from 2000 to 2005 (some issues are available to download at: http://www.linc.ie/magazine/index.html) and research published by LASI since 2002: http://www.lasionline.org/.
13 See www.irishqueerarchive.com for further information.

11

The Brundtland Committee's
Our Common Future
Hilary Tovey

Introduction

The book this chapter discusses revolutionised how environmental discourse is framed, globally and in Ireland. It is widely credited with giving the world the term 'sustainable development', described by McNaghten and Urry (1998: 212) as 'the most significant attempt to reconfigure society–nature relations' of recent years. *Our Common Future*, the report of the UN-established World Commission on Environment and Development, and widely known as 'the Brundtland Report' after its Chairwoman, the ex-Prime Minister of Norway Gro Brundtland, was published in 1987. It reached its thirteenth impression in 1991 and still sells today at a slow but steady pace. Like many others, probably, who read *Our Common Future* I came to the book backwards: as an environmental sociologist, finding myself overwhelmed by the array of competing meanings attached to sustainable development, I decided to go back to the 'source' in search of some certainty. I did not find it, but instead found a book which is more complex, rich and interesting than many later commentators suggest, and more open to radical interpretation than most policy discourses on sustainability allow.

Environmental issues of course existed, in Ireland as elsewhere, well before 'sustainable development' emerged to re-orient public thinking about them, but in many developed countries in the early 1980s, environmental movements had retreated into a period of acquiescence. According to Jamison (2001: 93), *Our Common Future* signalled the re-emergence of environmental politics into the public sphere, but in 'a more global and more professional guise'. Over the next decade, he wrote, the focus would shift from local concerns to a set of new environmental problems such as climate change, ozone depletion and biodiversity; environmental politics would move from confrontation to co-operation as the international context opened up to de-regulation and globalisation of business. Environmental non-government organisations, business and governments would work together to achieve a new kind of development, one that would take into account the environmental costs of economic development projects and practices. *Our Common Future* both internationalised the environmental agenda and opened up environmental debate to new constituencies, new expertises, and new considerations.

Jamison (2001: 94) also says the quest for sustainable development initiated by Brundtland significantly opened up environmentalism to the social sciences: the 'comprehensive program of global recovery' which the Report laid out needed the support of a knowledge base which would include many other areas of expertise than just the (previously hegemonic) natural sciences. Whether the knowledge base for sustainable development really has been opened up in this way, it is certainly true that the Report, and the first UN Earth Summit which followed at Rio De Janeiro in 1992, provoked an agenda for research within environmental sociology, politics and economics – around citizen engagement, participation and public consultation, around expertise and knowledge, around integrating ecology and economy, and around relations between society and nature in general – which still shapes much research and theorising within the social sciences today. What might surprise the authors of the Report is the extent of disagreement that has emerged around these issues.

The topic of this chapter is the reception within Ireland of *Our Common Future* and the idea of 'sustainable development' it sponsored over the two decades since its publication. I suggest that in the Irish context, at least, the history of 'sustainable development' has been a good deal less predictable than Jamison allows. Although the medium has generally been enthusiastically endorsed, particularly among certain groups of actors on environmental affairs, the message has had a more complex and even divisive impact. But to explain how that may have arisen and taken the form it has, we need first to consider the contents of the book in somewhat more detail.

The text

Our Common Future was and remains distinctive in its concern to offer an inclusive voice on environmental problems. The report was put together by a 21-member Commission with a large representation from the developing world: only 7 members were from North America and Europe (and two of these came from Eastern Europe), while the rest (including the Vice-Chair) came from Africa, Asia, South America and the USSR. The organisers wanted the Commission to be constituted by 'a clear majority of members from the developing countries' in order 'to reflect world realities' (World Commission on Environment and Development (WCED), 1987: xii) and to include people from a range of different disciplines ('Foreign ministers, finance and planning officials, policymakers in agriculture, science and technology' – Ibid.). During the course of its work, the Commission travelled to many different parts of the world, looking for inputs and comments from a wider social grouping than its own, some of which are reproduced in the Report in the form of separate text boxes.

Today *Our Common Future* is remembered mainly for its popularisation of the term 'sustainable development', and in particular for its definition: sustainable development 'meets the needs of the present without compromising the ability of future generations to meet their own needs' (WCED, 1987: 8, 43). The idea is echoed every time people speak of their concern about the world they will be leaving to their children and grandchildren. Less often remembered is the way the Commission elaborated this idea in the following paragraphs. Sustainable development, as they understood it, crucially refers to equity – not only between generations but within the same generation: 'meeting essential needs requires not only a new era of economic growth for nations in which the majority are poor, but an assurance that those poor get their fair share of the resources required to sustain that growth' (WCED, 1987: 8). In turn, that is most likely to happen in political systems which 'secure effective citizen participation in decision making' (Ibid.). It is hard now to imagine how transformative the concept seemed at the time, promising to reconcile many great global cleavages – most importantly, between environmental protection and economic growth, but also between rich and poor, developed and developing countries, and West and East in the dying years of the Cold War. It shed inspirational and innovative lights on many different areas, some of which are briefly elaborated below.

For me, most inspirational is the broad, humanist and inclusive interpretation it offers of its key terms: 'the environment' is 'where we all live', 'development' is 'what we all do in attempting to improve our lot' (WCED, 1987: xi) – language that seems to offer an escape from narrow, scientised definitions of sustainability in terms of conserving or protecting biophysical resources, or flows of energy and materials. The report often talks of 'sustainable development paths' in the plural, recognising that no one policy framework can be laid down for every country in the world to follow: 'No single blueprint of sustainability will be found, as economic and social systems and ecological conditions differ widely among countries. Each nation will have to work out its own policy objectives' (WCED, 1987: 40).

From the start *Our Common Future* argues that inequality is the world's main environmental as well as socioeconomic problem. It insists that poverty is as much a cause of environmental degradation as wealth or overconsumption: the world cannot move to a sustainable form of development without addressing the causes of poverty. Environmental degradation erodes the possibilities for economic development and the heaviest burden is borne by the poorest people (WCED, 1987: 35); overriding priority must be given to meeting 'the essential needs of the world's poor' (WCED, 1987: 43). While this may express the sensibilities of developing world members on the Commission, it is also a plea to Western environmentalists to consider the poor and their livelihoods, not just 'nature', in their actions and reasoning for environmental protection.

Our Common Future is permeated by a concern for democracy in environmental decision-making. It attempts to involve not just governments, scientists, and private enterprise but 'first and foremost ... people' (WCED, 1987: xiv). To bring about the 'extensive social changes' that are needed to avert ecological catastrophe, we must 'reach the minds and hearts' of 'citizen's groups and NGOs' as well as 'educational institutions and the scientific community', who all have a crucial part to play in setting the world on sustainable development paths (Ibid.). Throughout, citizen participation and democracy are put forward as key to equitable solutions to environmental problems. 'Sustainability requires the enforcement of wider responsibilities for the impacts of decisions', and while that requires changes in legal and institutional frameworks, law alone cannot enforce the common interest: that

> principally needs community knowledge and support, which entails greater public participation in the decisions that affect the environment. This is best secured by de-centralising the management of resources upon which local communities depend, and giving these communities an effective say over the use of these resources. It will also require promoting citizens' initiatives, empowering people's organizations, and strengthening local democracy. (WCED, 1987: 63)

Finally, *Our Common Future* is inspirational in addressing as interconnected a range of problems more usually treated as discrete issues: the position of women in society, population pressures and population loss, food security, the loss of species and genetic resources, energy, industry and human settlement patterns. These must be considered together because 'economy' and 'ecology' are tightly intertwined. Economic development in its current forms is unsustainable because 'those responsible for managing natural resources and protecting the environment are institutionally separated from those responsible for managing the economy. The real world of interlocked economic and ecological systems will not change; the policies and institutions must' (WCED, 1987: 9).

The report was described by its Chair as 'unanimous'. Its language is suffused with consensual expressions , with 'we ' and 'our' – sometimes referring to the Commission itself, more often to 'everyone', 'all citizens of the world', 'the people', 'the community'; the future it addresses is 'our common future', which is shared by 'us all', and in which we all have 'a common interest'. Reading the text, however, we start to notice many points at which voices contradict each other, or issues are reconciled with the overall argument only by fudging their analysis. 'Sustainable development' emerges as not just an inspirational but also a confused concept; faultlines become visible to which we can trace later disagreements and contrasting interpretations, some of which are evident within environmental discourses and policies in Ireland today. Arguably, the most contentious areas have to do with knowledge, the role of citizens, and the place of 'the local' within environmental management.

Against the 'catastrophe' predictions of publications like the 'Club of Rome' Report (Meadows *et al.*, 1972), *Our Common Future* sets out its faith in human ingenuity to provide for both continuing economic growth and environmental protection. Science and technology can reconcile these:

natural limits are not the obstacle to development but rather 'limitations imposed by the present state of technology and social organisation on environmental resources' (WCED, 1987: 8). Other pages, however, emphasise the fragility as well as the bountifulness of nature and how, if we cross certain thresholds, we 'endanger the basic integrity of the system' (WCED, 1987: 32, 33). A rather unsatisfactory attempt at resolution emerges later, distinguishing between 'set limits' and 'ultimate limits': there are no 'set limits' (e.g. population size or resource use) to growth and 'the accumulation of knowledge and the development of technology can enhance the carrying capacity of the resource base', but there are 'ultimate limits', and 'long before these are reached, the world must ensure equitable access to the constrained resource and reorient technological efforts to relieve the pressure' (WCED, 1987: 45).

Contradictions around science and technological development and their role in sustainable development surface repeatedly. 'The gap in science and technological capacities [between less developed and industrialised countries] is particularly wide in areas of direct relevance to the objectives of sustainable development, including biotechnological and genetic engineering, new energy sources, new materials and substitutes, and low-waste and non-polluting technologies' (WCED, 1987: 87); narrowing this gap 'must be supported by international assistance especially in such key areas as biotechnology' (WCED, 1987: 88). But some ten pages earlier the report argues against exporting technologically intensive forms of food production into developing countries and in favour of supports for 'sustainable, regenerative agriculture' (WCED, 1987: 77), and a later chapter – 'Food security: sustaining the potential' (WCED, 1987: 118 ff) – opens with the claim that what we require are policies 'to ensure that the food is produced where it is needed and in a manner that sustains the livelihoods of the rural poor'. This chapter identifies the three major solutions to contemporary food security problems as: shifting food production to where it is most needed (food-deficit countries or regions within countries); securing the livelihoods of the rural poor; and conserving natural resources.

Throughout the report, moreover, it is evidently assumed that there is no conflict between what science and technology can give us to resolve environmental problems, and what people want and will ask for if given a chance to participate democratically. If anything has been learnt from environmental social science research in the intervening years, it is that this assumption is unsound. Attempts to introduce incineration into different parts of Ireland as a way of dealing with waste management problems provide an obvious illustration. In the same year as *Our Common Future* was published, another publication also appeared which has had a huge subsequent influence on environmental sociologists, if less so on policy-makers and institutional actors – Ulrich Beck's (1992) *Risk Society*. For Beck, science and technology must be recognised as part of the problem rather than as the solution to the multiplication of environmental risks in industrial society, and a 'Risk

Society' is one in which 'authoritative knowledge' and 'scientific expertise' become a focus of social dissent and debate ('definitional struggle'), as the citizen-victims of these risks struggle to have their own experiences and values articulated and heard in decision-making settings.

Our Common Future is addressed first and foremost to 'people', yet this is constantly qualified by the idea that 'people' need to be 'informed', producing a subterranean ambiguity around the relations between 'expertise' and 'community (or local, lay, traditional etc) knowledge'. The public whose 'rights, roles and participation in development planning, decision making and project implementation should be expanded' (WCED, 1987: 21) must be 'informed'. Yet at the same time, the problem is to get political and economic institutions to recognise 'the people's' concerns: 'We found everywhere deep public concern for the environment, concern that has led not just to protests but often to changed behaviour. The challenge is to ensure that these new values are more adequately reflected in the principles and operations of political and economic structures' (WCED, 1987: 28). Similar ambiguities arise around 'participation'. Direct citizen participation is said to be essential to sustainable environmental decision-making, yet for 'some large-scale projects' a different kind of participation (the kind later given force in the Aarhus Convention) is needed: public inquiries and hearings, access to relevant information, availability of alternative sources of technical expertise 'can provide an informed basis for public discussions' (WCED, 1987: 64).

Better environmental education is the way to produce a more informed citizenry: 'Many people base their understanding of environmental processes and development on traditional beliefs or on information provided by a conventional education. Many thus remain ignorant about ways in which they could improve traditional production practices and better protect the natural resource base' (WCED, 1987: 113). On the next page, however, there is a discussion of 'indigenous or tribal peoples' as communities which 'are the repositories of vast accumulations of traditional knowledge and experience. Their disappearance is a loss for the wider society, which could learn a great deal from their traditional skills in sustainably managing very complex ecological systems' (WCED, 1987: 114). The report calls for protection of their traditional land rights and local institutions as 'crucial for maintaining the harmony with nature and the environmental awareness characteristic of the traditional way of life'; these local communities must be given 'a decisive voice in the decisions about resource use in their area ... Their marginalisation is a symptom of a style of development that tends to neglect both human and environmental considerations. Hence a more careful and sensitive consideration of their interests is a touchstone of sustainable development policy' (WCED, 1987: 116).

How we are to recognise which 'indigenous communities' fit this account (and which are simply 'ill-informed') is not explained. Alongside an insufficient account of human knowledge we could also note the report's mechanistic and undertheorised idea of 'shared human needs' (Redclift, 1997). In a discussion of poverty in the first chapter, a quote appears in a text box from a person attending the Commission's roadshow in Jakarta: 'I think this Commission should give attention on how to look into the question of more participation for those people who are the object of development. Their basic needs include the right to preserve their cultural identity, and their right not to be alienated from their own society, and their own community'. There is no comment on this contribution within the text itself, despite the fact that it crucially undermines the assumption that there are 'basic human needs' which can be defined in a culture-neutral way.

A central question for the Commission is: 'how are individuals in the real world to be persuaded or made to act in the common interest?' (WCED, 1987: 46). Laws, education, taxes, subsidies and other incentives are important, but '[m]ost important, effective participation in decision-making processes by local communities can help them articulate and effectively enforce their common interest' (WCED, 1987: 47). But it recognises that this is a local-level response; international responses are also needed. *Our Common Future* offers a rather poor analysis of how local and global are intertwined, despite an interesting sketch of global capitalism as a system characterised by monopolistic control over resources, unequal capacities to commandeer 'free' resources, and inequitable distribution of pollution. 'Local' is often equated with 'national', or it is assumed that the national level will adequately recognise and incorporate local particularities in its environmental policies. More insightful criticisms are offered of international aid systems than of international trade, yet even here, criticism is often unexpectedly mild. Throughout, promoting the expansion of international trade is justified as necessary to economic growth in less developed countries, despite recognition of the environmental damage it can cause. Economic globalisation is making the world more interdependent: the actions of one nation affect the possibilities of others, for both economic growth and environmental protection. The solution offered is that developing and developed countries should follow different strategies: reviving growth is central for the developing world, while developed countries need to 'change the quality' of their growth, making it 'less material- and energy-intensive and more equitable in its impact' (WCED, 1987: 52). How lowering consumption in the developed world may affect the growth possibilities of developing countries is not discussed.

Our Common Future lays down the outlines for two rather different discourses of sustainable development. The definition in terms of inter- and intra-generational equity at the outset of the Report is suffused with overtones of social justice, a humanitarian concern for the livelihoods of the world's poorest, and a recognition of the environmental wisdom often secreted within their cultures. But as the text develops, a discourse about harmonising environmental management with economic progress also gains momentum. A strategy for sustainable development unfolds which is about integrating production and growth with conservation and enhancement: 'In essence, sustainable development is a process of change in which the exploitation of resources, the direction of investments, the orientation of technological development and institutional change are all in harmony and enhance both current and future potential to meet human needs and aspirations' (WCED, 1987: 46). The emphasis on 'provision for all of an adequate livelihood base and adequate access to resources' (WCED, 1987: 40) is weakened in this new discourse of technological management of growth-associated risks. Technological development has to pay greater attention to environmental factors and environmental resource concerns (WCED, 1987: 61); new technologies should produce 'social goods' not just market value, public policy should bring this about 'through incentives and disincentives', and we need 'new techniques and technologies – as well as legal and institutional mechanisms – for safety design and control, accident prevention, damage mitigation' (Ibid.). 'Merging environment and economics in decision making' must become the central element in the strategy for sustainable development (WCED, 1987, 62). Within the text, these two discourses are still thought of as interrelated and compatible; over the period since, however, it has become increasingly evident how technological advances in resource use have a capacity to remove equitable access to resources, and how merging environment and economics in decision-making can undermine equitable access to decision-making.

The Brundtland Report has been described by some commentators as reproducing a deeply 'modernist' tradition of thought, portraying a world in which citizens trust in expert systems, national governments command wide public support, individuals are rational actors more than social beings, and belief is still widespread in the Enlightenment project of 'progress' in which scientific advances in the mastery of nature are the basis for economic development and civilisation (see e.g. McNaghten and Urry, 1998; Irwin, 2001). Such comments imply that *Our Common Future* profoundly misread the 'postmodern' social and cultural world into which it was to be launched at the end of the 1980s. Yet while there are undoubted elements of 'modernism' in the report, a fairer comment might be that there is much less agreement between its various authors than they claim. We can detect in the text an ongoing disagreement between a 'modernising' perspective on development and a 'small is beautiful' (Schumacher, 1973) perspective; or between two environmental narratives, one probably more associated with the global North, the other with the South (Bruckmeier and Kopytina, 2006), one of which is about scientific advances, technological expertise, and an informed and disciplined citizenry, while the other is about citizen empowerment, environmental justice, local control over local resources, and the development of local cultures and knowledge systems as an alternative or supplement to Western science.

'Sustainable development' is both a 'narrative' and a 'project' (Irwin, 2001); it is both an attempt to say what environmental problems we face, and an attempt to mobilise action around new normative goals for our relations with nature. Academics have passed many pleasurable years in trying to tie down the definition of this slippery or 'essentially contested' concept (see Baker *et al.*, 1997). Its generality and inclusiveness make it inevitable that it would inspire many different kinds of social actor and a range of different interpretations (Jamison, 2001). While professionals in business and government and within mainstream environmental NGOs transformed the quest for sustainable development into instrumental terms, for many local activists it took on more ethical and moral connotations (Sachs, 1999); many Marxist and critical environmentalists rejected it wholesale as a smokescreen for 'capitalism as usual'. Much recent discussion suggests that a definition is impossible, and it is better to see 'sustainable development' simply as a 'discourse coalition' (Hajer, 1996) or 'platform concept' (Bruckmeier and Tovey, 2009) where different social groups often pursuing very different agendas can assemble together and make common cause. In Europe, and as I argue below, in Ireland, 'sustainable development' has paved the way for the triumph of an ecological modernisation discourse which celebrates Western science and technology as the solution to both environmental and developmental problems through the building of an integrated 'knowledge society'. But residues of the subaltern discourse can be found in Ireland too, particularly in the language of local environmental activist groups.

Sustainable development discourses in Ireland

Reception of Our Common Future in Ireland

During the late 1970s and 1980s in Ireland, what came gradually to be described as 'environmental' controversies gained a high profile (Allen and Jones, 1990; Baker, 1990; Tovey, 1993). Conflicts broke out in both agrarian and industrial Ireland, around the building of a nuclear power plant in County Wexford, gold mining in North Mayo, fishing rights on rivers, salmon farming, the contamination of farmland in South Tipperary by a large chemical multinational company, asbestos factories, the development of the chemicals industry in Ringaskiddy in County Cork, and the planning permission given to Dow Chemicals to site a branch plant in East Cork, among others (Peace, 1993; Allen, 2004). These battles, in which risks from industrial pollution to the health and livelihoods of rural populations were often the overt target, have been explained as a type of 'atavistic' rural response to the experience of incorporation into a global economic system which threatened to undermine the autonomy of local communities (Allen, 2004; Leonard, 2006), or as part of a broader split around how the 'modernity project' should be realised in Ireland (Tovey, 1993). The first Green Party TD was elected in 1989, and this could be taken as the start of a new type of environmental politics, in which environmental issues were both more frequently named as such and became less contentious as environmental discourses became more 'mainstreamed' or 'normalised'. Survey research into environmental attitudes among the general population in 1992 and 2002 found that responses to broadly the same set of questions asked on both dates showed little change in levels of support for environment-friendly policies, but there was a marked shift in the range of responses, with fewer people in 2002 offering either of the more extreme positions ('strongly agree', 'strongly disagree') than in 1992 (Motherway *et al.*, 2003). This normalising of environmental concerns seemed to reflect changes in the way environmental issues were perceived, framed and debated: on one hand, awareness and talk about the environment increased in Irish society over the period; on the other the discourse shifted, from 'environment versus jobs and economy, and pollution as an isolated, abstract problem, to a more integrated view, as extolled in the concept of sustainable development' (Motherway *et al.*, 2003: 10).

It seems unlikely that many people in Ireland sat down and read the Brundtland Report in the late 1980s and early 1990s. The movement of sustainable development language and ideas into mainstream currency appears to have been more an effect of the global publicity given to the 1992 Rio Conference, contacts with EU environmental policy-makers and NGOs, and the various international agreements on environmental issues to which the Rio Conference led and in many of which Ireland, either individually or as part of the EU, participated. An early official nod towards the concept appears with the decision by the Haughey government to define the 1990 Irish Presidency of the EU as a 'Green presidency'. The 1993 *Report of the Green 2000 Advisory Group* suggested that 'nature conservation' be redefined as 'the sustainable use of nature' (Green 2000 Advisory Group, 1993: 292). Sustainable development discourse intensified in the 1997 Report *Sustainable Development – a Strategy for Ireland,* which, while clearly prioritising economic growth, went through the Irish economy sector by sector and set out recommendations for integration of environmental sustainability into the growth strategies of each. 'Continued economic growth is essential to meet people's legitimate ambitions for a better life and to provide the resources for implementing environmental protection measures. But we should not tolerate development that is inefficient, that is excessive in its consumption of natural resources or that unduly pressurises the environment' (1997, Foreword). This set the tone for many later policy statements, including the *Green Paper on Sustainable Energy* (1999), the *National Climate Change Strategy* (2000) and the Planning and Development Act (2000). Sustainable development language even began to suffuse Partnership agreements like the 1999 *Programme for Prosperity and Fairness.*

Institutional changes in environmental management began to emerge in line with the new discourse. The Environmental Protection Agency (Ireland) was established in 1993; Comhar, the 'Sustainable Development Partnership', was set up to 'advance the national agenda for sustainable development and contribute to the formation of a national consensus regarding this process' (publicity statement, 2002) in 1999. Environmental Impact Assessments, Integrated Pollution Control licensing, and the Rural Environmental Protection Scheme began to transform Irish environmental regulatory practices, even if substantially driven by EU developments, and some movement by the state towards integrating environmental goals into economic growth became evident in regulatory arrangements which crossed some government department boundaries. The emergence into the Irish public sphere of sustainable development as a way of thinking about problems in nature and in nature–society relations coincided with a new debate about 'partnership and governance' as a separate but related force for change (Motherway *et al.*, 2003). Partnership language symbolised that 'a broader set of actors are seen to be at the policy making table, and a set of issues broader than pure economics' (Motherway *et al.*, 2003: 8). From the late 1990s, partnership at national level began to be disseminated down to local government, although many environmentalists felt that their inclusion at the decision-making tables, national and local, remained largely tokenistic. Some limited adoption of the Rio Conference's Local Agenda 21 emerged at county council level, as part of local government reforms.

'Mainstreaming' environmental issues in these ways did not pass by without criticism. For Taylor (2001), the goal of this emergent Irish environmental policy regime was not protection of the environment but rather, management of public perceptions and the establishment of 'acceptable levels' of pollution. A publication by a group of environmental and community groups (Earth Summit Ireland, 2002), put together in advance of the second Earth Summit in Johannesburg, described implementation and enforcement in Irish environmental policy as 'patchy and weakly applied' (Earth Summit Ireland, 2002: 11) and argued that ongoing environmental damage from economic growth remained greater than any gains which may have been won by the integration of sustainability concerns into development policy processes.

Sustainable Development and Ecological Modernisation
Colonisation of the sustainable development 'platform' by the language of ecological modernisation appears to be so advanced now that Irish environmental researchers rarely differentiate between the two. In 2003, Motherway *et al.* (2003: ix) were arguing that 'Political discourses about the environment have evolved significantly in the past 10 years, particularly through the advent of the politics of sustainable development as embodied in the ecological modernisation paradigm. Sustainable development has become the dominant language of political talk about the environment – including the paradigm of ecological modernisation in which environmental and economic goals are seen as aligned'. By 2006, Leonard (2006: 26) made no distinction between sustainable development and ecological modernisation as policy discourses, referring to the argument that the environment can be 'managed' in conjunction with industrial development as a 'viewpoint'

that 'includes theories such as Ecological Modernisation and Sustainable Development ... The development of Ecological Modernisation theory has been linked to the publication of the Brundtland report (WCED, 1987) and other events such as the UNCED conference on environment and development (1997)'. But ignoring the presence of two competing versions of Brundtland makes much of the discourse and practices of environmentalism in Ireland opaque and unintelligible.

Ecological modernisation is a thesis about social change which is associated in particular with the work of German social theorist Joseph Huber and two Dutch sociologists, Arthur Mol and Gert Spaargaren (see e.g. Spaargaren and Mol, 1995). It argues that environmental protection can be achieved not by abandoning our current path of economic and social modernisation but by further modernisation – a form of modernisation which both 'ecologises the economy' and 'economises ecology'. Furthermore, it predicts that this extended modernisation will be adopted because it is rational – it meets the interests of both business and capital, and of those environmental NGOs and movements who are prepared to behave responsibly towards environmental regulation and policy. This theory of social change is increasingly substantiated *de facto*, as the ideas it contains are taken up and transformed into policy by governments across Europe and in particular at the EU level itself (Baker, 1997; Young, 2000), although the claim that ecological modernisation policy does in fact benefit the environment has been challenged (Buttel, 2000). Ecological modernisation protagonists understand themselves as simply translating 'sustainable development' into practical policy terms, and there is no doubt that some elements within *Our Common Future* legitimise this claim, notably passages such as those cited above that '[m]erging environment and economics in decision making' must become the central element in the strategy for sustainable development, and development policy must come to recognise 'economic and ecological interdependence' (WCED, 1987: 62–3). But the translation comes at significant cost, particularly to its more radically democratic and empowering aspects.

In Ireland, it was probably the 1997 government report *Sustainable Development – A Strategy for Ireland* which established the dominance of ecological modernisation discourse here. This report emphasised three themes central to ecological modernisation policy formation: a view of environmental protection policy as primarily about achieving efficiency in the use of energy and materials and in the management of pollution; a conception of environmental management as a technical project, to be devised and implemented by technical experts; and an argument that environmental protection creates new economic opportunities through both the enhanced efficiencies and cost-saving it delivers and the new business growth areas in environmental technologies which it opens up. The discourse has many attractions. It presupposes a consensus on what 'the environment' is which can guide regulatory policy. It offers a place within the decision-making process to environmental NGOs, provided they are prepared to work within its framework, to bring their own technical expertise (for example, in areas such as alternative energy generation) to the table, thus reducing potential dissent and conflict from environmental movements. Most attractive of all, it requires no transformative changes in the organisation of the economy, distribution of resources, or consumption practices, just an incremental 'rationalisation' of these so that over time they fit better with ecological limitations. There is considerable potential for mutual support and interaction between an ecological modernisation approach to resolving environmental problems and the economic growth strategy targeted at realising a 'knowledge society' or 'knowledge-based economy' (Johnson, 2004; Tovey, 2008) which is enthusiastically endorsed by both the EU Lisbon Strategy and successive Irish governments: both policy projects understand 'useful knowledge' in the same way, as the potential of science to deliver technological advances which realise profits through their 'smart' use of environmental resources.

The language of environmental activism in Ireland

Despite a mainstreaming of environmental discourse and the emergence of apparent consensus around the mutually supportive roles of government, business and environmental NGOs in furthering environmental well being, more than a decade of 'sustainable development' talk using the language of ecological modernisation has not reduced environmental activism in Ireland. Rather, it has split the environmental movement further between those groups who find advantages for themselves in this language, and those who voice their frustrations, through other vocabularies, at what is happening to the Irish environment. Across the developed world, indeed, there appears to be a common pattern of response to ecological modernisation policy and practices, whereby some sectors of environmental movements professionalise in response to expanding opportunities to influence environmental policy-making, while others (Jamison, 2001, calls them 'community' activists) try to uphold the original democratic ambitions of *Our Common Future* (Fischer, 2000). What makes the Irish version of this split distinctive, perhaps, has been the general weakness of the 'professional' element of the movement. In terms of capacity to influence policy and planning outcomes, the 'community' element has been no less weak, but as an open-ended, polymorphous and continually self-regenerating movement it can be seen as rather strong.

The proliferation of local controversies and mobilisations, and of locally based and locally oriented activist groups, makes the Irish environmental movement more similar to those found in other 'peripheral' areas of Southern Europe than to 'core' countries like Germany, the Netherlands, Sweden and perhaps Britain (Tovey, 2007). Kousis (1999) argues that grassroots activism and local-level mobilisations are the characteristic form which environmental movements have taken in Spain, Greece and Portugal, in contrast to the large, institutionalised organisations with formalised memberships found in other EU countries. Spain in the 1990s, for example, had the lowest per capita level of environmental association membership of any EU country, but the highest level of 'unconventional mobilisations'. These are countries in which associational culture is weak, but community and resistance cultures are strong (Ibid.). It is worth noting also that it was in the 'core' countries that most efforts to implement Agenda 21 took place, mandating environmental NGOs to play their part in local projects such as protecting urban ecologies. In Southern Europe, however, while substantial efforts were made by community-based activists to highlight and address serious local problems, '[o]fficial responses to these local citizen and environmental activists' were 'primarily negative' (Jamison, 2001: 155).

The presence of substantial grassroots environmental mobilisation thus appears to be related to high levels of authoritarianism within state and expert circles which close down citizen opportunities for participation. Grassroots mobilisations also draw on and articulate cultural positions which are often stigmatised as 'ignorant' or 'irrational' by these same authorities. Fischer (2005) argues that relations between environmental scientists, policy-makers and developers on one side, and affected publics on the other, are frequently complicated by the presence of different 'cultural rationalities' which produce very different analyses of risk and risk management. An emphasis on cultural conflict runs through much recent work on environmental mobilisations in Ireland. Leonard (2006), for example, depicts grassroots environmentalism as an expression of agrarian fundamentalism or traditionalist rural populism. He frames the cases he studies as a 'wider contest between grassroots community campaigns and the technocratic alliance between industry and the state over the introduction of major projects or policies'. His own 'bottom-up' analysis represents Irish environmentalism as formed out of 'rural sentiment', 'community politics' and 'a traditionalist discourse which embraces local values over the modernisation projects of colonisers, state officials or EU bureaucrats ... a rural mindset that holds self-sufficiency and local wisdom drawn from interaction with the hinterland in higher regard than the conventional wisdom of the representatives of politics or industry' (Leonard, 2006: 41).

We find similar interpretations in other recent work. Kelly's (2007) study found that focus groups made up of environmental regulators and policy-makers generally assumed that the neutral, generalisable 'facts' discovered by science are most appropriate for solving environmental problems, but groups made up of environmental activists, farmers, and even some from the general public were inclined to question this 'idealisation of science' and prioritise instead their own local, sensory and common-sense knowledge. 'In doing this, they also drew on deeply felt cultural themes which questioned the right of "outsiders", "they", "Dublin" to superior knowledge and their right to dominate and make decisions for their local area' (Kelly, 2007: 202). An analysis of the Corrib gas dispute traces its history as a process of amplification of 'cultural misunderstandings' between the two sides. On one side are the companies, whose 'various corporate claims suggest allegiance to an ecological modernisation discourse' that represents maximising development and achieving environmental protection as compatible objectives (Garavan, 2008: 69). On the other is a distinctive local discourse about 'the good life', which became even more distinctive over the course of the dispute as the local community had to go through an extended process of 'clarifying issues usually left unexamined' and protesters 'came to frame what had initially been a series of inchoate and visceral reactions to the proposed processing plant into rhetorically effective language' (Garavan, 2008: 65; see also Chapter 8 of this volume). Moran, in her analysis of the environmental culture found among people in East Connemara, similarly argues that local people's view of sustainability are formed out of

> intimate knowledge of people and place ... which in turn informs environmental decision-making practices. Local perceptions of sustainability incorporate ideas about the rich socio-cultural fabric of East Connemara and the ways in which local knowledge of the physical and social environment may be carried into the future. The desire to ensure that this way of life is sustained is central to local neighbouring practices. Protecting long-established social relationships is fundamental to ensuring that this knowledge can survive, as it is seen as necessary to sustain future generations who may inhabit the local area. (2008: 149)

While Garavan suggests that we can interpret the Corrib gas dispute as a direct conflict over the ecological modernisation claim that economic development and environmental protection are mutually compatible, Moran suggests the problem is rather that the local culture is simply different from and incommensurate with ecological modernisation discourse 'advanced by national and supranational (EU) government' (Moran, 2008: 127).

Highlighting how various local communities around Ireland understand 'sustainability' or 'the good life' differently from how it is understood in state and regulatory discourses produces often very illuminating analyses. The danger lies in exaggerating the extent to which local or 'grassroots' environmental discourse is some sort of historic inheritance from a once culturally different (i.e. rural) Ireland, unaffected by ideas which have come from outside. First, this suggests that Irish local environmental cultures are somehow unique, inherited from a unique rural and perhaps Gaelic cultural past. As we have seen, however, Kousis identifies very similar themes within Southern European environmentalism. In her view, this specific type of environmentalism is a struggle against 'ecological marginalisation': the threatened 'take-over of local natural resources by powerful private, state or supra-state interests and the gradual or immediate ecosystem disorganisation that results' (Kousis, 1999: 173). Second, it suggests that local environmental mobilisations occur in Ireland in a disconnected way, ignoring the extent to which local groups network with each other and with activist groups in other countries and seek support through sharing languages and worldviews as well as information on resistance strategies and tactics, and downplaying the extent to which experienced environmental activists circulate between local mobilisations, drawn there either directly by the existence of a fight to be fought or simply, since this is a small country, by accident of work or other mobility (Tovey, 2007). These conflicts might better be seen as economically and politically as much as culturally based: different discourses of sustainable development articulate and draw on fundamentally different understandings of the politics of economic development and of 'natural resource' use.

Analyses of local environmental conflicts as 'culture-clash' often counterpose the 'abstract' concepts of "the environment"' (Garavan, 2008: 78) typical of policy discourses to the immediacy of 'local place' and 'local knowledge'. But there is no obvious reason why 'environment' must always be 'abstract', in the sense that it ignores the local. While *Our Common Future* clearly understands 'sustainable development' as a global project in which all people should engage, it treats environmental problems repeatedly as local problems – problems of 'communities', especially of poor communities whose access to and control over their own resources is under threat. It is true that the meaning of 'the local' remains vague and its relations with the global are poorly worked through in the Brundtland Report. But when Ryan (2008: 303) claims that '[a]t the heart of the matter is a conception of "place" which cannot be reduced to dominant interpretations of "ecology" or "development"', his complaint makes sense only if we are thinking of environmental discourse as ecological modernisation discourse. What emerges from these accounts of local environmental mobilisations and discourses is an account of 'local place' as local ecologies, local livelihoods, local social relations and local knowledges. Suggesting that these themes are not found in 'environmental' discourse, and that environmental discursive frames cannot adequately capture such local concerns is effectively surrendering the battle over whose discourse of sustainable development is to be accepted as 'truth'.

The term 'sustainable development' is not widely used within the community form of Irish environmentalism. Kelly's 2007 study of Irish environmental discourses found that it was used by only one group out of eleven 'general public' focus groups conducted. Some of the 'activist' focus groups did 'explore and clarify what sustainable development in an Irish context would mean' (Kelly, 2007: 171), but even they passed rather rapidly from trying to define the concept to complaining about state actions – e.g. the government decision to transfer decision-making powers in relation to waste management from local councillors to county managers – as anti-democratic and not in keeping with the Irish state's claimed commitment to sustainable development. For many of the groups involved, particularly activists and farmers, it was participatory democracy which emerged as a major theme, in the form of complaints about decisions which had environmental consequences for a local community being taken by outside interests without adequate consultation, especially by business and political elites, bureaucrats and 'suits' (Kelly, 2007: 209). The marginalisation of the term 'sustainable development' among activists may reflect its appropriation into a form of discourse they find alien; it does not mean that the themes which characterise sustainable development discourse in its subaltern version are not strongly present in their talk.

Conclusion

'Alternative' environmental activists might find it an empowering experience to go back and read the Brundtland Report, to reclaim and reframe the concept of 'sustainable development' which, even in confused form, it set out. It has often been easy for regulators and the media in Ireland to dismiss the form of environmental mobilisation found here as 'populist' or 'NIMBYist' , but this misunderstands both the discourses it draws on and the context in which it has grown. As *Our Common Future* reminds us, the 'environment' is where people live. The term 'environmental' does not belong to any one group, and there are no universal definitions of environmental sustainability. Local environmental mobilisations open up and extend its meaning in important ways; in their hands, it becomes a discourse about local livelihoods and the complex local ecologies on which they depend, local community relations and knowledges, and also and profoundly a discourse about democratic rights to participate in the protection of one's own local place. All of these themes can be traced back in some form to *Our Common Future*.

What transforms local livelihood and ecological concerns into collective activism and protest appears to be the experience community activists routinely have of being left outside local development decision-making processes. They endure repeated difficulties over long periods in accessing decision-making processes and having their own voices heard. Feelings of anger and injustice at their marginalisation, despite their considerable local ecological knowledge and the huge efforts they make to educate themselves about the predictable effects of proposed developments on local ecological and economic conditions, appear to exercise a strong binding force, uniting small groups of disparate individuals into a self-defined environmental group (Tovey, 2007). Kelly (2007: 14) notes that lack of consultation about how local areas are to be used for economic development is often 'an emblem for wider grievances'. Equally, lack of consultation can be understood as itself an 'environmental' grievance. If environmentalism is about sustainable development, it is centrally about expanding democracy: the first comprehensive articulation of 'sustainable development' clearly states that this must be development which 'secures effective citizen participation in decision making' (WCED, 1987: 8).

Concluding remarks
Fiona Dukelow and Orla O'Donovan

> Don't be 'practical' in politics. To be practical ... means that you have schooled yourself to think along the lines, and in the grooves of those who rob you would desire you to think. (Connolly, ([1909]1997: 5)

When the ideas that have shaped this book were first being sketched out in mid-2007, our thoughts were focused on what seemed to be the unassailable capitalist orthodoxies of our times. Three years later, in 2010, the landscape has shifted considerably and the unstable, contradictory nature of contemporary global capitalism has again become more visible, as the economic crisis triggered by the subprime mortgage crisis which emerged in the USA in 2008 has had repercussions across the world. These repercussions mean severe hardship and insecurity for people and regions least able to cope with the vagaries of financial speculation and the debt-fuelled consumption boom which are symptomatic of the current crisis. Feted only a few years ago as the 'Celtic Tiger' and Europe's economic star performer, Ireland has seen its transformation by the current crisis in capitalism, according to the *Financial Times* (Murray Brown, 2009), into 'Dire Land' as tax revenue from property transactions halved between 2006 and 2008 and the government began the introduction of the 'most severe austerity programme' since the foundation of the state. Against this economic background, José Manuel Barroso, the president of the European Commission who celebrated the EU as a 'non-imperial empire', urged voters in the 2009 Irish referendum on the Lisbon Treaty to be pragmatic and vote yes, not least to boost investor confidence. In a similar vein, the Taoiseach Brian Cowen argued that opponents of the Treaty needed to 'get real' as a 'yes' vote was fundamental to economic recovery. It seems we are entering a period in which those on the left who oppose modern empires – which like those of old, are invariably built on exploitation, violence and destruction – will increasingly be told to 'be practical'.

Yet the economic crisis also presents a moment of political opportunity for movements against capitalism. It provides an opening for alternative ideas which have the potential to mobilise against what, for the moment at least, has been exposed as the problematic nature of the relationship between state and capital, and the unjust, volatile and ultimately unsustainable nature of contemporary capitalism. The current crisis exposes the ineffectiveness of contemporary modes of neo-liberal state regulation and the simultaneous contradictory, yet unstinting, propensity for the state to uphold the system when things go wrong, in other words, 'socialism for the rich'.

While not all of the texts considered in this book directly address the problems of capitalism, they all by various means offer alternative ways of thinking and acting against oppression and inequality. Importantly, each of them rejects appeals to a circumscribed 'practical' politics. Furthermore, while the current crisis may invoke the need for a new wave of radical ideas, much of what is new is a re-articulation and re-invigoration of past ideas and texts of thinkers whose legacies endure and whose critical imagination, values, and vision continue to inspire, mobilise and show us possible ways to 'reorder the co-ordinates of the present' (Duncombe, 2007a: 498). The texts considered in this book may also be thought of as part of a broader inventory of 'resources of hope' (Brah, 2002: 39); their hopefulness and alterity coming closer to realisation at moments and in spaces when and where dominant paradigms can be more openly contested and challenged. The fact that the texts, written across two centuries from 1791 to 1987, remain inspirational points to their significance, not solely as sources of historical lineage for various contemporary social movements, but also insofar as the issues and ideals dealt within them are recursive. The origins of many of the texts are specific to political and cultural situations at particular points in time. However, their analytical purchase, their creative imagination and their language have the ability in various ways to transcend and translate across boundaries of time and space and continue to speak to the problems of our times and contribute to the imagination of alternatives. The manner in which the contemporary economic crisis has emerged, how it is being handled and its differentiated effects are a manifestation of structural problems of societies built upon the oppressive intersections of class, 'race', gender and sexuality, together with environmental exploitation and feeble forms of democracy. While gains against various forms of oppression have been made over time, in many respects – to borrow the words Bernadette McAliskey borrows from Leonard Cohen – 'nothing much has happened since but closing time' with regard to the problems identified in many of the texts. In this respect therefore, they also serve to remind us of the illusory nature of the pervasive sense of 'endism' (Gamble, 2000) characterising contemporary political discourse, which refers to the notion that we live after the 'end of history', the 'end of politics', or that we are living in post-feminist or post-racist times, with no need nor space for contestation.

In this context the remainder of these concluding remarks attempt to bring together some of the ways in which the chapters in this book offer resources and insights for contemporary social movements; by acting as problem posing texts, by envisioning alternatives, and offering a language by which both problems and alternative worlds can be articulated; and by offering insights into the problems and potential of oppositional political strategies.

Problem posing

A number of the texts operate principally as problem-posing texts, they articulate and analyse a problem around which collective meaning and action can be framed. On a broad scale, as these texts show, oppression may be understood to be rooted in problems of power and knowledge. Paine's *The Rights of Man*, which concerns the nature of state power and the rights of citizens, and the problem of the usurpation of power, continues to be a touchstone for critique of the state and its use and misuse of power. While Paine posed the problem of state power in revolutionary times when democratic forms of statehood were an emergent form, the challenge of that text is still clear in the ways in which democracy has evolved in practice and diverged from Paine's conception. In the recent Irish context for example, re-staging a referendum until the 'right' result is generated, as with the Nice Treaty rejected in 2001 but accepted in a second referendum in 2002, and in relation to the Lisbon Treaty, rejected in 2008 and put to vote again in 2009, is clearly in contravention of Paine's concept of the rights of citizens. Another challenge generated by Paine's text, as McAliskey notes, is 'if the process by which the state is created excludes the interest and perspective of those marginalised due to class, gender, 'race', and so on , then every state in Europe needs a new constitution'. Again in the Irish case this marginalisation is clearly evident in a case discussed later in the book, namely in comments made by Shell to Sea protesters, as documented in Mark Garavan's chapter on Freire's *Pedagogy of the Oppressed*. While the comment made here specifically contrasts the marginalisation of local interests against the interests of the multinational energy companies, the same could be said of many local campaigns and movements that struggle against the state's championing of private interests over public welfare:

> It was hard to accept that our government was willing to let this happen. You'd feel that the government should be there to protect the citizens and they weren't doing it. They were helping out a multi-national oil and gas company above ordinary Irish citizens. It's hard to accept that kind of thing. You'd feel like you shouldn't really have to put up a fight. We weren't only fighting the gas company we were fighting the government and even lower levels of the State such as the county council. (See page 134 of this volume)

Other texts bring notice to problems within a philosophical as opposed to a political frame, by demonstrating the connections between particular experiences of subordination or oppression and the ontological and epistemological bases of the social world. In so doing they help to speak truth to power. Perhaps the definitive classic text in this sense is Freire's *Pedagogy of the Oppressed*, which offers a methodology and conceptual toolkit for the development of a critical consciousness about the nature of the world and the potential of human agency. In a substantive sense texts which pose problems and challenge knowledge in a particular field include Szasz's *The Myth of Mental Illness* and Beauvoir's *The Second Sex*. These texts draw attention to knowledge as myth in the case of mental illness and femininity respectively, and demonstrate how the generation and use of knowledge within particular paradigms, or within scientised and patriarchal ways of knowing, is intimately connected with the oppression of particular groups of people. Problematising knowledge in this way allows for a re-framing of particular problems and identities, as in Szasz's conceptualisation of mental illness as 'problems of living' or as in ways by which Beauvoir's book became a conduit for women to liberate themselves from the myths of femininity. Essentially by problematising the construction or the mythological bases of knowledge, texts such as these become resources, as Orla McDonnell points out, for the 'uprising of the slaves' in opposing and contesting the coercive uses to which that knowledge is put and the individual and collective consequences of this.

Envisioning alternatives

As Skrimshire (2006: 202–3) suggests 'most if not all, popular movements against a dominant power require some reference to the imagination of life outside that system, whether it be an imminent and tangible possibility ... or something more literally utopian'. In terms of large-scale thinking, perhaps the text which offers the most in this direction is Illich's *Tools for Conviviality*. Illich's imagining of a convivial world, as Orla O'Donovan suggests, offers 'big picture revisioning and rethinking injustice' and a stimulus in contemporary times when many movements of the left seem stymied by a lack of vision and seem to be locked into a pattern of simply opposing the ideas and the proposals of the political mainstream. This is to the neglect of cultivating, clarifying and being sustained by their own vision, desires and aspirations for an alternative world. 'Big vision' texts, such as Illich's, help in James Connolly's (1987: 5) words to free the mind from thinking in 'the grooves of those who rob you would desire you to think'.

The notion of alternative vision is also evident in James Connolly's *Labour in Irish History*, as Fintan Lane discusses. This work shows how texts may offer an alternative vision, not by imagining an alternative future, but by re-imagining the past in order to galvanise movements of the present. In Connolly's case, as Lane shows, his writing of history was clearly instrumental and engaged; by inscribing the role and perspective of the working class into Irish history and thus challenging historical orthodoxies, his intention was to draw his working-class readership into the socialist movement.

Big-vision thinking can also be communicated in very achievable terms, contrary to those who tell us that utopian or alternative thinking is impractical and should be abandoned in favour of the need to 'get practical' or 'get real', as already mentioned (except, of course, when we are told 'to think outside the box'). As Eileen O'Carroll's chapter demonstrates, while William Thompson was known for his utopian socialism, he also serves as a model of how to connect vision with very a detailed consideration of how to realise it. This was evident to a degree in his early letters concerning the provision of education in Cork city, and more fully realised in his later work *Labor Rewarded*, which deals with how to make his ideal of an alternative co-operative way of living and working happen, and thereby followed through on his critique of the unequal distribution of wealth.

Language

All of the texts provide in some way a mobilising language which is central to social movements – to articulate grievances and solutions to those grievances, to create identities, and to strategise. In the case of *Black Power* for example, Robbie McVeigh shows how the book, by naming racism and developing the concept of institutional racism, offered black people a language to articulate the problem of their subordination by virtue of their colour whilst at the same time implicating a particular politics of liberation. In a similar way, Tina O'Toole's discussion of Adrienne Rich's essay 'On Compulsory Heterosexuality and Lesbian Existence' shows how the concept of lesbian continuum offered a powerful expression of identity, at both an individual and a collective level, as well as a strategy of political engagement. More broadly, movement language can also serve as an important tool to maintain identity and vision against the nullifying and stultifying effects of mainstream discourse or contemporary versions of *The Daily Chloroform*, the aptly named popular newspaper in Robert Tressell's *The Ragged Trousered Philanthropists* as discussed in Rosie Meade's chapter.

However, many of the chapters also demonstrate the problems social movements encounter when the transformative potential of their language and its political implications becomes disarmed in some way. Crucially this does not necessarily mean the disappearance of a concept, although in some circumstances this is the case, as for example when Garavan remarks that 'officially, we don't have "oppressed" people in Ireland'. More often the potency of particular expressions and concepts is colonised when the concepts remain in use and when they permeate policy documents and mainstream media discourse, but in ways which involve a distortion or dilution of their movement meaning. This is clearly demonstrated in McVeigh's chapter when he traces the afterlife of Ture and Hamilton's formulation of institutional racism, now 'hegemonic and state-sanctioned institutional racism-lite'. Here this concept, along with many others generated by movement intellectuals, becomes so diluted that it bears none of its radical impulse and allows state institutions to claim their effective management or elimination of the problem against what therefore appear as the unreal and unreasonable claims of minorities. Hilary Tovey's chapter on *Our Common Future* illustrates another way in which the value of a concept becomes diluted. The concept of sustainable development, as she shows, did not have a clear cut meaning in the Brundtland report, and over time the potentially contested nature of the concept has been submerged by quite a conservative interpretation of what it means, with the result, as Tovey notes, that 'makes much of the discourse and practices of environmentalism in Ireland opaque and unintelligible'. In situations such as these, McVeigh's chapter points to one of the simplest ways in which mobilising texts remain a necessity, by continuing to provide a template or a source for clarifying concepts, resisting their uncritical meanings, and reinforcing particular activist strategies.

Political strategy

Meade's chapter alerts us to the ways in which the colonisation of movement language and concepts is symptomatic of problems at a more fundamental level for left-wing political strategies, namely the difficulties encountered by activists when the dominant capitalist hegemony manages to invert reality and colonise imagination. As Meade shows, this problem, which Tressell explored creatively in *The Ragged Trousered Philanthropists*, has strong parallels with contemporary neo liberalism. Here it seems almost impossible to create and communicate any form of radical, creative and counter-cultural language, argument or strategy without coming up against its commodification in some way, or its use bounded by economised and marketised interpretations. In this context, movements that desire an alternative world and pursue a politics of liberation seem estranged from the wider population, and their strategies aimed at convincing people that alternatives are desirable and possible seem ineffective. As Meade suggests, there are no easy solutions to these problems, but taking seriously the question of why it is 'that despite having a compelling analysis and people's best interests at heart, the left seems bereft of imagination and allure' is an important part of addressing them. The current economic crisis, particularly as it unfolds in Ireland, presents an opportune time when perhaps the disconnect between movements of the left and the wider population narrows and spaces are opened where there is greater receptivity to the alternative assessments of the crisis and its resolution as offered by the left. However, it remains to be seen if the opportunity can be harnessed to successfully mobilise against what, for the moment at least, are the no-longer unassailable orthodoxies of capitalism.

Bibliography

Alldred, P. (1999) 'Not making a virtue of a necessity: Nancy Fraser on postsocialist politics', in T. Jordan and A. Lent (eds), *Storming the Millennium. The New Politics of Change*, London: Lawrence & Wishart, pp. 127–39.

Allen, K. (1990) *The Politics of James Connolly*, London: Bookmarks.

Allen, K. (1997) *Fianna Fáil and Irish Labour: 1926 to the Present*, London: Pluto Press.

Allen, R. (2004) *No Global: The People of Ireland versus the Multinationals*, London: Pluto Press.

Allen, R., and T. Jones (1990) *Guests of the Nation: People of Ireland Versus the Multinationals*, London: Earthscan.

Althusser, L. (2008) *On Ideology*, London: Verso.

Anderson, W. K. (1994) *James Connolly and the Irish Left*, Dublin: Irish Academic Press.

An Garda Síochána (2005) *Garda Action Plan for the Implementation of the Garda Human Rights Audit Report*, Dublin: An Garda Síochána.

Ascher, C. (1987) 'Simone de Beauvoir – mother of us all', *Social Text*, 17: 107–9.

Bair, D. (1990) *Simone de Beauvoir*, London: Jonathon Cape.

Baker, S. (1990) 'The evolution of the Irish ecology movement', in W. Rudig (ed.), *Green Politics One*, Edinburgh: Edinburgh University Press.

Baker, S. (1997) *The Politics of Sustainable Development: Theory, Policy and Practice within the European Union*, London/NY: Routledge.

Baker, S., M. Kousis, D. Richardson and S. Young (1997) 'Introduction', in S. Baker *et al.* (eds), *The Politics of Sustainable Development*, London: Routledge.

Ball, F.C. (1979) *One of the Damned*, London: Lawrence and Wishart.

Barthes, R. (1993) *Mythologies*, London: Vintage.

Baud, M., and R. Rutten (eds) (2004) *Popular Intellectuals and Social Movements. Framing Protest in Asia, Africa, and Latin America*, Cambridge: Cambridge University Press.

Bauer, N. (2004) 'Must we read Simone de Beauvoir?', in E. Grosholz (ed.), *The Legacy of Simone de Beauvoir*, Oxford: Oxford University Press.

Beauvoir, S. de (1968) *Force of Circumstance*, London: Penguin.

Beauvoir, S. de (1974) *All Said and Done*, London: André Deutsch and Weidenfeld and Nicolson.

Beauvoir, S. de (1997) *The Second Sex*, London: Vintage.

Beaven, B. (2005) *Leisure, Citizenship and Working-Class Men in Britain, 1850–1945*, Manchester: Manchester University Press.

Beck, U. (1992) *Risk Society – Towards a New Modernity*, London: Sage (German edition first published 1987).

Bello, W. (2006) 'The capitalist conjuncture: over-accumulation, financial crises, and the retreat from globalisation', *Third World Quarterly*, 27 (8): 1345–67.

Benford, R., and D. Snow (2000) 'Framing processes and social movements: an overview and assessment', *Annual Review of Sociology*, 26: 611–39.

Bentall, R.P., and D. Pilgrim (1993) 'Thomas Szasz, crazy talk and the myth of mental illness, *British Journal of Medical Psychology*, 66 (1): 69–76.

Boltanski, L., and E. Chiapello (2005a) 'The new spirit of capitalism', *International Journal of Politics, Culture and Society*, 18 (3–4): 161–88.

Boltanski, L., and E. Chiapello (2005b) *The New Spirit of Capitalism*, London: Verso.

Boston Women's Health Collective (1976) *Our Bodies, Ourselves*, New York, NY: Simon and Schuster.

Bowles, G. (1983) 'Introduction: the context', *Gender Issues*, 3 (1): 3–6.

Bracken, P., and P. Thomas (2005) *Postpsychiatry: Mental Health in a Postmodern World*, Oxford: Oxford University Press.

Brah, A. (2002) 'Global modalities, local predicaments: globalisation and the critical imagination', *Feminist Review*, 70: 30–45.

Bridenthal, R., and C. Koonz (eds) (1977) *Becoming Visible: Women in European History*, Boston, MA: Houghton Mifflin.

Browne, I.W. (1964) 'American psychiatry and the cult of psychoanalysis', *Journal of the Irish Medical Association*, 54: 11–17.

Browne, I. (2008) *Music and Madness*, Cork: Atrium, Cork University Press.

Bruckmeier, K., and M. Kopytina (2006) 'Sustainable rural development – how does it affect rural societies in Europe and the southern hemisphere?' in V. Majerova (ed.), *Countryside – Our World*, Proceedings of the conference in Cesky Krumlov, Czech Republic, 1–3 March 2006, pp. 42–71.

Bruckmeier, K., and H. Tovey (2009) 'Natural resource management for sustainable development', Introduction to K. Bruckmeier and H. Tovey (eds), *Rural Sustainable Development in the Knowledge Society*, Farnham, Surrey: Ashgate.

Bulbeck, C. (1999) 'Simone de Beauvoir and generations of feminists', *Hecate*, 25 (2): 5–21.

Buttel, F. (2000) 'Classical theory and contemporary environmental sociology', in G. Spaargaren, A. Mol and F. Buttel (eds), *Environment and Global Modernity*, London: Sage.

Byrne, K. (1976) 'Mechanics institutes in Ireland before 1855', unpublished M.Ed. dissertation, University College Cork.

Carmichael, S. (2007) *Stokely Speaks: From Black Power to Pan-Africanism*, Chicago, IL: Lawrence Hill Books.

Carmichael, S., and E. Thelwell (2003) *Ready for Revolution: The Life and Struggles of Stokely Carmichael (Kwame Ture)*, New York, NY: Scribner.

Cayley, D. (ed.) (1992) *Ivan Illich in Conversation*, Concord, Ontario: House of Anansi Press.

Chodorow, N. (1978) *The Reproduction of Mothering*, Berkeley, CA: University of California Press.

Claeys, G. (1989) *Citizens and Saints: Politics and Anti-Politics in early British Socialism*, Cambridge: Cambridge University Press.

Claeys, G. (ed.) (1993) *Selected Works of Robert Owen*, Farnham: Ashgate Publishing.

Clare, A. (1976) *Psychiatry in Dissent: Controversial Issues in Thought and Practice*, London: Tavistock.

Cohen, C.I., and S. Timimi (eds) (2008) *Liberatory Psychiatry: Philosophy, Politics, and Mental Health*, Cambridge: Cambridge University Press.

Connolly, J. ([1909]1987) *Workshop Talks*, Dublin: Repsol.

Connolly, J. (1910) *Labour in Irish History*, Dublin: Maunsel & Co.

Connolly, J. (1922) *Labour in Ireland, Labour in Irish History: The Reconquest of Ireland*, Dublin and London: Maunsel and Roberts Ltd.

Connolly, L. (2002) *The Irish Women's Movement: From Revolution to Devolution*, London: Palgrave.

Connolly, L., and T. O'Toole (2005) *Documenting Irish Feminisms The Second Wave*, Dublin: Woodfield Press.

Conroy, R. (1980) 'Images of Irish Women Bibliography', *Crane Bag*, 4 (1): 586–93.

Craig, E. (1983) *An Irish Commune: The Experiment at Ralahine, County Clare, 1831–1833*, Dublin: Irish Academic Press.

Crone, J. (1980) 'Lesbians in the Irish feminist movement', *Elektra* (Trinity College Dublin Women's Group Magazine), Nov., n.p.

Crone, J. (1995) 'Lesbians: the lavender women of Ireland', in I. O'Caroll and E. Collins, (eds) *Lesbian and Gay Visions of Ireland, Towards the Twenty-first Century*, London: Cassell, pp. 60–70.

Cronin, M. (2000) '"Of one mind?" O'Connellite crowds in the 1830s and 1840s', in P. Jupp and E. Magennis (eds), *Crowds in Ireland, c.1720–1920*, Basingstoke: Macmillan.

Crossley, N. (2002) *Making Sense of Social Movements*, Maidenhead: Open University Press.

Dáil Éireann (1983) Eighth Amendment of the Constitution Bill, 1982: Second Stage (Resumed), vol. 340, 17 February.

Daily Mirror (2009) 'It's the first day in his new job, he's at his desk by 8.35am, and already the new President is ... TAKING CARE OF BUSINESS', 21 January.

Daly, M. ([1979] 1991) *Gyn/Ecology: The Metaethics of Radical Feminism*, London: The Women's Press.

Department of the Environment (1987) *Sustainable Development – a Strategy for Ireland*, Dublin: Government Stationery Office.

Department of Health and Children (2006) *A Vision for Change: Report of the Expert Group on Mental Health Policy*, Dublin: Stationery Office.

Department of Justice and Equality (2005) *National Action Plan against Racism*, Dublin: Department of Justice and Equality.

Dinnerstein, D. (1976) *The Mermaid and the Minotaur: Sexual Arrangements and the Human Malaise*, New York, NY: Harper and Row.

Donzelot, J. (1991) 'Pleasure in Work', in G. Burchell, C. Gordon and P. Miller (eds) *The Foucault Effect*, Chicago: University of Chicago Press, pp. 251–80.

Dooley, D. (1996) *Equality in Community: Sexual Equality in the Writings of William Thompson and Anna Doyle Wheeler*, Cork: Cork University Press.

Dooley, D. (ed.) (1997) *William Thompson, Appeal (1825)*, Cork: Cork University Press.

Dorcey, M. (1995) 'Interview', in Í. O'Carroll and E. Collins (eds) *Lesbian and Gay Visions of Ireland: Towards the Twenty-First Century*, London: Cassell, pp. 25–44.

Duncombe, S. (2007a) '(From) Cultural resistance to community development',

Community Development Journal, 42 (4): 490–500.

Duncombe, S. (2007b) *Dream: Re-Imagining Progressive Politics in an Age of Fantasy*, New York: The New Press.

Dunphy, R. (2005) 'Fianna Fáil and the working class, 1926–38', in F. Lane and D. Ó Drisceoil (eds), *Politics and the Irish Working Class, 1830–1945*, Basingstoke: Macmillan.

Du Plessix Gray, F. (1970) *Divine Disobedience. Profiles in Catholic Radicalism*, London: Hamish Hamilton.

Eagleton, T. (2000) 'The Radicalism of William Thompson', *The Irish Review*, 26: 80–8.

Earth Summit Ireland (2002) *Telling It Like It Is – Ten Years of Unsustainable Development in Ireland*, Dublin: Earth Summit Ireland Ltd.

Edmondson, R.,and H. Rau (eds) (2008) *Environmental Argument and Cultural Difference*, Bern, Switzerland: Peter Lang.

Ehrenrich, B., and D. English (1978) *For Her Own Good: 150 Years of the Experts' Advice to Women*, New York: Doubleday, Anchor.

Ellis, P. B. (1972) *A History of the Irish Working Class*, London: Victor Gollancz.

Ellmann, R. (1982) *James Joyce*, Oxford and New York: Oxford University Press.

Esteva, G. (1992) 'Development', in W. Sachs (ed.), *The Development Dictionary: A Guide to Knowledge as Power*, London: Zed Books, pp. 6–25.

Evans, M. (ed.) (2009) *Simone de Beauvoir's* The Second Sex: *New Interdisciplinary Essays*, Manchester: Manchester University Press.

Expert Group on Mental Health Policy (2004a) *Speaking Your Mind: A Report on the Public Consultation Process*, Dublin: Department of Health and Children.

Expert Group on Mental Health Policy (2004b) *What We Heard: A Report on the Service User Consultation Process*, Dublin: Department of Health and Children.

Eyerman, R., and A. Jamieson (1991) *Social Movements: A Cognitive Approach*, Cambridge: Polity.

Felstiner, M. L. (1980) '"*The Second Sex*" through the second wave' *Feminist Studies*, 6 (2): 247–76.

Fischer, F. (2000) *Citizens, Experts and the Environment: the Politics of Local Knowledge*, Durham: Duke University Press.

Fischer, F. (2005) 'Are scientists irrational? Risk assessment in practical reason', in M. Leach, I. Scoones and B. Wynne (eds), *Science and Citizens*, London: Zed Books, pp. 54–65.

Foucault, M. (1980) *Power/Knowledge: Selected Interviews and Other Writings, 1972–77*, C. Gordon (ed), New York, NY: Pantheon Books.

Frank, T. (2001) *One Market Under God*, New York, NY: Anchor Books.

Freire, P. (1972) *Pedagogy of the Oppressed*, Harmondsworth: Penguin.

Fricker, M. (2007) *Epistemic Injustice. Power and the Ethics of Knowing*, Oxford: Oxford University Press.

Fromm, E. (2001) 'Introduction', in I. Illich, *Celebration of Awareness. A Call for Institutional Reform*, London: Marion Boyars, pp. 7–10.

Gamble, A. (2000) *Politics and Fate*, Cambridge: Polity Press.

Garavan, M. (ed.) (2006) *The Rossport Five. Our Story*, Dublin: Small World Media.

Garavan, M. (2008) 'Problems in Achieving Dialogue – Cultural Misunderstandings in the Corrib Gas Dispute', in R. Edmondson and H. Rau (eds): *Environmental Argument and Cultural Difference – Locations, Fractures and Deliberations*, Bern, Switzerland: Peter Lang, pp. 65–92.

Garber, L. (2001) *Identity Poetics: Race, Class, and the Lesbian-Feminist Roots of Queer Theory*, New York, NY: Columbia University Press.

George, S. (2008) *We the Peoples of Europe*, London: Pluto Press.

Gerrassi, J. (1976) 'Simone de Beauvoir: *The Second Sex* 25 years later', Interview with Simone de Beauvoir, *Society*, 13 (2): 79–85.

Glaser, F.B. (1965) 'The dichotomy game: a further consideration of the writings of Dr. Thomas Szasz', *American Journal of Psychiatry*, 121: 1069–74.

Glazer, S. (2007) 'A Second Sex', *Bookforum*, April/May 2007. www.bookforum. com/inprint/014_01/113 (retrieved 15 April 2010).

Gramsci, A. (1977) *Antonio Gramsci, Selections from Political Writings (1910–1920)*, Q. Hoare and J. Matthews (eds), New York, NY: International Publishers.

Greaves, C. D. (1961) *The Life and Times of James Connolly*, London: Lawrence and Wishart.

Greally, H. ([1971] 2008) *Bird's Nest Soup*, Cork: Attic Press.

Green 2000 Advisory Group (1993) *Report to the Taoiseach Mr. Albert Reynolds*, Dublin: Stationery Office.

Hajer, M. (1996) 'Ecological modernisation as cultural politics', in S. Lash, B. Szerszynski and B. Wynne (eds), *Risk, Environment and Modernity: Towards a New Ecology*, London: Sage.

Hardon, A. (2006) 'Contesting contraceptive innovation – Reinventing the script', *Social Science & Medicine*, 62: 614–27.

Harker, D. (2003) *Tressell – The Real Story of the Ragged Trousered Philanthropists*, London: Zed.

Haugaard, M. (1997) *The Constitution of Power – A Theoretical Analysis of Power, Knowledge and Structure*, Manchester: Manchester University Press.

Hobsbawm, E.J. (1987) *Industry and Empire: From 1750 to the Present Day*, Harmondsworth: Penguin.

Hochschild, A. (1983) 'Illich: the ideologue in scientist's clothing', *Gender Issues*, 3: 6–11.

Hoinacki, L., and C. Mitcham (eds) (2002) *The Challenges of Ivan Illich: A Collective Reflection*, New York, NY: State University of New York Press.

Hollingshead, A.B., and F.C. Redlich (1958) *Social Class and Mental Illness: A Community Study*, New York, NY: John Wiley.

Hopton, J. (2006) 'The future of critical psychiatry', *Critical Social Policy*, 26 (1): 57–73.

Horkheimer, M., and T. Adorno, (1973) *Dialectic of Enlightenment*, London: Allen Lane.

Howell, D. (1986) *A Lost Left: Three Studies in Socialism and Nationalism* (Manchester: Manchester University Press.

Hunt, T. (2004) 'Introduction', in Robert Tressell, *The Ragged Trousered Philanthropists*, London: Penguin Classics, pp. vii–xxxi

Illich, I. (1973) *Tools for Conviviality*, New York, NY: Harper & Row.

Illich, I. (1976) *Limits to Medicine – Medical Nemesis: The Expropriation of Health*, Middlesex: Penguin.

Illich, I. (2002) 'The cultivation of conspiracy', in L. Hoinacki and C. Mitcham (eds), *The Challenges of Ivan Illich: A Collective Reflection*, New York, NY: State University of New York Press, pp. 233–42.

Imbert, C. (2004) 'Simone de Beauvoir: a woman philosopher in the context of her generation', in E. Grosholz, (ed.), *The Legacy of Simone de Beauvoir*, Oxford:

Oxford University Press.

Independent Monitoring Commission (2006) *Eighth Report of the Independent Monitoring Commission*, presented to the Government of the United Kingdom and the Government of Ireland under Articles 4 and 7 of the International Agreement establishing the Independent Monitoring Commission. Ordered by the House of Commons to be printed 1 February 2006.

Ionann Management Consultants (2004) *An Garda Síochána Human Rights Audit: Report from Ionann Management Consultants*, Dublin: Ionann Management Consultants Limited.

Irish Examiner (2005) 'Force's recruitment drive to include anti-racism training for members', 7 October.

Irish Family Planning Association (2000) *The Irish Journey. Women's Stories of Abortion*, Dublin: Irish Family Planning Association.

Irwin, A. (2001) *Sociology and the Environment*, Cambridge: Polity Press.

Jamison, A. (2001) *The Making of Green Knowledge – Environmental Politics and Cultural Transformation*. Cambridge: Cambridge University Press.

Jasanoff, S. (2005) *Designs on Nature. Science and Democracy in Europe and the United States*, Princeton, NJ: Princeton University Press.

Johnson, D. (2004) 'Ecological modernisation, globalisation and Europeanisation: a mutually reinforcing nexus?', in J. Barry, B. Baxter and R. Dunphy (eds), *Europe, Globalisation and Sustainable Development*, London: Routledge, pp. 152–67.

Kahn, R. (2009) 'Anarchic epimetheanism: the pedagogy of Ivan Illich', in R. Amster, A. DeLeon, L. Fernandez, A. Nocella and D. Shannon (eds), *Contemporary Anarchist Studies. An Introductory Anthology of Anarchy in the Academy*, London: Routledge, pp. 125–35.

Kahn, R., and D. Kellner (2007) 'Paulo Freire and Ivan Illich: technology, politics and the reconstruction of education', *Policy Futures in Education*, 5 (4): 431–48.

Kaufmann, D. (1986) 'Simone de Beauvoir: questions of difference and generation', *Yale French Studies*, 72: 121–31.

Keating, C. (1977) 'The Second Sex', *St. Stephen's*, 3 (4): 19–22.

Kelley, R. (1996) *Race Rebels*, New York, NY: The Free Press

Kelly, M. (2007) *Environmental Debates and the Public in Ireland*, Dublin: IPA.

Kirby, P. (2006) 'Theorising globalisation's social impact: proposing the concept of vulnerability', *Review of International Political Economy*, 13 (4): 632–55.

Klein, N. (2000) *No Logo*, London: Flamingo.

Klein, N. (2007) *The Shock Doctrine*, London: Penguin.

Kousis, M. (1999) 'Sustaining local environmental mobilisations: groups, actions and claims in Southern Europe', in C. Rootes (ed.), *Environmental Movements: Local, National and Global*, London: Frank Cass, pp. 171–90.

Kruks, S. (1992) 'Gender and subjectivity: Simone de Beauvoir and contemporary feminism', *Signs*, 18 (1): 89–110.

Kruks, S. (2005) 'Beauvoir's time/our time: the renaissance in Simone de Beauvoir studies', *Feminist Studies*, 31 (2): 286–309.

Kuhn, T. (1962) *The Structure of Scientific Revolutions*, Chicago, IL: University of Chicago Press.

Lane, F. (1997) *The Origins of Modern Irish Socialism, 1881–1896*, Cork: Cork University Press.

Lane, F. (2000) 'James Connolly's 1901 census return', *Saothar*, 25: 103–6.

Lane, F. (2001) *In Search of Thomas Sheahan: Radical Politics in Cork, 1824–1836*,

Dublin: Irish Academic Press.

Lather, P. (1994) 'The absent presence: patriarchy, capitalism, and the nature of teacher work', in L. Stone and G. Masuchika Boldt (eds), *The Education Feminism Reader.* London: Routledge.

Leonard, L. (2006) *Green Nation – The Irish Environmental Movement from Carnsore Point to the Rossport Five.* Drogheda: Choice Publishing.

Levine, J. (1982) *Sisters: The Personal Story of an Irish Feminist*, Dublin: Ward River Press.

Levitt, P. (2001) *The Transnational Villagers*, Berkeley, CA: University of California Press.

Lynch, T. (2001) *Beyond Prozac: Healing Mental Suffering Without Drugs*, Dublin: Marino Books.

Lyons, T. (2003) *The Education Work of Richard Lovell Edgeworth, Irish Educator and Inventor, 1744–1817*, Lampeter: Edwin Mellen Press.

McAuley, M., and S. Tiernan (2008) *Tribades, Tommies and Transgressives: Histories of Sexualities*, Cambridge: Cambridge Scholars Publishing.

McAvoy, S. (2008) 'From anti-amendment campaigns to demanding reproductive justice: the changing landscape of abortion rights activism in Ireland, 1983–2008', in J. Schweppe (ed.) *The Unborn Child, Article 40.3.3 and Abortion in Ireland Twenty Five Years of Protection?*, Dublin: The Liffey Press.

McCafferty, N. (2004) *Nell*, Dublin: Penguin Ireland.

Mac Eoin, S. (1982) 'Co-operatives and job creation', in M. Linehan (ed.), *Co-operatives and the Law. Papers Presented at the Colloquium on Co-operatives and the Law*, Cork: Bank of Ireland Centre for Co-operative Studies, pp. 54–62.

McGill, P., and Q. Oliver (2002) *A Wake Up Call on Race: Implications of the Macpherson Report for Institutional Racism in Northern Ireland: A Report for the Equality Commission for Northern Ireland*, Belfast: Equality Commission for Northern Ireland.

McNaghten, P., and J. Urry (1998) *Contested Natures*, London: Sage.

MacPherson, W. (1999) *The Stephen Lawrence Inquiry: Report of an Inquiry by Sir William MacPherson of Cluny: advised by Tom Cook, the Right Reverend Dr John Sentamu, Dr Richard Stone.* Presented to Parliament by the Secretary of State for the Home Department February 1999 Cm 4262-I.

McRobbie, A. (2004) 'Post-feminism and popular culture', *Feminist Media Studies*, 4 (3): 255–64.

Maddock, M. (2008) 'Coercion in psychiatry', MindFreedom Ireland, http://mindfreedomireland.com (retrieved 24 May 2010).

Madsen, C. (2000) 'The thin thread of conversation: an interview with Mary Daly', *Cross Currents*, 50 (3): 332–48.

Maguire, A. (2005) *Rock the Sham! The Irish Lesbian and Gay Organisations Battle to March in the New York City St. Patrick's Day Parade*, New York, NY: Street Level Press.

Mayo, P. (2008) 'Antonio Gramsci and his relevance for the education of adults', *Educational Philosophy and Theory*, 40 (3): 418–35.

Marlowe, N. (ed.) (1918) *James Fintan Lalor: Collected Writings,* Dublin: Maunsel & Co.

Marx, K. (1979) *Capital. A Critique of Political Economy*, Harmondsworth: Penguin.

Marx, K., and F. Engels (1970) *The German Ideology*, London: Lawrence & Wishart.

Meadows, D.H., D.L. Meadows, J. Randers and W.W. Behrens (1972) *Limits to Growth*, London: Earth Island.

Miles, P. (1984) 'The painter's Bible and the British workman: Robert Tressell's literary activism', in J. Hawthorn (ed.), *The British Working-Class Novel in the Twentieth Century*, London: Edward Arnold, pp. 1–18.

Miller, J. (1976) *Toward a New Psychology of Women*, Boston, MA: Beacon.

Millet, K. (1989) 'Kate Millet', in P. Forster and I. Sutton (eds), *Daughters of de Beauvoir*, London: Women's Press, pp. 17–31.

Mitcham, C. (2002) 'The challenges of this collection', in L. Hoinacki and C. Mitcham (eds), *The Challenges of Ivan Illich: A Collective Reflection*, New York, NY: State University of New York Press, pp. 9–32.

Moi, T. (2004) 'While we wait: notes on the English translation of *The Second Sex*', in E. Grosholz (ed.), *The Legacy of Simone de Beauvoir*, Oxford: Oxford University Press.

Moi, T. (2008) *Simone de Beauvoir: The Making of an Intellectual Woman* (2nd edn), Oxford: Oxford University Press.

Moran, L. (2008) 'Local knowledge and conceptions of neighbourliness in environmental disputes: evidence from Connemara', in R. Edmondson and H. Rau (eds), *Environmental Argument and Cultural Difference*, Bern, Switzerland: Peter Lang, pp. 125–50.

Morgan, A. (1988) *James Connolly: A Political Biography*, Manchester: Manchester University Press.

Morris, W. (1944) 'Useful work versus useless toil', in G. D. H. Cole (ed.), *William Morris Selected Works*, London: Nonesuch Press, pp. 603–23.

Motherway, B., M. Kelly, P. Faughnan and H. Tovey (2003) *Trends in Irish Environmental Attitudes between 1993 and 2002*. First report of the research programme on environmental attitudes, values and behavours in Ireland, www.ucd.ie/~environ/home.htm (retrieved 24 May 2010).

Murray Brown, J. (2009) 'Dire land', *Financial Times*, 30 August.

Murtagh, T. (1980) 'Simone's story', *The Irish Times*, 18 April.

Nahuis, R., and H. van Lente (2008) 'Where are the politics? Perspectives on democracy and technology', *Science, Technology & Human Values*, 33 (5): 559–81.

Nazareth, P. (1967) 'A committed novel', *Transition*, 29 (Feb–Mar): 35–8.

Negri, A. (1999) *Insurgencies*, Minneapolis, MN: University of Minnesota Press.

Nestle, J. (2003) *A Restricted Country*, San Francisco, CA: Cleis Press.

Nevin, D. (2005) *James Connolly: 'A Full Life'*, Dublin: Gill & Macmillan.

Nevin, D. (ed.) (2007) *Between Comrades: James Connolly, Letters and Correspondence, 1889–1916*, Dublin: Gill & Macmillan.

Newton, H. (2009) *Revolutionary Suicide*, London: Penguin Classics.

Ní Chuilleanáin, E. (1988) 'The politics of moral citizenship' *Index on Censorship*, 17 (4): 24–5.

Obama, B. (2009) 'Remarks by the President to the NAACP Centennial Convention', The White House, Office of the Press Secretary, 17 July 2009. http://blogs.suntimes.com/sweet/2009/07/obamas_naacp_speech.html (retrieved 29 July 2009).

Ó Broin, E. (2009) *Sinn Féin and the Politics of Left Republicanism*, London: Pluto Press.

O'Caroll, I., and E. Collins (eds) (1995) *Lesbian and Gay Visions of Ireland, Towards the Twenty-first Century*, London: Cassell.

Ó Cathasaigh, A. (2002) 'James Connolly and the writing of *Labour in Irish History* (1910)', *Saothar*, 27, 103–8.

Ó Gráda, C. (1983) 'The Owenite community at Ralahine, County Clare, 1831–33: a reassessment', in E. Craig (ed.), *An Irish Commune: The Experiment at Ralahine, County Clare, 1831–1833*, Dublin: Irish Academic Press.

Okely, J. (1986) *Simone de Beauvoir: A Re-reading*, London: Virago.

Olson, K. (ed.) (2008) *Adding Insult to Injury: Nancy Fraser and her Critics*, London: Verso.

Paine, T. (1987) *The Rights of Man. Being an answer to Mr. Burke's attack on the French Revolution*, New York, NY: Prometheus Books.

Pankhurst, R. (1991) *William Thompson (1775–1833): Pioneer Socialist*, London: Pluto Press, 1991.

Peace, A. (1993) 'Environmental protest, bureaucratic closure: the politics of discourse in rural Ireland', in K. Milton (ed.), *Environmentalism – the View from Anthropology*, London: Routledge, pp. 181–204.

Phelan, S. (1989) *Identity Politics: Lesbian Feminism and the Limits of Community*. Philadephia, PA: Temple University Press.

Pilgrim, D., and Rogers A. (2005) 'The troubled relationship between psychiatry and sociology', *International Journal of Social Psychiatry*, 51 (3): 228–41.

Police Ombudsman for Northern Ireland (2007) Statement by the Police Ombudsman for Northern Ireland on her investigation into the circumstances surrounding the death of Raymond McCord Jnr and related matters, Belfast: Police Ombudsman for Northern Ireland.

Price, R. (1789) *A Discourse on the Love of Our Country*, London: T. Cadell.

Puirséil, N. (2007) *The Irish Labour Party, 1922–73*, Dublin: UCD Press.

Ransom, B. (1980) *Connolly's Marxism*, London: Pluto Press.

Raymond, J. (1989) 'Putting the politics back into lesbianism', *Women's Studies International Forum*, 12 (2): 149–56.

Redclift, M. (1997) 'Frontiers of consumption – sustainable rural economies and societies in the next century?', in H. de Haan, B. Kasimis and M. Redclift (eds), *Sustainable Rural Development*. Aldershot: Ashgate.

Reed Jr., A. (2000) *Class Notes*, New York, NY: The New Press.

Rich, A. (1977) *Of Woman Born: Motherhood as Experience and Institution*, London: Virago.

Rich, A. (1986) 'On compulsory heterosexuality and lesbian existence', in *Blood, Bread and Poetry: Selected Prose 1979–1985*. London: Virago, pp. 23–75.

Rich, W. (2004) 'From Muskogee to Morningside Heights: political scientist Charles V. Hamilton' *Living Legacies*, www.columbia.edu/cu/alumni/Magazine/Spring2004/hamilton.html (retrieved 24 May 2010).

Ritzer, G. (1993) *The McDonaldization of Society. An Investigation into the Changing Character of Contemporary Social Life*, Thousand Oaks, CA: Pine Forge Press.

Rodgers, C. (1998) 'The influence of *The Second Sex* on the French feminist scene', in R. Evans (ed.), *Simone de Beauvoir's* The Second Sex: *New Interdisciplinary Essays*, Manchester: Manchester University Press.

Ross, B. (1995) *The House that Jill Built*, Toronto: University of Toronto Press.

Rossiter, A. (2009) *Ireland's Hidden Diaspora: The 'Abortion Trail' and the Making of a London-Irish Underground, 1980–2000*, London: IASC Publishing.

Rowan, B. (2006) 'Loyalist White a police informer: Special Branch recruited killer'

Belfast Telegraph, 21 February.

Ryan, K. (2008) 'Environmental conflict and democracy: between reason and hegemony', in R. Edmondson and R. Henrike (eds), *Environmental Argument and Cultural Difference,* Bern, Switzerland: Peter Lang, pp. 307–35.

Sachs, W. (1999) *Planet Dialectics: Explorations in Environment and Development*, London: Zed Books.

Schumacher, E. F. (1973) *Small Is Beautiful – Economics as if People Mattered*, London: Blond and Briggs.

Schwartz Cowan, R. (1976) 'The "industrial revolution" in the home: household technology and social change in the 20th century', *Technology and Culture*, 17 (1): 1–23.

Schwartz Cowan, R. (1983) *More Work for Mother: The Ironies of Household Technology from the Open Hearth to the Microwave*, New York, NY: Basic Books.

Scott, J.C. (1990) *Domination and the Arts of Resistance*, New Haven, CT: Yale University Press.

Seanad Éireann (1977) Employment Equality Bill, 1975: Second and Subsequent Stages, vol. 86, 25 May.

Seanad Éireann (1985) Health (Family Planning) (Amendment) Bill, 1985: Second Stage Resumed, vol. 107, 6 March.

Secomb, L. (1999) 'Beauvoir's minoritarian philosophy', *Hypatia*, 14 (4): 96–113.

Share, B. (2003) 'Maunsel and Company (1905–25)', in B. Lalor (ed.), *The Encyclopaedia of Ireland*, Dublin: Gill & Macmillan.

Sillitoe, A. (1991) 'Introduction', in Robert Tressell, *The Ragged Trousered Philanthropists*, London: Paladin, pp. 7–10.

Simon, B. (1960) *Studies in the History of Education 1780–1870*, London: Lawrence and Wishart.

Simon, B. (1985) *Does Education Matter?*, London: Lawrence and Wishart.

Simons, M. (1983) 'The silencing of Simone de Beauvoir: guess what's missing from *The Second Sex?*', *Women's Studies International Forum*, 6 (5): 559–64.

Sismondo, S. (2008) 'Science and technology studies and an engaged program', in E. Hackett, O. Amsterdamska, M. Lynch and J. Wajcman (eds), *The Handbook of Science and Technology Studies* (3rd edn), Cambridge, MA: MIT Press, pp. 13–31.

Skrimshire, S. (2006) 'Another *what* is possible? Ideology and utopian imagination in anti-capitalist resistance', *Political Theology*, 7 (2): 201–21.

Small Firms Association (2008a) 'Free SFA seminar on enhancing work-life balance within your organisation', www.sfa.ie/Sectors/SFA/SFAEvents.nsf/vPages/2008-6-5~Free-SFA-Seminar-on-Enhancing-Work-Life-Balance-within-your-Organisation?OpenDocument (retrieved 24 May 2010).

Small Firms Association (2008b) 'SFA calls for decrease in minimum wage', www.ibec.ie/Sectors/SFA/SFA.nsf/vPages/Press_Centre~sfa-calls-for-decrease-in-minimum-wage-15-07-2008?OpenDocument (retrieved 24 May 2010).

Smith, D. (2008) 'Google, 10 years in: big, friendly giant or a greedy Goliath?' *The Observer*, 17 August.

Snow, D., and R. Benford (2000) 'Framing processes and social movements: an overview and assessment', *Annual Review of Sociology*, 26: 611–39.

Sobrino, Jon (2008) *The Eye of the Needle*, London: Norton Longman & Todd.

Spaargaren, G., and A. P. J. Mol (1995) 'Sociology, environment and modernity: ecological modernisation as a theory of social change', in M. Redclift and

G. Woodgate (eds), *The Sociology of the Environment*, vol. 3, part IV, Aldershot: Edward Elgar.

Spivak, G. (1988) 'Subaltern studies: deconstructing historiography', in R. Guha and G. Spivak (eds), *Selected Subaltern Studies*, Oxford: Oxford University Press, pp. 197–221.

Stavro, E. (1999) 'The use and abuse of Simone de Beauvoir: re-evaluating the French poststructuralist critique', *European Journal of Women's Studies*, 6: 263–80.

Steinberg, M. (1999) 'The talk and back talk of collective action: a dialogic analysis of repertoires of discourse among nineteenth-century English cotton spinners', *American Journal of Sociology*, 105 (3): 736–80.

Stopper, A. (2006) *Monday at Gaj's: The Story of the Irish Women's Liberation Movement*, Dublin: Liffey Press.

Szasz, T. (1960) 'The myth of mental illness', *American Psychologist*, 15 (February): 113–18.

Szasz, T. (1961) *The Myth of Mental Illness: Foundations of a Theory of Personal Conduct*, New York, NY: Paul B. Hoeber.

Szasz, T. ([1961] 1974 rev. edn) *The Myth of Mental Illness: Foundations of a Theory of Personal Conduct*, New York: Harper Collins.

Szasz, T. (1997) 'Thomas Szasz in conversation with Alan Kerr', *Psychiatric Bulletin*, 21: 39–44.

Szasz, T. (2000) 'Curing the therapeutic state: Thomas Szasz on the medicalisation of American life' (Interview with Jacob Sullum), *Reason*, 32 (July): 26–34.

Szasz, T. (2002) 'Mental illness: From shame to pride', *Ideas on Liberty*, 52 (November): 37–8.

Szasz, T. (2004) 'An autobiographical sketch', in J.A. Schaler (ed.), *Szasz Under Fire: The Psychiatric Abolitionist Faces His Critics*, Chicago: Open Court, pp. 1–28.

Szasz, T. (2007) *Coercion as Cure: A Critical History of Psychiatry*, New Brunswick, NJ: Transaction Publishers.

Taylor, G. (2001) *Conserving the Emerald Tiger – The Politics of Environmental Regulation in Ireland*, Galway: Arlen House.

Thomas, P., and P. Bracken (2008) 'Power, freedom, and mental health: a post-psychiatry perspective', in C.I. Cohen and S. Timimi (eds), *Liberatory Psychiatry: Philosophy, Politics, and Mental Health*, Cambridge: Cambridge University Press. pp. 35–53.

Thompson, W. (1818a) *Practical Education for the South of Ireland, in Letters addressed to the Proprietors of the Cork Institution, on the Propriety and Necessity of Directing its Funds to their Proper Object, the Diffusion of Knowledge, by a Useful and Practical System of Education, Applying Science to the Common Purposes of Life*, Cork: West and Coldwells.

Thompson, W. (1818b) 'To the proprietors of the Cork Institution', *The Southern Reporter* 16, 19, 23, 26, 28, May; 13, 18, 25, 27 June; 18 July; 5 November 1818.

Thompson, W. (1824) *An Inquiry into the Principles of the Distribution of Wealth most Conducive to Human Happiness; Applied to the Newly Proposed System of Voluntary Equality of Wealth*, London: Longman, Hurst, Rees, Orme, Brown & Green.

Thompson, W. (1825) *Appeal of One-Half of the Human Race, Women, Against the Pretensions of the Other Half, Men, to Retain them in Political and Thence in Civil and Domestic Slavery*, London: Longman, Hurst, Rees, Orme, Brown &

Green.

Thompson, W. (1827) *Labor Rewarded. The Claims of Labor and Capital Concili-ated: or How to Secure to Labor the Whole Products of its Exertions*, London: Hunt and Clarke.

Thompson, W. (1830) *Practical Directions for the Speedy and Economical Estab-lishment of Communities, on the Principles of Mutual Co-operation, United Possessions and Equality*, London: Strange and E. Wilson.

Tidd, U. (2008) 'État présent: Simone de Beauvoir Studies', *French Studies*, 63 (2): 200–8.

Tijmes, P. (2002) *In memoriam: Ivan Illich* (obituary), www.pudel.uni-bremen.de/pdf/tijmes.pdf (retrieved 9 November 2009).

Time (2001) 'Why she's arguably the world's most influential woman', *Global Influentials*, www.time.com/time/2001/influentials/yboprah.html (retrieved 20 November 2008).

Tovey, H. (1993) 'Environmentalism in Ireland: two versions of development and modernity', *International Sociology*, 8 (4): 413–30.

Tovey, H. (2007) *Environmentalism in Ireland: Movement and Activists*, Dublin: IPA.

Tovey, H. (2008) Guest Editor, 'Rural Sustainable Development in the Era of Know-ledge Society', Special Issue, *Sociologia Ruralis*, 48 (3).

Tressell, R. (2004) *The Ragged Trousered Philanthropists*, London: Penguin Classics.

Tucker, V. (1983) 'A history of workers' co-operatives in Ireland and the UK', in M. Linehan and V. Tucker (eds), *Workers' Co-operatives. Potential and Problems*, Cork: University College Cork Bank of Ireland Centre for Co-operative Studies, pp. 26–43.

Ture, K., and C.V. Hamilton (1992) *Black Power: The Politics of Liberation: With New Afterwords by the Authors*, New York, NY: Vintage Books.

United States Congress (1976a) *Hearings before the Select Committee to Study Governmental Operations with Respect to Intelligence Activities. Final report of the Select Committee to Study Governmental Operations with Respect to Intel-ligence Activities. Volume 6: Federal Bureau of Investigation*, Washington, DC: US Government Printing Office.

United States Congress (1976b) *Final Report of the Select Committee to Study Governmental Operations with Respect to Intelligence Activities, United States Senate. Book II: Intelligence Activities and the Rights of Americans*, Washington, DC: US Government Printing Office.

United States Congress (1976c) *Final Report of the Select Committee to Study Governmental Operations with Respect to Intelligence Activities. Book III: Sup-plementary Detailed Staff Reports on Intelligence Activities and the Rights of Americans*, Washington, DC: US Government Printing Office.

Van Dijk, T.A. (1998) *Ideology: A Multidisciplinary Approach*, London: Sage.

Vintges, K. (1999) 'Simone de Beauvoir: a feminist thinker for our times', *Hypatia*, 14 (4): 133–44.

Walter, N. (1998) *The New Feminism*, London: Little, Brown.

Wardle, D. (1970) *English Popular Education 1780–1970*, Cambridge: Cambridge University Press.

Whelehan, I. (1995) *Modern Feminist Thought: From the Second Wave to 'Post-Feminism'*, Edinburgh: Edinburgh University Press.

Williams, R. (1983) *Writing in Society*, London: Verso.

Wittig, M. (1992) 'One is not born a woman', in *The Straight Mind and Other Essays*, Boston, MA: Beacon Press.

Woggon, H. (2005) 'Interpreting James Connolly, 1916–23', in F. Lane and D. Ó Drisceoil (eds), *Politics and the Irish Working Class, 1830–1945*, Basingstoke: Palgrave Macmillan.

World Commission on Environment and Development (1987) *Our Common Future*, Oxford: Oxford University Press.

Yamin, R. (2002) 'Children's strikes, parents' rights: Paterson and Five Points', *International Journal of Historical Archaeology*, 6 (2): 113–26.

Young, J.D. (1985) 'Militancy, English socialism and the ragged trousered philanthropists', *Journal of Contemporary History*, 20 (2): 283–303.

Young, S. (ed.) (2000) *The Emergence of Ecological Modernisation – Integrating the Environment and the Economy?* London: Routledge.

Zimmerman, B. (1997) 'What has never been: an overview of Lesbian literary criticism', in R. Warhol and D. Price Herndl (eds), *Feminisms*, New Jersey, NJ: Rutgers University Press, pp. 76–96.

Index